Programming in Lua
Third Edition

Programming in Lua
Third Edition

Roberto Ierusalimschy

PUC-Rio, Brazil

Lua.org

Rio de Janeiro

Programming in Lua, Third Edition
by Roberto Ierusalimschy

ISBN 978-85-903798-5-0

The author can be contacted at roberto@lua.org.

Book cover by Luiza Novaes. Lua logo design by Alexandre Nako. Typeset by the author using LaTeX.

CIP – Biblioteca do Departamento de Informática, PUC-Rio

	Ierusalimschy, Roberto
I22	Programming in Lua / Roberto Ierusalimschy. – 3th ed. – Rio de Janeiro, 2013.
	xviii, 348 p. : 25 cm.
	Includes index.
	ISBN 978-85-903798-5-0
	1. Lua (Programming language). I. Title.
	005.133 – dc20

to Ida, Noemi, and Ana Lucia

Contents

Preface

When Waldemar, Luiz, and I started the development of Lua, back in 1993, we could hardly imagine that it would spread as it did. Started as an in-house language for two specific projects, currently Lua is widely used in all areas that can benefit from a simple, extensible, portable, and efficient scripting language, such as embedded systems, mobile devices, and, of course, games.

We designed Lua, from the beginning, to be integrated with software written in C/C++ and other conventional languages. This integration brings many benefits. Lua is a tiny and simple language, partly because it does not try to do what C is already good for, such as sheer performance, low-level operations, and interface with third-party software. Lua relies on C for these tasks. What Lua does offer is what C is not good for: a good distance from the hardware, dynamic structures, no redundancies, and ease of testing and debugging. For these goals, Lua has a safe environment, automatic memory management, and good facilities for handling strings and other kinds of data with dynamic size.

Part of the power of Lua comes from its libraries. This is not by chance. After all, one of the main strengths of Lua is its extensibility. Many features contribute to this strength. Dynamic typing allows a great degree of polymorphism. Automatic memory management simplifies interfaces, because there is no need to decide who is responsible for allocating and deallocating memory, or how to handle overflows. Higher-order functions and anonymous functions allow a high degree of parameterization, making functions more versatile.

More than an extensible language, Lua is also a *glue language*. Lua supports a component-based approach to software development, where we create an application by gluing together existing high-level components. These components are written in a compiled, statically typed language, such as C or C++; Lua is the glue that we use to compose and connect these components. Usually, the components (or objects) represent more concrete, low-level concepts (such as widgets and data structures) that are not subject to many changes during program development, and that take the bulk of the CPU time of the final program. Lua gives the final shape of the application, which will probably change a lot during the life cycle of the product. However, unlike other glue technologies, Lua is a full-fledged language as well. Therefore, we can use Lua not only to glue components, but also to adapt and reshape them, and to create completely new components.

Of course, Lua is not the only scripting language around. There are other languages that you can use for more or less the same purposes. Nevertheless, Lua offers a set of features that makes it your best choice for many tasks and gives it a unique profile:

Extensibility: Lua's extensibility is so remarkable that many people regard Lua not as a language, but as a kit for building domain-specific languages. We designed Lua from scratch to be extended, both through Lua code and through external C code. As a proof of concept, Lua implements most of its own basic functionality through external libraries. It is really easy to interface Lua with C/C++, and Lua has been used integrated with several other languages as well, such as Fortran, Java, Smalltalk, Ada, C#, and even with other scripting languages, such as Perl and Python.

Simplicity: Lua is a simple and small language. It has few (but powerful) concepts. This simplicity makes Lua easy to learn and contributes to its small size. Its complete distribution (source code, manual, plus binaries for some platforms) fits comfortably in a floppy disk.

Efficiency: Lua has a quite efficient implementation. Independent benchmarks show Lua as one of the fastest languages in the realm of scripting languages.

Portability: When we talk about portability, we are talking about running Lua on all platforms we have ever heard about: all flavors of UNIX and Windows, PlayStation, Xbox, Mac OS X and iOS, Android, Kindle Fire, NOOK, Haiku, QUALCOMM Brew, IBM mainframes, RISC OS, Symbian OS, Rabbit processors, Raspberry Pi, Arduino, and many more. The source code for each of these platforms is virtually the same. Lua does not use conditional compilation to adapt its code to different machines; instead, it sticks to the standard ANSI (ISO) C. This way, you do not usually need to adapt it to a new environment: if you have an ANSI C compiler, you just have to compile Lua, out of the box.

Audience

Lua users typically fall into three broad groups: those that use Lua already embedded in an application program, those that use Lua stand alone, and those that use Lua and C together.

Many people use Lua embedded in an application program, such as Adobe Lightroom, Nmap, or World of Warcraft. These applications use the Lua–C API to register new functions, to create new types, and to change the behavior of some language operations, configuring Lua for their specific domains. Frequently, the users of such applications do not even know that Lua is an independent language adapted for a particular domain. For instance, many developers of plug-ins for Lightroom do not know about other uses of the language;

Nmap users tend to think of Lua as the language of the Nmap Scripting Engine; players of World of Warcraft may regard Lua as a language exclusive to that game.

Lua is useful also as a stand-alone language, not only for text-processing and one-shot little programs, but increasingly for medium-to-large projects, too. For such uses, the main functionality of Lua comes from libraries. The standard libraries, for instance, offer basic pattern matching and other functions for string handling. As Lua improves its support for libraries, there has been a proliferation of external packages. Lua Rocks, a deployment and management system for Lua modules, currently features more than 150 packages.

Finally, there are those programmers that work on the other side of the bench, writing applications that use Lua as a C library. Those people will program more in C than in Lua, although they need a good understanding of Lua to create interfaces that are simple, easy to use, and well integrated with the language.

This book has much to offer to all these people. The first part covers the language itself, showing how we can explore all its potential. We focus on different language constructs and use numerous examples and exercises to show how to use them for practical tasks. Some chapters in this part cover basic concepts, such as control structures, while others cover topics more advanced, such as iterators and coroutines.

The second part is entirely devoted to tables, the sole data structure in Lua. Its chapters discuss data structures, persistence, packages, and object-oriented programming. There we will unveil the real power of the language.

The third part presents the standard libraries. This part is particularly useful for those that use Lua as a stand-alone language, although many other applications also incorporate all or part of the standard libraries. This part devotes one chapter to each standard library: the mathematical library, the bitwise library, the table library, the string library, the I/O library, the operating system library, and the debug library.

Finally, the last part of the book covers the API between Lua and C, for those that use C to get the full power of Lua. The flavor of this part is necessarily quite different from the rest of the book. There, we will be programming in C, not in Lua; therefore, we will be wearing a different hat. For some readers, the discussion of the C API may be of marginal interest; for others, it may be the most relevant part of this book.

About the Third Edition

This book is an updated and expanded version of the second edition of *Programming in Lua* (also known as the *PiL 2 book*). Although the book structure is virtually the same, this new edition has substantial new material.

First, I have updated the whole book to Lua 5.2. Of particular relevance is the chapter about environments, which was mostly rewritten. I also rewrote several examples to show how to benefit from the new features offered by Lua 5.2.

Nevertheless, I clearly marked the differences from Lua 5.1, so you can use the book for that version too.

Second, and more important, I have added exercises to all chapters of the book. These exercises range from simple questions about the language to full small-size projects. Several exercises illustrate important aspects of programming in Lua and are as important as the examples to expand your toolbox of useful techniques.

As we did with the first and second editions of *Programming in Lua*, we self-published this third edition. Despite the limited marketing, this avenue brings several benefits: we have total control over the book contents; we keep the full rights to offer the book in other forms; we have freedom to choose when to release another edition; and we can ensure that the book does not go out of print.

Other Resources

The reference manual is a must for anyone who wants to really learn a language. This book does not replace the Lua reference manual. Quite the opposite, they complement each other. The manual only describes Lua. It shows neither examples nor a rationale for the constructs of the language. On the other hand, it describes the whole language; this book skips over seldom-used dark corners of Lua. Moreover, the manual is the authoritative document about Lua. Wherever this book disagrees with the manual, trust the manual. To get the manual and more information about Lua, visit the Lua site at http://www.lua.org.

You can also find useful information at the Lua users' site, kept by the community of users at http://lua-users.org. Among other resources, it offers a tutorial, a list of third-party packages and documentation, and an archive of the official Lua mailing list.

This book describes Lua 5.2, although most of its contents also apply to Lua 5.1 and Lua 5.0. The few differences between Lua 5.2 and older Lua 5 versions are clearly marked in the text. If you are using a more recent version (released after the book), check the corresponding manual for occasional differences between versions. If you are using a version older than 5.2, this is a good time to consider an upgrade.

A Few Typographical Conventions

The book encloses "literal strings" between double quotes and single characters, such as 'a', between single quotes. Strings that are used as patterns are also enclosed between single quotes, like '[%w_]*'. The book uses a typewriter font both for chunks of code and for identifiers. For **reserved words**, it uses a boldface font. Larger chunks of code are shown in display style:

```
-- program "Hello World"
print("Hello World")          --> Hello World
```

The notation --> shows the output of a statement or, occasionally, the result of an expression:

```
print(10)      --> 10
13 + 3         --> 16
```

Because a double hyphen (--) starts a comment in Lua, there is no problem if you include these annotations in your programs. Finally, the book uses the notation <--> to indicate that something is equivalent to something else:

```
this      <-->      that
```

Running the Examples

You will need a Lua interpreter to run the examples in this book. Ideally, you should use Lua 5.2, but most of the examples run also on Lua 5.1 without modifications.

The Lua site (http://www.lua.org) keeps the source code for the interpreter. If you have a C compiler and a working knowledge of how to compile C code in your machine, you should try to install Lua from its source code; it is really easy. The *Lua Binaries* site (search for luabinaries) offers precompiled Lua interpreters for most major platforms. If you use Linux or another UNIX-like system, you may check the repository of your distribution; several distributions already offer a package with Lua. For Windows, a good option is *Lua for Windows* (search for luaforwindows), which is a "batteries-included environment" for Lua. It includes the interpreter and an integrated text editor, plus many libraries.

If you are using Lua embedded in an application, such as WoW or Nmap, you may need to refer to the application manual (or to a "local guru") to learn how to run your programs. Nevertheless, Lua is still the same language; most things that we will see in this book are valid regardless of how you are using Lua. Nevertheless, I recommend that you start your study of Lua using the stand-alone interpreter to run your first examples and experiments.

Acknowledgments

It is almost ten years since I published the first edition of this book. Several friends and institutions have helped me along this journey.

As always, Luiz Henrique de Figueiredo and Waldemar Celes, Lua coauthors, offered all kinds of help. André Carregal, Asko Kauppi, Brett Kapilik, Diego Nehab, Edwin Moragas, Fernando Jefferson, Gavin Wraith, John D. Ramsdell, and Norman Ramsey provided invaluable suggestions and useful insights for diverse editions of this book.

Luiza Novaes, head of the Arts & Design Department at PUC-Rio, managed to find some time in her busy schedule to create an ideal cover for this edition.

Lightning Source, Inc. proved a reliable and efficient option for printing and distributing the book. Without them, the option of self-publishing the book would not be an option.

The Center for Latin American Studies at Stanford University provided me with a much-needed break from regular work, in a stimulating environment, during which I did most of the work for this third edition.

I also would like to thank the Pontifical Catholic University of Rio de Janeiro (PUC-Rio) and the Brazilian National Research Council (CNPq) for their continuous support to my work.

Finally, I must express my deep gratitude to Noemi Rodriguez, for all kinds of help (technical and non-technical) and for illumining my life.

Part I

The Language

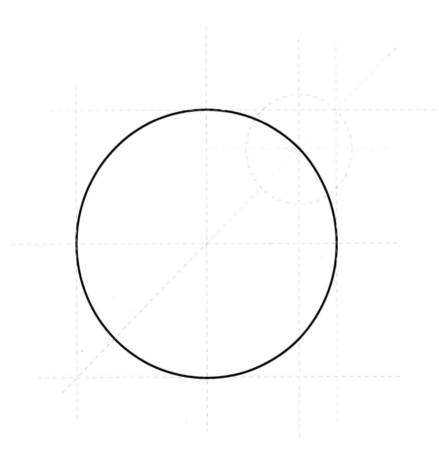

1
Getting Started

To keep with the tradition, our first program in Lua just prints "Hello World":

```
print("Hello World")
```

If you are using the stand-alone Lua interpreter, all you have to do to run your first program is to call the interpreter — usually named lua or lua5.2 — with the name of the text file that contains your program. If you save the above program in a file hello.lua, the following command should run it:

```
% lua hello.lua
```

As a more complex example, the next program defines a function to compute the factorial of a given number, asks the user for a number, and prints its factorial:

```
-- defines a factorial function
function fact (n)
  if n == 0 then
    return 1
  else
    return n * fact(n-1)
  end
end

print("enter a number:")
a = io.read("*n")          -- reads a number
print(fact(a))
```

3

1.1 Chunks

Each piece of code that Lua executes, such as a file or a single line in interactive mode, is called a *chunk*. A chunk is simply a sequence of commands (or statements).

Lua needs no separator between consecutive statements, but you can use a semicolon if you wish. My personal convention is to use semicolons only to separate two or more statements written in the same line. Line breaks play no role in Lua's syntax; for instance, the following four chunks are all valid and equivalent:

```
a = 1
b = a*2

a = 1;
b = a*2;

a = 1; b = a*2

a = 1  b = a*2    -- ugly, but valid
```

A chunk can be as simple as a single statement, such as in the "Hello World" example, or it can be composed of a mix of statements and function definitions (which are actually assignments, as we will see later), such as the factorial example. A chunk can be as large as you wish. Because Lua is used also as a data-description language, chunks with several megabytes are not uncommon. The Lua interpreter has no problems at all with large chunks.

Instead of writing your program to a file, you can run the stand-alone interpreter in interactive mode. If you call `lua` without any arguments, you will get its prompt:

```
% lua
Lua 5.2  Copyright (C) 1994-2012 Lua.org, PUC-Rio
>
```

Thereafter, each command that you type (such as `print "Hello World"`) executes immediately after you enter it. To exit the interactive mode and the interpreter, just type the end-of-file control character (`ctrl-D` in UNIX, `ctrl-Z` in Windows), or call the `exit` function, from the Operating System library — you have to type `os.exit()`.

In interactive mode, Lua usually interprets each line that you type as a complete chunk. However, if it detects that the line does not form a complete chunk, it waits for more input, until it has a complete chunk. This way, you can enter a multi-line definition, such as the `factorial` function, directly in interactive mode. However, it is usually more convenient to put such definitions in a file and then call Lua to run the file.

You can use the `-i` option to instruct Lua to start an interactive session after running the given chunk:

```
% lua -i prog
```

A command line like this one will run the chunk in file prog and then prompt you for interaction. This is especially useful for debugging and manual testing. At the end of this chapter, we will see other options for the stand-alone interpreter.

Another way to run chunks is with the dofile function, which immediately executes a file. For instance, suppose you have a file lib1.lua with the following code:

```
function norm (x, y)
  return (x^2 + y^2)^0.5
end

function twice (x)
  return 2*x
end
```

Then, in interactive mode, you can type

```
> dofile("lib1.lua")      -- load your library
> n = norm(3.4, 1.0)
> print(twice(n))         --> 7.0880180586677
```

The dofile function is useful also when you are testing a piece of code. You can work with two windows: one is a text editor with your program (in a file prog.lua, say) and the other is a console running Lua in interactive mode. After saving a modification in your program, you execute dofile("prog.lua") in the Lua console to load the new code; then you can exercise the new code, calling its functions and printing the results.

1.2 Some Lexical Conventions

Identifiers (or names) in Lua can be any string of letters, digits, and underscores, not beginning with a digit; for instance

```
i         j         i10       _ij
aSomewhatLongName   _INPUT
```

You should avoid identifiers starting with an underscore followed by one or more upper-case letters (e.g., _VERSION); they are reserved for special uses in Lua. Usually, I reserve the identifier _ (a single underscore) for dummy variables.

In older versions of Lua, the concept of what is a letter depended on the locale. However, such letters make your program unsuitable to run in systems that do not support that locale. Lua 5.2 accepts only the ranges A-Z and a-z as letters to be used in identifiers.

The following words are reserved; we cannot use them as identifiers:

```
and       break     do        else      elseif
end       false     goto      for       function
if        in        local     nil       not
or        repeat    return    then      true
until     while
```

Lua is case-sensitive: **and** is a reserved word, but And and AND are two other different identifiers.

A comment starts anywhere with a double hyphen (--) and runs until the end of the line. Lua also offers block comments, which start with --[[and run until the next]].[1] A common trick to comment out a piece of code is to enclose the code between --[[and --]], like here:

```
--[[
print(10)          -- no action (commented out)
--]]
```

To reactivate the code, we add a single hyphen to the first line:

```
---[[
print(10)          --> 10
--]]
```

In the first example, the --[[in the first line starts a block comment, and the double hyphen in the last line is still inside that comment. In the second example, the sequence ---[[starts an ordinary, single-line comment, so that the first and the last lines become independent comments. In this case, the print is outside comments.

1.3   Global Variables

Global variables do not need declarations; you simply use them. It is not an error to access a non-initialized variable; you just get the value nil as the result:

```
print(b)   --> nil
b = 10
print(b)   --> 10
```

If you assign nil to a global variable, Lua behaves as if the variable had never been used:

```
b = nil
print(b)   --> nil
```

After this assignment, Lua can eventually reclaim the memory used by the variable.

1.4   The Stand-Alone Interpreter

The stand-alone interpreter (also called lua.c due to its source file, or simply lua due to its executable) is a small program that allows the direct use of Lua. This section presents its main options.

---

[1]Block comments can be more complex than that, as we will see in Section 2.4.

When the interpreter loads a file, it ignores its first line if this line starts with a hash ('#'). This feature allows the use of Lua as a script interpreter in UNIX systems. If you start your script with something like

```
#!/usr/local/bin/lua
```

(assuming that the stand-alone interpreter is located at /usr/local/bin), or

```
#!/usr/bin/env lua
```

then you can call the script directly, without explicitly calling the Lua interpreter.

The usage of lua is

```
lua [options] [script [args]]
```

Everything is optional. As we have seen already, when we call lua without arguments the interpreter enters in interactive mode.

The -e option allows us to enter code directly into the command line, like here:

```
% lua -e "print(math.sin(12))"    --> -0.53657291800043
```

(UNIX needs the double quotes to stop the shell from interpreting the parentheses.)

The -l option loads a library. As we saw previously, -i enters interactive mode after running the other arguments. Therefore, the next call will load the lib library, then execute the assignment x=10, and finally present a prompt for interaction.

```
% lua -i -llib -e "x = 10"
```

In interactive mode, you can print the value of any expression by writing a line that starts with an equal sign followed by the expression:

```
> = math.sin(3)               --> 0.14112000805987
> a = 30
> = a                         --> 30
```

This feature helps to use Lua as a calculator.

Before running its arguments, the interpreter looks for an environment variable named LUA_INIT_5_2 or else, if there is no such variable, LUA_INIT. If there is one of these variables and its content is @*filename*, then the interpreter runs the given file. If LUA_INIT_5_2 (or LUA_INIT) is defined but it does not start with '@', then the interpreter assumes that it contains Lua code and runs it. LUA_INIT gives us great power when configuring the stand-alone interpreter, because we have the full power of Lua in the configuration. We can preload packages, change the path, define our own functions, rename or delete functions, and so on.

A script can retrieve its arguments in the predefined global variable arg. In a call like %lua script a b c, the interpreter creates the table arg with all the command-line arguments, before running the script. The script name goes into index 0, its first argument ("a" in the example) goes to index 1, and so on. Preceding options go to negative indices, as they appear before the script. For instance, consider this call:

```
% lua -e "sin=math.sin" script a b
```

The interpreter collects the arguments as follows:

```
arg[-3] = "lua"
arg[-2] = "-e"
arg[-1] = "sin=math.sin"
arg[0] = "script"
arg[1] = "a"
arg[2] = "b"
```

More often than not, a script uses only the positive indices (arg[1] and arg[2], in the example).

Since Lua 5.1, a script can also retrieve its arguments through a vararg expression. In the main body of a script, the expression ... (three dots) results in the arguments to the script. (We will discuss vararg expressions in Section 5.2.)

Exercises

Exercise 1.1: Run the factorial example. What happens to your program if you enter a negative number? Modify the example to avoid this problem.

Exercise 1.2: Run the twice example, both by loading the file with the -l option and with dofile. Which way do you prefer?

Exercise 1.3: Can you name other languages that use -- for comments?

Exercise 1.4: Which of the following strings are valid identifiers?

```
___    _end    End    end    until?    nil    NULL
```

Exercise 1.5: Write a simple script that prints its own name without knowing it in advance.

2

Types and Values

Lua is a dynamically typed language. There are no type definitions in the language; each value carries its own type.

There are eight basic types in Lua: *nil*, *boolean*, *number*, *string*, *userdata*, *function*, *thread*, and *table*. The type function gives the type name of any given value:

```
print(type("Hello world"))   --> string
print(type(10.4*3))          --> number
print(type(print))           --> function
print(type(type))            --> function
print(type(true))            --> boolean
print(type(nil))             --> nil
print(type(type(X)))         --> string
```

The last line will result in "string" no matter the value of X, because the result of type is always a string.

Variables have no predefined types; any variable can contain values of any type:

```
print(type(a))    --> nil    ('a' is not initialized)
a = 10
print(type(a))    --> number
a = "a string!!"
print(type(a))    --> string
a = print         -- yes, this is valid!
a(type(a))        --> function
```

Notice the last two lines: functions are first-class values in Lua; so, we can manipulate them like any other value. (We will see more about this facility in Chapter 6.)

Usually, when you use a single variable for different types, the result is messy code. However, sometimes the judicious use of this facility is helpful, for instance in the use of nil to differentiate a normal return value from an abnormal condition.

2.1 Nil

Nil is a type with a single value, **nil**, whose main property is to be different from any other value. Lua uses nil as a kind of non-value, to represent the absence of a useful value. As we have seen, a global variable has a nil value by default, before its first assignment, and you can assign nil to a global variable to delete it.

2.2 Booleans

The boolean type has two values, *false* and *true*, which represent the traditional boolean values. However, booleans do not hold a monopoly of condition values: in Lua, any value can represent a condition. Conditional tests (e.g., conditions in control structures) consider both the boolean **false** and nil as false and anything else as true. In particular, Lua considers both zero and the empty string as true in conditional tests.

Throughout this book, I will type "false" to mean any false value, that is, the boolean **false** or nil. When I mean specifically the boolean value, I will type "**false**". The same holds for "true" and "**true**".

2.3 Numbers

The number type represents real (double-precision floating-point) numbers. Lua has no integer type.

Some people fear that even a simple increment or comparison can go weird with floating-point numbers. Reality, however, is not like that. Virtually all platforms nowadays follow the IEEE 754 standard for floating-point representation. Following this standard, the only possible source of errors is a representation error, which happens when a number cannot be exactly represented. An operation rounds its result only if that result has no exact representation. Any operation with a result that has an exact representation must give that exact result.

The fact is that any integer up to 2^{53} (approximately 10^{16}) has an exact representation as a double-precision floating-point number. When you use a double to represent an integer, there is no rounding error at all, unless the number has an absolute value greater than 2^{53}. In particular, a Lua number can represent any 32-bit integer without rounding problems.

Of course, fractional numbers can have representation errors. The situation here is not different from what happens with pen and paper. If we want to write 1/7 in decimal, we will have to stop somewhere. If we use ten digits to represent a number, 1/7 becomes rounded to 0.142857142. If we compute 1/7*7 using ten digits, the result will be 0.999999994, which is different from 1. Moreover, numbers that have a finite representation in decimal can have an infinite representation in binary. For instance, 12.7-20+7.3 is not exactly zero when computed with doubles, because both 12.7 and 7.3 do not have an exact finite representation in binary (see Exercise 2.3).

Before we go on, remember: integers do have exact representations and therefore do not have rounding errors.

Most modern CPUs do floating-point arithmetic as fast as (or even faster than) integer arithmetic. Nevertheless, it is easy to compile Lua so that it uses another type for numbers, such as longs or single-precision floats. This is particularly useful for platforms without hardware support for floating point, such as embedded systems. See file luaconf.h in the distribution for details.

We can write numeric constants with an optional decimal part, plus an optional decimal exponent. Examples of valid numeric constants are:

```
4       0.4      4.57e-3      0.3e12      5E+20
```

Moreover, we can also write hexadecimal constants, prefixing them with 0x. Since Lua 5.2, hexadecimal constants can also have a fractional part and a binary exponent (prefixed by 'p' or 'P'), as in the following examples:

```
0xff (255)      0x1A3 (419)      0x0.2 (0.125)      0x1p-1 (0.5)
0xa.bp2 (42.75)
```

(For each constant, we added its decimal representation in parentheses.)

2.4 Strings

Strings in Lua have the usual meaning: a sequence of characters. Lua is eight-bit clean and its strings can contain characters with any numeric code, including embedded zeros. This means that you can store any binary data into a string. You can also store Unicode strings in any representation (UTF-8, UTF-16, etc.). The standard string library that comes with Lua offers no explicit support for those representations. Nevertheless, we can handle UTF-8 strings quite reasonably, as we will discuss in Section 21.7.

Strings in Lua are immutable values. You cannot change a character inside a string, as you can in C; instead, you create a new string with the desired modifications, as in the next example:

```
a = "one string"
b = string.gsub(a, "one", "another")   -- change string parts
print(a)        --> one string
print(b)        --> another string
```

Strings in Lua are subject to automatic memory management, like all other Lua objects (tables, functions, etc.). This means that you do not have to worry about allocation and deallocation of strings; Lua handles this for you. A string can contain a single letter or an entire book. Programs that manipulate strings with 100K or 1M characters are not unusual in Lua.

You can get the length of a string using the prefix operator '#' (called the *length operator*):

```
a = "hello"
print(#a)              --> 5
print(#"good\0bye")    --> 8
```

Literal strings

We can delimit literal strings by matching single or double quotes:

```
a = "a line"
b = 'another line'
```

They are equivalent; the only difference is that inside each kind of quote you can use the other quote without escapes.

As a matter of style, most programmers always use the same kind of quotes for the same kind of strings, where the "kinds" of strings depend on the program. For instance, a library that manipulates XML may reserve single-quoted strings for XML fragments, because those fragments often contain double quotes.

Strings in Lua can contain the following C-like escape sequences:

\a	bell
\b	back space
\f	form feed
\n	newline
\r	carriage return
\t	horizontal tab
\v	vertical tab
\\	backslash
\"	double quote
\'	single quote

The following examples illustrate their use:

```
> print("one line\nnext line\n\"in quotes\", 'in quotes'")
one line
next line
"in quotes", 'in quotes'

> print('a backslash inside quotes: \'\\\'')
a backslash inside quotes: '\'

> print("a simpler way: '\\'")
a simpler way: '\'
```

We can specify a character in a string also by its numeric value through the escape sequences *ddd* and \\x*hh*, where *ddd* is a sequence of up to three decimal digits and *hh* is a sequence of exactly two hexadecimal digits. As a somewhat complex example, the two literals "alo\n123\"" and '\97lo\10\04923"' have the same value, in a system using ASCII: 97 is the ASCII code for 'a', 10 is the code for newline, and 49 is the code for the digit '1'. (In this example we must write 49 with three digits, as \049, because it is followed by another digit; otherwise Lua would read the number as 492.) We can also write that same string as '\x61\x6c\x6f\x0a\x31\x32\x33\x22', representing each character by its hexadecimal code.

Long strings

We can delimit literal strings also by matching double square brackets, as we do with long comments. Literals in this bracketed form can run for several lines and do not interpret escape sequences. Moreover, this form ignores the first character of the string when this character is a newline. This form is especially convenient for writing strings that contain large pieces of code, as in the following example:

```
page = [[
<html>
<head>
  <title>An HTML Page</title>
</head>
<body>
  <a href="http://www.lua.org">Lua</a>
</body>
</html>
]]

write(page)
```

Sometimes, you may want to enclose a piece of code containing something like a=b[c[i]] (notice the]] in this code), or you may need to enclose some code that already has some code commented out. To handle such cases, you can add any number of equal signs between the two open brackets, as in [===[. After this change, the literal string ends only at the next closing brackets with the same number of equal signs in between (]===], in our example). The scanner ignores pairs of brackets with a different number of equal signs. By choosing an appropriate number of signs, you can enclose any literal string without having to add escapes into it.

This same facility is valid for comments, too. For instance, if you start a long comment with --[=[, it extends until the next]=]. This facility allows you easily to comment out a piece of code that contains parts already commented out.

Long strings are the ideal format to include literal text in your code, but you should not use them for non-text literals. Although literal strings in Lua can contain arbitrary characters, it is not a good idea to use them in your code: you may have problems with your text editor; moreover, end-of-line sequences like "\r\n" may change to "\n" when read. Instead, it is better to code arbitrary binary data using numeric escape sequences, either in decimal or in hexadecimal, such as "\x13\x01\xA1\xBB". However, this poses a problem for long strings, because they would result in quite long lines.

For those situations, Lua 5.2 offers the escape sequence \z: it skips all subsequent characters in the string until the first non-space character. The next example illustrates its use:

```
data = "\x00\x01\x02\x03\x04\x05\x06\x07\z
        \x08\x09\x0A\x0B\x0C\x0D\x0E\x0F"
```

The \z at the end of the first line skips the following end-of-line and the indentation of the next line, so that the byte \x07 is directly followed by \x08 in the resulting string.

Coercions

Lua provides automatic conversions between numbers and strings at run time. Any numeric operation applied to a string tries to convert the string to a number:

```
print("10" + 1)          --> 11
print("10 + 1")          --> 10 + 1
print("-5.3e-10"*"2")    --> -1.06e-09
print("hello" + 1)       -- ERROR (cannot convert "hello")
```

Lua applies such coercions not only in arithmetic operators, but also in other places that expect a number, such as the argument to math.sin.

Conversely, whenever Lua finds a number where it expects a string, it converts the number to a string:

```
print(10 .. 20)          --> 1020
```

(The .. is the string concatenation operator in Lua. When you write it right after a numeral, you must separate them with a space; otherwise, Lua thinks that the first dot is a decimal point.)

Today we are not sure that these automatic coercions were a good idea in the design of Lua. As a rule, it is better not to count on them. They are handy in a few places, but add complexity both to the language and to programs that use them. After all, strings and numbers are different things, despite these conversions. A comparison like 10=="10" is false, because 10 is a number and "10" is a string.

If you need to convert a string to a number explicitly, you can use the function tonumber, which returns nil if the string does not denote a proper number:

```
line = io.read()      -- read a line
n = tonumber(line)    -- try to convert it to a number
if n == nil then
  error(line .. " is not a valid number")
else
  print(n*2)
end
```

To convert a number to a string, you can call the function `tostring`, or concatenate the number with the empty string:

```
print(tostring(10) == "10")    --> true
print(10 .. "" == "10")        --> true
```

These conversions are always valid.

2.5 Tables

The table type implements associative arrays. An associative array is an array that can be indexed not only with numbers, but also with strings or any other value of the language, except nil.

Tables are the main (in fact, the only) data structuring mechanism in Lua, and a powerful one. We use tables to represent ordinary arrays, sets, records, and other data structures in a simple, uniform, and efficient way. Lua uses tables to represent packages and objects as well. When we write `io.read`, we think about "the `read` function from the `io` module". For Lua, this expression means "index the table `io` using the string `read` as the key".

Tables in Lua are neither values nor variables; they are *objects*. If you are familiar with arrays in Java or Scheme, then you have a fair idea of what I mean. You may think of a table as a dynamically allocated object; your program manipulates only references (or pointers) to them. Lua never does hidden copies or creation of new tables behind the scenes. Moreover, you do not have to declare a table in Lua; in fact, there is no way to declare one. You create tables by means of a *constructor expression*, which in its simplest form is written as {}:

```
a = {}                -- create a table and store its reference in 'a'
k = "x"
a[k] = 10             -- new entry, with key="x" and value=10
a[20] = "great"       -- new entry, with key=20 and value="great"
print(a["x"])    --> 10
k = 20
print(a[k])      --> "great"
a["x"] = a["x"] + 1     -- increments entry "x"
print(a["x"])    --> 11
```

A table is always anonymous. There is no fixed relationship between a variable that holds a table and the table itself:

```
a = {}
a["x"] = 10
b = a                -- 'b' refers to the same table as 'a'
print(b["x"])        --> 10
b["x"] = 20
print(a["x"])        --> 20
a = nil              -- only 'b' still refers to the table
b = nil              -- no references left to the table
```

When a program has no more references to a table, Lua's garbage collector will eventually delete the table and reuse its memory.

Each table can store values with different types of indices, and it grows as needed to accommodate new entries:

```
a = {}      -- empty table
-- create 1000 new entries
for i = 1, 1000 do a[i] = i*2 end
print(a[9])      --> 18
a["x"] = 10
print(a["x"])  --> 10
print(a["y"])  --> nil
```

Note the last line: like global variables, table fields evaluate to nil when not initialized. Also like global variables, you can assign nil to a table field to delete it. This is not a coincidence: Lua stores global variables in ordinary tables. We will discuss this subject further in Chapter 14.

To represent records, you use the field name as an index. Lua supports this representation by providing a.name as syntactic sugar for a["name"]. Therefore, we could write the last lines of the previous example in a cleaner manner as follows:

```
a.x = 10             -- same as a["x"] = 10
print(a.x)           -- same as print(a["x"])
print(a.y)           -- same as print(a["y"])
```

For Lua, the two forms are equivalent and can be intermixed freely. For a human reader, however, each form may signal a different intention. The dot notation clearly shows that we are using the table as a record, where we have some set of fixed, predefined keys. The string notation gives the idea that the table can have any string as a key, and that for some reason we are manipulating that specific key.

A common mistake for beginners is to confuse a.x with a[x]. The first form represents a["x"], that is, a table indexed by the string "x". The second form is a table indexed by the value of the variable x. See the difference:

```
a = {}
x = "y"
a[x] = 10                    -- put 10 in field "y"
print(a[x])    --> 10        -- value of field "y"
print(a.x)     --> nil       -- value of field "x" (undefined)
print(a.y)     --> 10        -- value of field "y"
```

To represent a conventional array or a list, you simply use a table with integer keys. There is neither a way nor a need to declare a size; you just initialize the elements you need:

```
-- read 10 lines, storing them in a table
a = {}
for i = 1, 10 do
  a[i] = io.read()
end
```

Given that you can index a table with any value, you can start the indices of an array with any number that pleases you. However, it is customary in Lua to start arrays with one (and not with zero, as in C) and several facilities in Lua stick to this convention.

Usually, when you manipulate a list you must know its length. It can be a constant or it can be stored somewhere. Often we store the length of a list in a non-numeric field of the table; for historical reasons, several programs use the field "n" for this purpose.

Often, however, the length is implicit. Remember that any non-initialized index results in nil; you can use this value as a sentinel to mark the end of the list. For instance, after you read 10 lines into a list, it is easy to know that its length is 10, because its numeric keys are $1, 2, \ldots, 10$. This technique only works when the list does not have *holes*, which are nil elements inside it. We call such a list without holes a *sequence*.

For sequences, Lua offers the length operator '#'. It returns the last index, or the length, of the sequence. For instance, you could print the lines read in the last example with the following code:

```
-- print the lines
for i = 1, #a do
  print(a[i])
end
```

Because we can index a table with any type, when indexing a table we have the same subtleties that arise in equality. Although we can index a table both with the number 0 and with the string "0", these two values are different and therefore denote different entries in a table. Similarly, the strings "+1", "01", and "1" all denote different entries. When in doubt about the actual types of your indices, use an explicit conversion to be sure:

```
i = 10; j = "10"; k = "+10"
a = {}
a[i] = "one value"
a[j] = "another value"
a[k] = "yet another value"
print(a[i])           --> one value
print(a[j])           --> another value
print(a[k])           --> yet another value
print(a[tonumber(j)]) --> one value
print(a[tonumber(k)]) --> one value
```

You can introduce subtle bugs in your program if you do not pay attention to this point.

2.6   Functions

Functions are first-class values in Lua: programs can store functions in variables, pass functions as arguments to other functions, and return functions as results. Such facilities give great flexibility to the language; a program can redefine a function to add new functionality, or simply erase a function to create a secure environment when running a piece of untrusted code (such as code received through a network). Moreover, Lua offers good support for functional programming, including nested functions with proper lexical scoping; just wait until Chapter 6. Finally, first-class functions play a key role in Lua's object-oriented facilities, as we will see in Chapter 16.

Lua can call functions written in Lua and functions written in C. Typically, we resort to C functions both to achieve better performance and to access facilities not easily accessible directly from Lua, such as operating-system facilities. All the standard libraries in Lua are written in C. They comprise functions for string manipulation, table manipulation, I/O, access to basic operating system facilities, mathematical functions, and debugging.

We will discuss Lua functions in Chapter 5 and C functions in Chapter 27.

2.7   Userdata and Threads

The userdata type allows arbitrary C data to be stored in Lua variables. It has no predefined operations in Lua, except assignment and equality test. Userdata are used to represent new types created by an application program or a library written in C; for instance, the standard I/O library uses them to represent open files. We will discuss more about userdata later, when we get to the C API.

We will explain the thread type in Chapter 9, where we discuss coroutines.

Exercises

Exercise 2.1: What is the value of the expression `type(nil)==nil`? (You can use Lua to check your answer.) Can you explain this result?

Exercise 2.2: Which of the following are valid numerals? What are their values?

```
.0e12    .e12    0.0e    0x12    0xABFG    0xA    FFFF    0xFFFFFFFF
0x    0x1P10    0.1e1    0x0.1p1
```

Exercise 2.3: The number 12.7 is equal to the fraction 127/10, where the denominator is a power of ten. Can you express it as a common fraction where the denominator is a power of two? What about the number 5.5?

Exercise 2.4: How can you embed the following piece of XML as a string in Lua?

```
<![CDATA[
  Hello world
]]>
```

Show at least two different ways.

Exercise 2.5: Suppose you need to format a long sequence of arbitrary bytes as a string literal in Lua. How would you do it? Consider issues like readability, maximum line length, and performance.

Exercise 2.6: Assume the following code:

```
a = {};   a.a = a
```

What would be the value of a.a.a.a? Is any a in that sequence somehow different from the others?

Now, add the next line to the previous code:

```
a.a.a.a = 3
```

What would be the value of a.a.a.a now?

3

Expressions

Expressions denote values. Expressions in Lua include the numeric constants and string literals, variables, unary and binary operations, and function calls. Expressions include also the unconventional function definitions and table constructors.

3.1 Arithmetic Operators

Lua supports the usual arithmetic operators: the binary '+' (addition), '-' (subtraction), '*' (multiplication), '/' (division), '^' (exponentiation), '%' (modulo), and the unary '-' (negation). All of them operate on real numbers. For instance, x^0.5 computes the square root of x, while x^(-1/3) computes the inverse of its cubic root.

The following rule defines the modulo operator:

```
a % b == a - math.floor(a/b)*b
```

For integer operands, it has the usual meaning, with the result always having the same sign as the second argument. For real operands, it has some extra uses. For instance, x%1 is the fractional part of x, and so x - x%1 is its integer part. Similarly, x - x%0.01 is x with exactly two decimal digits:

```
x = math.pi
print(x - x%0.01)        --> 3.14
```

As another example of the use of the modulo operator, suppose you want to check whether a vehicle turning a given angle will start to backtrack. If the angle is given in degrees, you can use the following formula:

```
local tolerance = 10
function isturnback (angle)
  angle = angle % 360
  return (math.abs(angle - 180) < tolerance)
end
```

This definition works even for negative angles:

```
print(isturnback(-180))          --> true
```

If we want to work with radians instead of degrees, we simply change the constants in our function:

```
local tolerance = 0.17
function isturnback (angle)
  angle = angle % (2*math.pi)
  return (math.abs(angle - math.pi) < tolerance)
end
```

The operation `angle%(2*math.pi)` is all we need to normalize any angle to a value in the interval $[0, 2\pi)$.

3.2   Relational Operators

Lua provides the following relational operators:

```
<    >    <=   >=   ==   ~=
```

All these operators always produce a boolean value.

The `==` operator tests for equality; the `~=` operator is the negation of equality. We can apply both operators to any two values. If the values have different types, Lua considers them not equal. Otherwise, Lua compares them according to their types. Specifically, nil is equal only to itself.

Lua compares tables and userdata by reference, that is, two such values are considered equal only if they are the very same object. For instance, after the code

```
a = {}; a.x = 1; a.y = 0
b = {}; b.x = 1; b.y = 0
c = a
```

you have `a==c` but `a~=b`.

We can apply the order operators only to two numbers or to two strings. Lua compares strings in alphabetical order, which follows the locale set for Lua. For instance, with a Portuguese Latin-1 locale, we have `"acai"<"açaí"<"acorde"`. Values other than numbers and strings can be compared only for equality (and inequality).

When comparing values with different types, you must be careful: remember that `"0"` is different from 0. Moreover, `2<15` is obviously true, but `"2"<"15"` is false (alphabetical order). To avoid inconsistent results, Lua raises an error when you mix strings and numbers in an order comparison, such as `2<"15"`.

3.3   Logical Operators

The logical operators are **and**, **or**, and **not**. Like control structures, all logical
operators consider both the boolean **false** and nil as false, and anything else
as true. The **and** operator returns its first argument if it is false; otherwise, it
returns its second argument. The **or** operator returns its first argument if it is
not false; otherwise, it returns its second argument:

```
print(4 and 5)          --> 5
print(nil and 13)       --> nil
print(false and 13)     --> false
print(4 or 5)           --> 4
print(false or 5)       --> 5
```

Both **and** and **or** use short-cut evaluation, that is, they evaluate their second
operand only when necessary. Short-cut evaluation ensures that expressions
like (type(v) == "table" and v.tag == "h1") do not cause run-time errors: Lua
will not try to evaluate v.tag when v is not a table.

A useful Lua idiom is x = x or v, which is equivalent to

```
if not x then x = v end
```

That is, it sets x to a default value v when x is not set (provided that x is not set
to **false**).

Another useful idiom is (a and b) or c, or simply a and b or c, because **and**
has a higher precedence than **or**. It is equivalent to the C expression a?b:c,
provided that b is not false. For instance, we can select the maximum of two
numbers x and y with a statement like

```
max = (x > y) and x or y
```

When x > y, the first expression of the **and** is true, so the **and** results in its second
expression (x), which is always true (because it is a number), and then the **or**
expression results in the value of its first expression, x. When x > y is false, the
and expression is false and so the **or** results in its second expression, y.

The **not** operator always returns a boolean value:

```
print(not nil)      --> true
print(not false)    --> true
print(not 0)        --> false
print(not not 1)    --> true
print(not not nil)  --> false
```

3.4   Concatenation

Lua denotes the string concatenation operator by .. (two dots). If any operand
is a number, Lua converts this number to a string. (Some languages use the '+'
operator for concatenation, but 3+5 is different from 3..5.)

```
print("Hello " .. "World")   --> Hello World
print(0 .. 1)                --> 01
print(000 .. 01)             --> 01
```

Remember that strings in Lua are immutable values. The concatenation operator always creates a new string, without any modification to its operands:

```
a = "Hello"
print(a .. " World")   --> Hello World
print(a)               --> Hello
```

3.5   The Length Operator

The length operator works on strings and tables. On strings, it gives the number
of bytes in the string. On tables, it gives the length of the *sequence* represented
by the table.

The length operator provides several common Lua idioms for manipulating
sequences:

```
print(a[#a])      -- prints the last value of sequence 'a'
a[#a] = nil       -- removes this last value
a[#a + 1] = v     -- appends 'v' to the end of the list
```

As we saw in the last chapter, the length operator is unpredictable for lists
with holes (nils). It only works for sequences, which we defined as lists without
holes. More precisely, a *sequence* is a table where the numeric keys comprise a
set $1, \ldots, n$ for some n. (Remember that any key with value nil is actually not in
the table.) In particular, a table with no numeric keys is a sequence with length
zero.

Over the years, there have been many proposals to extend the meaning of the
length operator to lists with holes, but this extension is easier said than done.
The problem is that, because a list is actually a table, the concept of "length"
is somewhat fuzzy. For instance, consider the list resulting from the following
code:

```
a = {}
a[1] = 1
a[2] = nil    -- does nothing, as a[2] is already nil
a[3] = 1
a[4] = 1
```

It is easy to say that the length of this list is four, and that is has a hole at
index 2. However, what can we say about the next similar example?

```
a = {}
a[1] = 1
a[10000] = 1
```

Should we consider a as a list with 10 000 elements, where 9 998 of them are nil?
Now, the program does this:

```
a[10000] = nil
```

What is the list length now? Should it be 9999, because the program deleted the last element? Or maybe still 10000, as the program only changed the last element to nil? Or should the length collapse to 1?

Another common proposal is to make the # operator return the total number of elements in the table. This semantics is clear and well defined, but not useful at all. Consider all previous examples and think how useful would be such operator for real algorithms over lists or arrays.

Yet more troubling are nils at the end of the list. What should be the length of the following list?

```
a = {10, 20, 30, nil, nil}
```

Remember that, for Lua, a field with nil is indistinct from an absent field. Therefore, the previous table is equal to {10, 20, 30}; its length is 3, not 5.

You may consider that a nil at the end of a list is a very special case. However, many lists are built by adding elements one by one. Any list with holes that was built that way must have had nils at its end along the way.

Most lists we use in our programs are sequences (e.g., a file line cannot be nil) and, therefore, most of the time the use of the length operator is safe. If you really need to handle lists with holes, you should store the length explicitly somewhere.

3.6 Precedence

Operator precedence in Lua follows the table below, from the higher to the lower priority:

```
              ^
       not   #     -  (unary)
       *     /     %
       +     -
       ..
       <     >     <=    >=    ~=    ==
       and
       or
```

All binary operators are left associative, except for '^' (exponentiation) and '..' (concatenation), which are right associative. Therefore, the following expressions on the left are equivalent to those on the right:

```
a+i < b/2+1          <-->    (a+i) < ((b/2)+1)
5+x^2*8              <-->    5+((x^2)*8)
a < y and y <= z    <-->    (a < y) and (y <= z)
-x^2                <-->    -(x^2)
x^y^z               <-->    x^(y^z)
```

When in doubt, always use explicit parentheses. It is easier than looking it up in the manual and you will probably have the same doubt when you read the code again.

3.7   Table Constructors

Constructors are expressions that create and initialize tables. They are a distinctive feature of Lua and one of its most useful and versatile mechanisms.

The simplest constructor is the empty constructor, {}, which creates an empty table; we have seen it before. Constructors also initialize lists. For instance, the statement

```
days = {"Sunday", "Monday", "Tuesday", "Wednesday",
        "Thursday", "Friday", "Saturday"}
```

will initialize days[1] with the string "Sunday" (the first element of the constructor has index 1, not 0), days[2] with "Monday", and so on:

```
print(days[4])   --> Wednesday
```

Lua also offers a special syntax to initialize a table record-like, as in the next example:

```
a = {x=10, y=20}
```

This previous line is equivalent to these commands:

```
a = {}; a.x=10; a.y=20
```

The original expression, however, is faster, because Lua creates the table already with the right size.

No matter what constructor we use to create a table, we can always add fields to and remove fields from the result:

```
w = {x=0, y=0, label="console"}
x = {math.sin(0), math.sin(1), math.sin(2)}
w[1] = "another field"    -- add key 1 to table 'w'
x.f = w                   -- add key "f" to table 'x'
print(w["x"])             --> 0
print(w[1])               --> another field
print(x.f[1])             --> another field
w.x = nil                 -- remove field "x"
```

However, as I just mentioned, creating a table with a proper constructor is more efficient, besides being more elegant.

We can mix record-style and list-style initializations in the same constructor:

```
polyline = {color="blue",
            thickness=2,
            npoints=4,
            {x=0,   y=0},     -- polyline[1]
            {x=-10, y=0},     -- polyline[2]
            {x=-10, y=1},     -- polyline[3]
            {x=0,   y=1}      -- polyline[4]
           }
```

The above example also illustrates how we can nest constructors to represent more complex data structures. Each of the elements polyline[i] is a table representing a record:

```
print(polyline[2].x)    --> -10
print(polyline[4].y)    --> 1
```

Those two constructor forms have their limitations. For instance, you cannot initialize fields with negative indices, nor with string indices that are not proper identifiers. For such needs, there is another, more general, format. In this format, we explicitly write the index to be initialized as an expression, between square brackets:

```
opnames = {["+"] = "add", ["-"] = "sub",
           ["*"] = "mul", ["/"] = "div"}

i = 20; s = "-"
a = {[i+0] = s, [i+1] = s..s, [i+2] = s..s..s}

print(opnames[s])    --> sub
print(a[22])         --> ---
```

This syntax is more cumbersome, but more flexible too: both the list-style and the record-style forms are special cases of this more general syntax. The constructor {x=0,y=0} is equivalent to {["x"]=0, ["y"]=0}, and the constructor {"r","g","b"} is equivalent to {[1]="r", [2]="g", [3]="b"}.

You can always put a comma after the last entry. These trailing commas are optional, but are always valid:

```
a = {[1]="red", [2]="green", [3]="blue",}
```

This flexibility frees programs that generate Lua constructors from the need to handle the last element as a special case.

Finally, you can always use a semicolon instead of a comma in a constructor. I usually reserve semicolons to delimit different sections in a constructor, for instance to separate its list part from its record part:

```
{x=10, y=45; "one", "two", "three"}
```

Exercises

Exercise 3.1: What will the following program print?

```
for i = -10, 10 do
  print(i, i % 3)
end
```

Exercise 3.2: What is the result of the expression 2^3^4? What about 2^-3^4?

Exercise 3.3: We can represent a polynomial $a_n x^n + a_{n-1} x^{n-1} + \ldots + a_1 x^1 + a_0$ in Lua as a list of its coefficients, such as $\{a_0, a_1, \ldots, a_n\}$.
   Write a function that receives a polynomial (represented as a table) and a value for x and returns the polynomial value.

Exercise 3.4: Can you write the function from the previous item so that it uses at most n additions and n multiplications (and no exponentiations)?

Exercise 3.5: How can you check whether a value is a boolean without using the type function?

Exercise 3.6: Consider the following expression:

```
(x and y and (not z)) or ((not y) and x)
```

Are the parentheses necessary? Would you recommend their use in that expression?

Exercise 3.7: What will the following script print? Explain.

```
sunday = "monday"; monday = "sunday"
t = {sunday = "monday", [sunday] = monday}
print(t.sunday, t[sunday], t[t.sunday])
```

Exercise 3.8: Suppose that you want to create a table that associates each escape sequence for strings (see Section 2.4) with its meaning. How could you write a constructor for that table?

4

Statements

Lua supports an almost conventional set of statements, similar to those in C or Pascal. The conventional statements include assignment, control structures, and procedure calls. Lua also supports some not so conventional statements, such as multiple assignments and local variable declarations.

4.1 Assignment

Assignment is the basic means of changing the value of a variable or a table field:

```
a = "hello" .. "world"
t.n = t.n + 1
```

Lua allows *multiple assignment*, which assigns a list of values to a list of variables in one step. Both lists have their elements separated by commas. For instance, in the assignment

```
a, b = 10, 2*x
```

the variable a gets the value 10 and b gets 2*x.

In a multiple assignment, Lua first evaluates all values and only then executes the assignments. Therefore, we can use a multiple assignment to swap two values, as in the following examples:

```
x, y = y, x            -- swap 'x' for 'y'
a[i], a[j] = a[j], a[i]  -- swap 'a[i]' for 'a[j]'
```

Lua always adjusts the number of values to the number of variables: when
the list of values is shorter than the list of variables, the extra variables receive
nil as their values; when the list of values is longer, the extra values are silently
discarded:

```
a, b, c = 0, 1
print(a, b, c)          --> 0   1   nil
a, b = a+1, b+1, b+2    -- value of b+2 is ignored
print(a, b)             --> 1   2
a, b, c = 0
print(a, b, c)          --> 0   nil   nil
```

The last assignment in the above example shows a common mistake. To initialize a set of variables, you must provide a value for each one:

```
a, b, c = 0, 0, 0
print(a, b, c)          --> 0   0   0
```

Actually, most of the previous examples are somewhat artificial. I seldom
use multiple assignment simply to write several unrelated assignments in one
line. In particular, a multiple assignment is not faster than its equivalent
single assignments. Nevertheless, often we really need multiple assignment. We
already saw an example, to swap two values. A more frequent use is to collect
multiple returns from function calls. As we will discuss in detail in Section 5.1,
a function call can return multiple values. In such cases, a single expression can
supply the values for several variables. For instance, in the assignment a, b=f()
the call to f returns two results: a gets the first and b gets the second.

4.2   Local Variables and Blocks

Besides global variables, Lua supports local variables. We create local variables
with the **local** statement:

```
j = 10          -- global variable
local i = 1     -- local variable
```

Unlike global variables, local variables have their scope limited to the block
where they are declared. A *block* is the body of a control structure, the body of a
function, or a chunk (the file or string where the variable is declared):

```
x = 10
local i = 1          -- local to the chunk

while i <= x do
  local x = i*2      -- local to the while body
  print(x)           --> 2, 4, 6, 8, ...
  i = i + 1
end
```

```
if i > 20 then
  local x            -- local to the "then" body
  x = 20
  print(x + 2)       -- (would print 22 if test succeeded)
else
  print(x)           --> 10  (the global one)
end

print(x)             --> 10  (the global one)
```

Beware that this example will not work as expected if you enter it in interactive mode. In interactive mode, each line is a chunk by itself (unless it is not a complete command). As soon as you enter the second line of the example (local i=1), Lua runs it and starts a new chunk in the next line. By then, the **local** declaration is already out of scope. To solve this problem, we can delimit the whole block explicitly, bracketing it with the keywords **do–end**. Once you enter the **do**, the command completes only at the corresponding **end**, so Lua does not execute each line by itself.

These **do** blocks are useful also when you need finer control over the scope of some local variables:

```
do
  local a2 = 2*a
  local d = (b^2 - 4*a*c)^(1/2)
  x1 = (-b + d)/a2
  x2 = (-b - d)/a2
end            -- scope of 'a2' and 'd' ends here
print(x1, x2)
```

It is good programming style to use local variables whenever possible. Local variables help you avoid cluttering the global environment with unnecessary names. Moreover, the access to local variables is faster than to global ones. Finally, a local variable vanishes as soon as its scope ends, allowing the garbage collector to release its value.

Lua handles local-variable declarations as statements. As such, you can write local declarations anywhere you can write a statement. The scope of the declared variables begins after the declaration and goes until the end of the block. Each declaration can include an initial assignment, which works the same way as a conventional assignment: extra values are thrown away; extra variables get nil. If a declaration has no initial assignment, it initializes all its variables with nil:

```
local a, b = 1, 10
if a < b then
  print(a)   --> 1
  local a    -- '= nil' is implicit
  print(a)   --> nil
end          -- ends the block started at 'then'
print(a, b)  --> 1   10
```

A common idiom in Lua is

```
local foo = foo
```

This code creates a local variable, foo, and initializes it with the value of the global variable foo. (The local foo becomes visible only *after* its declaration.) This idiom is useful when the chunk needs to preserve the original value of foo even if later some other function changes the value of the global foo; it also speeds up the access to foo.

Because many languages force you to declare all local variables at the beginning of a block (or a procedure), some people think it is a bad practice to use declarations in the middle of a block. Quite the opposite: by declaring a variable only when you need it, you seldom need to declare it without an initial value (and therefore you seldom forget to initialize it). Moreover, you shorten the scope of the variable, which increases readability.

4.3   Control Structures

Lua provides a small and conventional set of control structures, with **if** for conditional execution and **while**, **repeat**, and **for** for iteration. All control structures have an explicit terminator: **end** terminates **if**, **for** and **while** structures; **until** terminates **repeat** structures.

The condition expression of a control structure can result in any value. Remember that Lua treats as true all values different from **false** and nil. (In particular, Lua treats both zero and the empty string as true.)

if then else

An **if** statement tests its condition and executes its *then-part* or its *else-part* accordingly. The else-part is optional.

```
if a < 0 then a = 0 end

if a < b then return a else return b end

if line > MAXLINES then
  showpage()
  line = 0
end
```

To write nested **if**s you can use **elseif**. It is similar to an **else** followed by an **if**, but it avoids the need for multiple **end**s:

```
if op == "+" then
  r = a + b
elseif op == "-" then
  r = a - b
elseif op == "*" then
  r = a*b
elseif op == "/" then
  r = a/b
else
  error("invalid operation")
end
```

Because Lua has no switch statement, such chains are somewhat common.

while

As the name implies, a **while** loop repeats its body while a condition is true. As usual, Lua first tests the **while** condition; if the condition is false, then the loop ends; otherwise, Lua executes the body of the loop and repeats the process.

```
local i = 1
while a[i] do
  print(a[i])
  i = i + 1
end
```

repeat

As the name implies, a **repeat–until** statement repeats its body until its condition is true. This statement does the test after the body, so that it always executes the body at least once.

```
-- print the first non-empty input line
repeat
  line = io.read()
until line ~= ""
print(line)
```

Unlike in most other languages, in Lua the scope of a local variable declared inside the loop includes the condition:

```
local sqr = x/2
repeat
  sqr = (sqr + x/sqr)/2
  local error = math.abs(sqr^2 - x)
until error < x/10000       -- local 'error' still visible here
```

Numeric for

The **for** statement has two variants: the *numeric* **for** and the *generic* **for**.
   A numeric **for** has the following syntax:

```
for var = exp1, exp2, exp3 do
  <something>
end
```

This loop will execute *something* for each value of var from exp1 to exp2, using exp3 as the *step* to increment var. This third expression is optional; when absent, Lua assumes 1 as the step value. As typical examples of such loops, we have

```
for i = 1, f(x) do print(i) end

for i = 10, 1, -1 do print(i) end
```

If you want a loop without an upper limit, you can use the constant math.huge:

```
for i = 1, math.huge do
  if (0.3*i^3 - 20*i^2 - 500 >= 0) then
    print(i)
    break
  end
end
```

   The **for** loop has some subtleties that you should learn in order to make good use of it. First, all three expressions are evaluated once, before the loop starts. For instance, in our first example, Lua calls f(x) only once. Second, the control variable is a local variable automatically declared by the **for** statement, and it is visible only inside the loop. A typical mistake is to assume that the variable still exists after the loop ends:

```
for i = 1, 10 do print(i) end
max = i         -- probably wrong! 'i' here is global
```

If you need the value of the control variable after the loop (usually when you break the loop), you must save its value into another variable:

```
-- find a value in a list
local found = nil
for i = 1, #a do
  if a[i] < 0 then
    found = i        -- save value of 'i'
    break
  end
end
print(found)
```

Third, you should never change the value of the control variable: the effect of such changes is unpredictable. If you want to end a **for** loop before its normal termination, use **break** (as we did in the previous example).

Generic for

The generic **for** loop traverses all values returned by an iterator function:

```
-- print all values of table 't'
for k, v in pairs(t) do print(k, v) end
```

This example uses pairs, a handy iterator function to traverse a table provided by the basic Lua library> For each step in that loop, k gets a key, while v gets the value associated with this key.

Despite its apparent simplicity, the generic **for** is powerful. With proper iterators, we can traverse almost anything in a readable fashion. The standard libraries provide several iterators, which allow us to iterate over the lines of a file (io.lines), the pairs of a table (pairs), the entries of a sequence (ipairs), the words of a string (string.gmatch), and so on.

Of course, we can write our own iterators. Although the use of the generic **for** is easy, the task of writing iterator functions has its subtleties; so, we will cover this topic later, in Chapter 7.

The generic loop shares two properties with the numeric loop: the loop variables are local to the loop body and you should never assign any value to them.

Let us see a more concrete example of the use of a generic **for**. Suppose you have a table with the names of the days of the week:

```
days = {"Sunday", "Monday", "Tuesday", "Wednesday",
        "Thursday", "Friday", "Saturday"}
```

Now you want to translate a name into its position in the week. You can search the table, looking for the given name. As you will learn soon, however, you seldom do searches in Lua. A more efficient approach is to build a reverse table, say revDays, which has the names as indices and the numbers as values. This table would look like this:

```
revDays = {["Sunday"] = 1,   ["Monday"] = 2,
           ["Tuesday"] = 3,   ["Wednesday"] = 4,
           ["Thursday"] = 5, ["Friday"] = 6,
           ["Saturday"] = 7}
```

Then, all you have to do to find the order of a name is to index this reverse table:

```
x = "Tuesday"
print(revDays[x])     --> 3
```

Of course, we do not need to declare the reverse table manually. We can build it automatically from the original one:

```
revDays = {}
for k,v in pairs(days) do
  revDays[v] = k
end
```

The loop will do the assignment for each element of days, with the variable k getting the key (1, 2, ...) and v the value ("Sunday", "Monday", ...).

4.4   break, return, and goto

The **break** and **return** statements allow us to jump out of a block. The **goto** statement allows us to jump to almost any point in a function.

We use the **break** statement to finish a loop. This statement breaks the inner loop (**for**, **repeat**, or **while**) that contains it; it cannot be used outside a loop. After the break, the program continues running from the point immediately after the broken loop.

A **return** statement returns occasional results from a function or simply finishes the function. There is an implicit return at the end of any function, so you do not need to write one if your function ends naturally, without returning any value.

For syntactic reasons, a **return** can appear only as the last statement of a block: in other words, as the last statement in your chunk or just before an **end**, an **else**, or an **until**. For instance, in the next example, **return** is the last statement of the **then** block.

```
local i = 1
while a[i] do
  if a[i] == v then return i end
  i = i + 1
end
```

Usually, these are the places where we use a **return**, because any other statement following it would be unreachable. Sometimes, however, it may be useful to write a **return** in the middle of a block; for instance, you may be debugging a function and want to avoid its execution. In such cases, you can use an explicit **do** block around the statement:

```
function foo ()
  return                --<< SYNTAX ERROR
  -- 'return' is the last statement in the next block
  do return end         -- OK
  <other statements>
end
```

A **goto** statement jumps the execution of a program to a corresponding label. There has been a long going debate about goto, with some people arguing even today that they are harmful to programming and should be banned from programming languages. Nonetheless, several current languages offer goto, with good reason. They are a powerful mechanism and, when used with care, can only improve the quality of your code.

In Lua, the syntax for a goto statement is quite conventional: it is the reserved word **goto** followed by the label name, which can be any valid identifier. The syntax for a label is a little more convoluted: it has two colons followed by the label name followed by more two colons, like in ::name::. This convolution is intentional, to make programmers think twice before using a goto.

Lua poses some restrictions to where you can jump with a goto. First, labels follow the usual visibility rules, so you cannot jump into a block (because a label inside a block is not visible outside it). Second, you cannot jump out of a function. (Note that the first rule already excludes the possibility of jumping *into* a function.) Third, you cannot jump into the scope of a local variable.

A typical and well-behaved use of a goto is to simulate some construction that you learned from another language but that is absent from Lua, such as continue, multi-level break, multi-level continue, redo, local error handling, etc. A continue statement is simply a goto to a label at the end of a loop block; a redo statement jumps to the beginning of the block:

```
while some_condition do
  ::redo::
  if some_other_condition then goto continue
  else if yet_another_condition then goto redo
  end
  <some code>
  ::continue::
end
```

A useful detail in the specification of Lua is that the scope of a local variable ends on the last *non-void* statement of the block where the variable is defined; labels are considered void statements. To see the usefulness of this detail, consider the next fragment:

```
while some_condition do
  if some_other_condition then goto continue end
  local var = something
  <some code>
  ::continue::
end
```

You may think that this goto jumps into the scope of variable var. However, the continue label appears after the last non-void statement of the block, and therefore it is not inside the scope of var.

The goto is also useful to write state machines. As an example, Listing 4.1 shows a program that checks whether its input has an even number of zeros. There are better ways to write this specific program, but this technique is useful if you want to translate a finite automata into Lua code automatically (think about dynamic code generation).

As another example, let us consider a simple maze game. The maze has several rooms, each with up to four doors: north, south, east, and west. At each step, the user enters a movement direction. If there is a door in this direction, the user goes to the corresponding room; otherwise, the program prints a warning. The goal is to go from an initial room to a final room.

This game is a typical state machine, where the current room is the state. We can implement this maze with one block for each room, using a goto to move from one room to another. Listing 4.2 shows how we could write a small maze with four rooms.

For this simple game, you may find that a data-driven program, where you describe the rooms and movements with tables, is a better design. However, if

Listing 4.1. An example of a state machine with **goto**:

```
::s1:: do
  local c = io.read(1)
  if c == '0' then goto s2
  elseif c == nil then print'ok'; return
  else goto s1
  end
end

::s2:: do
  local c = io.read(1)
  if c == '0' then goto s1
  elseif c == nil then print'not ok'; return
  else goto s2
  end
end

goto s1
```

the game has several special situations in each room, then this state-machine design is quite appropriate.

Exercises

Exercise 4.1:   Most languages with a C-like syntax do not offer an **elseif** construct. Why does Lua need this construct more than those languages?

Exercise 4.2:   Describe four different ways to write an unconditional loop in Lua. Which one do you prefer?

Exercise 4.3:   Many people argue that **repeat–until** is seldom used, and therefore it should not be present in a minimalistic language like Lua. What do you think?

Exercise 4.4:   Rewrite the state machine of Listing 4.2 without using goto.

Exercise 4.5:   Can you explain why Lua has the restriction that a goto cannot jump out of a function? (Hint: how would you implement that feature?)

Exercise 4.6:   Assuming that a goto could jump out of a function, explain what the program in Listing 4.3 would do. (Try to reason about the label using the same scoping rules used for local variables.)

Listing 4.2. A maze game:

```lua
goto room1        -- initial room

::room1:: do
  local move = io.read()
  if move == "south" then goto room3
  elseif move == "east" then goto room2
  else
    print("invalid move")
    goto room1        -- stay in the same room
  end
end

::room2:: do
  local move = io.read()
  if move == "south" then goto room4
  elseif move == "west" then goto room1
  else
    print("invalid move")
    goto room2
  end
end

::room3:: do
  local move = io.read()
  if move == "north" then goto room1
  elseif move == "east" then goto room4
  else
    print("invalid move")
    goto room3
  end
end

::room4:: do
  print("Congratulations, you won!")
end
```

Listing 4.3. A strange (and invalid) use of a **goto**:

```
function getlabel ()
  return function () goto L1 end
 ::L1::
  return 0
end

function f (n)
  if n == 0 then return getlabel()
  else
    local res = f(n - 1)
    print(n)
    return res
  end
end

x = f(10)
x()
```

5

Functions

Functions are the main mechanism for abstraction of statements and expressions in Lua. Functions can both carry out a specific task (what is sometimes called a *procedure* or a *subroutine* in other languages) or compute and return values. In the first case, we use a function call as a statement; in the second case, we use it as an expression:

```
print(8*9, 9/8)
a = math.sin(3) + math.cos(10)
print(os.date())
```

In both cases, a list of arguments enclosed in parentheses denotes the call; if the function call has no arguments, we still must write an empty list () to denote the call. There is a special case to this rule: if the function has one single argument and that argument is either a literal string or a table constructor, then the parentheses are optional:

```
print "Hello World"      <-->      print("Hello World")
dofile 'a.lua'           <-->      dofile ('a.lua')
print [[a multi-line     <-->      print([[a multi-line
 message]]                          message]])
f{x=10, y=20}            <-->      f({x=10, y=20})
type{}                   <-->      type({})
```

Lua also offers a special syntax for object-oriented calls, the colon operator. An expression like o:foo(x) is just another way to write o.foo(o, x), that is, to call o.foo adding o as a first extra argument. In Chapter 16, we will discuss such calls (and object-oriented programming) in more detail.

A Lua program can use functions defined both in Lua and in C (or in any other language used by the host application). For instance, all functions from the standard Lua library are written in C. However, when calling a function, there is no difference between functions defined in Lua and functions defined in C.

As we have seen in other examples, a function definition has a conventional syntax, like here:

```
-- add the elements of sequence 'a'
function add (a)
  local sum = 0
  for i = 1, #a do
    sum = sum + a[i]
  end
  return sum
end
```

In this syntax, a function definition has a *name* (add, in the example), a list of *parameters*, and a *body*, which is a list of statements.

Parameters work exactly as local variables, initialized with the values of the arguments passed in the function call. You can call a function with a number of arguments different from its number of parameters. Lua adjusts the number of arguments to the number of parameters, as it does in a multiple assignment: extra arguments are thrown away; extra parameters get nil. For instance, consider the next function:

```
function f (a, b) print(a, b) end
```

It has the following behavior:

```
f(3)          --> 3     nil
f(3, 4)       --> 3     4
f(3, 4, 5)    --> 3     4        (5 is discarded)
```

Although this behavior can lead to programming errors (easily spotted at run time), it is also useful, especially for default arguments. For instance, consider the following function, to increment a global counter:

```
function incCount (n)
  n = n or 1
  count = count + n
end
```

This function has 1 as its default argument; that is, the call incCount(), without arguments, increments count by one. When you call incCount(), Lua first initializes n with nil; the or expression results in its second operand and, as a result, Lua assigns a default 1 to n.

5.1 Multiple Results

An unconventional, but quite convenient feature of Lua is that functions can return multiple results. Several predefined functions in Lua return multiple values. An example is the `string.find` function, which locates a pattern in a string. This function returns two indices when it finds the pattern: the index of the character where the pattern match starts and the one where it ends. A multiple assignment allows the program to get both results:

```
s, e = string.find("hello Lua users", "Lua")
print(s, e)   --> 7    9
```

(Note that the first character of a string has index 1.)

Functions that we write in Lua also can return multiple results, by listing them all after the **return** keyword. For instance, a function to find the maximum element in a sequence can return both the maximum value and its location:

```
function maximum (a)
  local mi = 1          -- index of the maximum value
  local m = a[mi]       -- maximum value
  for i = 1, #a do
    if a[i] > m then
      mi = i; m = a[i]
    end
  end
  return m, mi
end

print(maximum({8,10,23,12,5}))    --> 23    3
```

Lua always adjusts the number of results from a function to the circumstances of the call. When we call a function as a statement, Lua discards all results from the function. When we use a call as an expression, Lua keeps only the first result. We get all results only when the call is the last (or the only) expression in a list of expressions. These lists appear in four constructions in Lua: multiple assignments, arguments to function calls, table constructors, and **return** statements. To illustrate all these cases, we will assume the following definitions for the next examples:

```
function foo0 () end               -- returns no results
function foo1 () return "a" end    -- returns 1 result
function foo2 () return "a", "b" end   -- returns 2 results
```

In a multiple assignment, a function call as the last (or only) expression produces as many results as needed to match the variables:

```
x,y = foo2()        -- x="a", y="b"
x = foo2()          -- x="a", "b" is discarded
x,y,z = 10,foo2()   -- x=10, y="a", z="b"
```

If a function has no results, or not as many results as we need, Lua produces nils for the missing values:

```
x,y = foo0()        -- x=nil, y=nil
x,y = foo1()        -- x="a", y=nil
x,y,z = foo2()      -- x="a", y="b", z=nil
```

A function call that is not the last element in the list always produces exactly one result:

```
x,y = foo2(), 20        -- x="a", y=20
x,y = foo0(), 20, 30    -- x=nil, y=20, 30 is discarded
```

When a function call is the last (or the only) argument to another call, all results from the first call go as arguments. We have seen examples of this construction already, with print. Because the print function can receive a variable number of arguments, the statement print(g()) prints all results returned by g.

```
print(foo0())          -->
print(foo1())          --> a
print(foo2())          --> a    b
print(foo2(), 1)       --> a    1
print(foo2() .. "x")   --> ax          (see next)
```

When the call to foo2 appears inside an expression, Lua adjusts the number of results to one; so, in the last line, the concatenation uses only the "a".

If we write f(g()) and f has a fixed number of arguments, Lua adjusts the number of results of g to the number of parameters of f, as we saw previously.

A constructor also collects all results from a call, without any adjustments:

```
t = {foo0()}           -- t = {}  (an empty table)
t = {foo1()}           -- t = {"a"}
t = {foo2()}           -- t = {"a", "b"}
```

As always, this behavior happens only when the call is the last expression in the list; calls in any other position produce exactly one result:

```
t = {foo0(), foo2(), 4}    -- t[1] = nil, t[2] = "a", t[3] = 4
```

Finally, a statement like return f() returns all values returned by f:

```
function foo (i)
  if i == 0 then return foo0()
  elseif i == 1 then return foo1()
  elseif i == 2 then return foo2()
  end
end

print(foo(1))    --> a
print(foo(2))    --> a  b
print(foo(0))    -- (no results)
print(foo(3))    -- (no results)
```

You can force a call to return exactly one result by enclosing it in an extra pair of parentheses:

```
print((foo0()))          --> nil
print((foo1()))          --> a
print((foo2()))          --> a
```

Beware that a **return** statement does not need parentheses around the returned value; any pair of parentheses placed there counts as an extra pair. Therefore, a statement like return(f(x)) always returns one single value, no matter how many values f returns. Sometimes this is what you want, sometimes not.

A special function with multiple returns is table.unpack. It receives an array and returns as results all elements from the array, starting from index 1:

```
print(table.unpack{10,20,30})     --> 10   20   30
a,b = table.unpack{10,20,30}      -- a=10, b=20, 30 is discarded
```

An important use for unpack is in a generic call mechanism. A generic call mechanism allows you to call any function, with any arguments, dynamically. In ANSI C, for instance, there is no way to code a generic call. You can declare a function that receives a variable number of arguments (with stdarg.h) and you can call a variable function, using pointers to functions. However, you cannot call a function with a variable number of arguments: each call you write in C has a fixed number of arguments, and each argument has a fixed type. In Lua, if you want to call a variable function f with variable arguments in an array a, you simply write this:

```
f(table.unpack(a))
```

The call to unpack returns all values in a, which become the arguments to f. For instance, consider the following call:

```
print(string.find("hello", "ll"))
```

You can dynamically build an equivalent call with the following code:

```
f = string.find
a = {"hello", "ll"}

print(f(table.unpack(a)))
```

Usually, unpack uses the length operator to know how many elements to return, so it works only on proper sequences. If needed, you can provide explicit limits to it:

```
print(table.unpack({"Sun", "Mon", "Tue", "Wed"}, 2, 3))
    --> Mon      Tue
```

Although the predefined unpack function is written in C, we could write it also in Lua, using recursion:

```
function unpack (t, i, n)
  i = i or 1
  n = n or #t
  if i <= n then
    return t[i], unpack(t, i + 1, n)
  end
end
```

The first time we call it, with a single argument, i gets 1 and n gets the length of the sequence. Then the function returns t[1] followed by all results from unpack(t,2,n), which in turn returns t[2] followed by all results from unpack(t,3,n), and so on, stopping after n elements.

5.2 Variadic Functions

A function in Lua can be *variadic*, that is, it can receive a variable number of arguments. For instance, we have already called print with one, two, and more arguments. Although print is defined in C, we can define variadic functions in Lua, too.

As a simple example, the following function returns the summation of all its arguments:

```
function add (...)
  local s = 0
  for i, v in ipairs{...} do
    s = s + v
  end
  return s
end

print(add(3, 4, 10, 25, 12))     --> 54
```

The three dots (...) in the parameter list indicate that the function is variadic. When we call this function, Lua collects all its arguments internally; we call these collected arguments the *extra arguments* of the function. A function can access its extra arguments using again the three dots, now as an expression. In our example, the expression {...} results in an array with all collected arguments. The function then traverses the array to add its elements.

We call the expression ... a *vararg expression*. It behaves like a multiple return function, returning all extra arguments of the current function. For instance, the command print(...) prints all extra arguments of the function. Likewise, the next command creates two local variables with the values of the first two optional arguments (or nil if there are no such arguments):

```
local a, b = ...
```

Actually, we can emulate the usual parameter-passing mechanism of Lua translating

```
function foo (a, b, c)
```

to

```
function foo (...)
  local a, b, c = ...
```

Those who fancy Perl's parameter-passing mechanism may enjoy this second form.

A function like the next one simply returns all arguments in its call:

```
function id (...) return ... end
```

It is a multi-value identity function. The next function behaves exactly like another function foo, except that before the call it prints a message with its arguments:

```
function foo1 (...)
  print("calling foo:", ...)
  return foo(...)
end
```

This is a useful trick for tracing calls to a specific function.

Let us see another useful example. Lua provides separate functions for formatting text (string.format) and for writing text (io.write). It is straightforward to combine both functions into a single variadic function:

```
function fwrite (fmt, ...)
  return io.write(string.format(fmt, ...))
end
```

Notice the presence of a fixed parameter fmt before the dots. Variadic functions can have any number of fixed parameters before the variadic part. Lua assigns the first arguments to these parameters; the rest (if any) goes as extra arguments. Below we show some examples of calls and the corresponding parameter values:

```
CALL                    PARAMETERS

fwrite()                fmt = nil, no extra arguments
fwrite("a")             fmt = "a", no extras
fwrite("%d%d", 4, 5)    fmt = "%d%d", extras = 4 and 5
```

(Note that the call fwrite() raises an error, because string.format needs a string as its first argument.)

To iterate over its extra arguments, a function can use the expression {...} to collect them all in a table, as we did in our definition of add.

In the rare occasions when the extra arguments can be valid nils, however, the table created with {...} may not be a proper sequence. For instance, there is no way to detect in such a table whether there were trailing nils in the original arguments. For these occasions, Lua offers the table.pack function.[1] This function receives any number of arguments and returns a new table with all its arguments, just like {...}; but this table has also an extra field "n", with the total number of arguments. The following function uses table.pack to test whether none of its arguments is nil:

---

[1]This function is new in Lua 5.2.

```
function nonils (...)
  local arg = table.pack(...)
  for i = 1, arg.n do
    if arg[i] == nil then return false end
  end
  return true
end

print(nonils(2,3,nil))    --> false
print(nonils(2,3))        --> true
print(nonils())           --> true
print(nonils(nil))        --> false
```

Remember, however, that {...} is cleaner and faster than `table.pack(...)` when the extra arguments cannot be nil.

5.3   Named Arguments

The parameter passing mechanism in Lua is *positional*: when we call a function, arguments match parameters by their positions. The first argument gives the value to the first parameter, and so on. Sometimes, however, it is useful to specify the arguments by name. To illustrate this point, let us consider the function `os.rename` (from the os library), which renames a file. Quite often, we forget which name comes first, the new or the old; therefore, we may want to redefine this function to receive two named arguments:

```
-- invalid code
rename(old="temp.lua", new="temp1.lua")
```

Lua has no direct support for this syntax, but we can have the same final effect, with a small syntax change. The idea here is to pack all arguments into a table and use this table as the only argument to the function. The special syntax that Lua provides for function calls, with just one table constructor as argument, helps the trick:

```
rename{old="temp.lua", new="temp1.lua"}
```

Accordingly, we define `rename` with only one parameter and get the actual arguments from this parameter:

```
function rename (arg)
  return os.rename(arg.old, arg.new)
end
```

This style of parameter passing is especially helpful when the function has many parameters and most of them are optional. For instance, a function that creates a new window in a GUI library may have dozens of arguments, most of them optional, which are best specified by names:

Listing 5.1. A function with named optional parameters:

```
function Window (options)
  -- check mandatory options
  if type(options.title) ~= "string" then
    error("no title")
  elseif type(options.width) ~= "number" then
    error("no width")
  elseif type(options.height) ~= "number" then
    error("no height")
  end

  -- everything else is optional
  _Window(options.title,
          options.x or 0,      -- default value
          options.y or 0,      -- default value
          options.width, options.height,
          options.background or "white",   -- default
          options.border      -- default is false (nil)
         )
end
```

Graphic window/widget (Tkinter-esque) stuff dues exist. fyi

```
w = Window{ x=0, y=0, width=300, height=200,
            title = "Lua", background="blue",
            border = true
          }
```

The Window function then has the freedom to check for mandatory arguments, add default values, and the like. Assuming a primitive _Window function that actually creates the new window (and that needs all arguments in a specific order), we could define Window as in Listing 5.1.

Exercises

Exercise 5.1: Write a function that receives an arbitrary number of strings and returns all of them concatenated together.

Exercise 5.2: Write a function that receives an array and prints all elements in that array. Consider the pros and cons of using table.unpack in this function.

Exercise 5.3: Write a function that receives an arbitrary number of values and returns all of them, except the first one.

Exercise 5.4: Write a function that receives an array and prints all combinations of the elements in the array. (Hint: you can use the recursive formula for combination: $C(n,m) = C(n-1,m-1) + C(n-1,m)$. To generate all $C(n,m)$ combinations of n elements in groups of size m, you first add the first element to the result and then generate all $C(n-1, m-1)$ combinations of the remaining elements in the remaining slots; then you remove the first element from the result and then generate all $C(n-1, m)$ combinations of the remaining elements in the free slots. When n is smaller than m, there are no combinations. When m is zero, there is only one combination, which uses no elements.)

6

More about Functions

Functions in Lua are first-class values with proper lexical scoping.

What does it mean for functions to be "first-class values"? It means that, in Lua, a function is a value with the same rights as conventional values like numbers and strings. We can store functions in variables (both global and local) and in tables, we can pass functions as arguments to and return them from other functions.

What does it mean for functions to have "lexical scoping"? It means that functions can access variables of their enclosing functions.[1] As we will see in this chapter, this apparently innocuous property brings great power to the language, because it allows us to apply in Lua many powerful programming techniques from the functional-language world. Even if you have no interest at all in functional programming, it is worth learning a little about how to explore these techniques, because they can make your programs smaller and simpler.

A somewhat confusing notion in Lua is that functions, like all other values, are anonymous; they do not have names. When we talk about a function name, such as print, we are actually talking about a variable that holds that function. Like any other variable holding any other value, we can manipulate such variables in many ways. The following example, although a little silly, shows the point:

```
a = {p = print}
a.p("Hello World")    --> Hello World
print = math.sin      -- 'print' now refers to the sine function
a.p(print(1))         --> 0.841470
sin = a.p             -- 'sin' now refers to the print function
sin(10, 20)           --> 10       20
```

---

[1]It also means that Lua properly contains the lambda calculus.

(Later we will see useful applications for this facility.)

If functions are values, are there expressions that create functions? Yes. In fact, the usual way to write a function in Lua, such as

```
function foo (x)  return 2*x  end
```

is just an instance of what we call *syntactic sugar*; it is simply a pretty way to write the following code:

```
foo = function (x)  return 2*x  end
```

Therefore, a function definition is in fact a statement (an assignment, more specifically) that creates a value of type "function" and assigns it to a variable. We can see the expression function (x) *body* end as a function constructor, just as {} is a table constructor. We call the result of such function constructors an *anonymous function*. Although we often assign functions to global variables, giving them something like a name, there are several occasions when functions remain anonymous. Let us see some examples.

The table library provides a function table.sort, which receives a table and sorts its elements. Such a function must allow unlimited variations in the sort order: ascending or descending, numeric or alphabetical, tables sorted by a key, and so on. Instead of trying to provide all kinds of options, sort provides a single optional parameter, which is the *order function*: a function that receives two elements and returns whether the first must come before the second in the sorted list. For instance, suppose we have a table of records like this:

```
network = {
  {name = "grauna",  IP = "210.26.30.34"},
  {name = "arraial", IP = "210.26.30.23"},
  {name = "lua",     IP = "210.26.23.12"},
  {name = "derain",  IP = "210.26.23.20"},
}
```

If we want to sort the table by the field name, in reverse alphabetical order, we just write this:

```
table.sort(network, function (a,b) return (a.name > b.name) end)
```

See how handy the anonymous function is in this statement.

A function that gets another function as an argument, such as sort, is what we call a *higher-order function*. Higher-order functions are a powerful programming mechanism, and the use of anonymous functions to create their function arguments is a great source of flexibility. Nevertheless, remember that higher-order functions have no special rights; they are a direct consequence of the ability of Lua to handle functions as first-class values.

To illustrate further the use of higher-order functions, we will write a naive implementation of a common higher-order function, the derivative. In an informal definition, the derivative of a function f in a point x is the value of $(f(x + d) - f(x))/d$ when d becomes infinitesimally small. According to this definition, we can compute an approximation of the derivative as follows:

```
function derivative (f, delta)
  delta = delta or 1e-4
  return function (x)
           return (f(x + delta) - f(x))/delta
         end
end
```

Given a function f, the call `derivative(f)` returns (an approximation of) its derivative, which is another function:

```
c = derivative(math.sin)
> print(math.cos(5.2), c(5.2))
  -->     0.46851667130038     0.46856084325086
print(math.cos(10), c(10))
  -->    -0.83907152907645    -0.83904432662041
```

Because functions are first-class values in Lua, we can store them not only in global variables, but also in local variables and in table fields. As we will see later, the use of functions in table fields is a key ingredient for some advanced uses of Lua, such as modules and object-oriented programming.

6.1 Closures

When we write a function enclosed in another function, it has full access to local variables from the enclosing function; we call this feature *lexical scoping*. Although this visibility rule may sound obvious, it is not. Lexical scoping, plus first-class functions, is a powerful concept in a programming language, but many languages do not support it.

Let us start with a simple example. Suppose you have a list of student names and a table that associates names to grades; you want to sort the list of names according to their grades, with higher grades first. You can do this task as follows:

```
names = {"Peter", "Paul", "Mary"}
grades = {Mary = 10, Paul = 7, Peter = 8}
table.sort(names, function (n1, n2)
  return grades[n1] > grades[n2]      -- compare the grades
end)
```

Now, suppose you want to create a function to do this task:

```
function sortbygrade (names, grades)
  table.sort(names, function (n1, n2)
    return grades[n1] > grades[n2]      -- compare the grades
  end)
end
```

The interesting point in the example is that the anonymous function given to sort accesses the parameter grades, which is local to the enclosing function sortbygrade. Inside this anonymous function, grades is neither a global variable nor a local variable, but what we call a *non-local variable*. (For historical reasons, non-local variables are also called *upvalues* in Lua.)

Why is this point so interesting? Because functions are first-class values, and therefore they can *escape* the original scope of their variables. Consider the following code:

```
function newCounter ()
  local i = 0
  return function ()        -- anonymous function
          i = i + 1
          return i
        end
end

c1 = newCounter()
print(c1())  --> 1
print(c1())  --> 2
```

In this code, the anonymous function refers to a non-local variable, i, to keep its counter. However, by the time we call the anonymous function, i is already out of scope, because the function that created this variable (newCounter) has returned. Nevertheless, Lua handles this situation correctly, using the concept of *closure*. Simply put, a closure is a function plus all it needs to access non-local variables correctly. If we call newCounter again, it will create a new local variable i, so we will get a new closure, acting over this new variable:

```
c2 = newCounter()
print(c2())  --> 1
print(c1())  --> 3
print(c2())  --> 2
```

So, c1 and c2 are different closures over the same function, and each acts upon an independent instantiation of the local variable i.

Technically speaking, what is a value in Lua is the closure, not the function. The function itself is just a prototype for closures. Nevertheless, we will continue to use the term "function" to refer to a closure whenever there is no possibility for confusion.

Closures provide a valuable tool in many contexts. As we have seen, they are useful as arguments to higher-order functions such as sort. Closures are valuable for functions that build other functions too, like our newCounter example or the derivative example; this mechanism allows Lua programs to incorporate sophisticated programming techniques from the functional world. Closures are useful for *callback* functions, too. A typical example here occurs when you create buttons in a conventional GUI toolkit. Each button has a callback function to be called when the user presses the button; you want different buttons to do slightly different things when pressed. For instance, a digital calculator needs ten similar buttons, one for each digit. You can create each of them with a function like this:

```
function digitButton (digit)
  return Button{ label = tostring(digit),
                 action = function ()
                             add_to_display(digit)
                          end
               }
end
```

In this example, we assume that `Button` is a toolkit function that creates new buttons; `label` is the button label; and `action` is the callback closure to be called when the button is pressed. The callback can be called a long time after `digitButton` did its task and after the local variable `digit` went out of scope, but it can still access this variable.

Closures are valuable also in a quite different context. Because functions are stored in regular variables, we can easily redefine functions in Lua, even predefined functions. This facility is one of the reasons why Lua is so flexible. Frequently, when you redefine a function you need the original function in the new implementation. For instance, suppose you want to redefine the function `sin` to operate in degrees instead of radians. This new function converts its argument and then calls the original `sin` function to do the real work. Your code could look like this:

```
oldSin = math.sin
math.sin = function (x)
  return oldSin(x*math.pi/180)
end
```

A slightly cleaner way to do this redefinition is as follows:

```
do
  local oldSin = math.sin
  local k = math.pi/180
  math.sin = function (x)
    return oldSin(x*k)
  end
end
```

Now, we keep the old version in a private variable; the only way to access it is through the new version.

You can use this same technique to create secure environments, also called *sandboxes*. Secure environments are essential when running untrusted code, such as code received through the Internet by a server. For instance, to restrict the files a program can access, we can redefine the `io.open` function using closures:

```
do
  local oldOpen = io.open
  local access_OK = function (filename, mode)
    <check access>
  end
  io.open = function (filename, mode)
    if access_OK(filename, mode) then
      return oldOpen(filename, mode)
    else
      return nil, "access denied"
    end
  end
end
```

What makes this example nice is that, after this redefinition, there is no way for
the program to call the unrestricted open function except through the new, restricted version. It keeps the insecure version as a private variable in a closure,
inaccessible from the outside. With this technique, you can build Lua sandboxes
in Lua itself, with the usual benefits: simplicity and flexibility. Instead of a one-
size-fits-all solution, Lua offers you a meta-mechanism, so that you can tailor
your environment for your specific security needs.

6.2   Non-Global Functions

An obvious consequence of first-class functions is that we can store functions not
only in global variables, but also in table fields and in local variables.

We have already seen several examples of functions in table fields: most Lua
libraries use this mechanism (e.g., io.read, math.sin). To create such functions
in Lua, we only have to put together the regular syntax for functions and for
tables:

```
Lib = {}
Lib.foo = function (x,y) return x + y end
Lib.goo = function (x,y) return x - y end

print(Lib.foo(2, 3), Lib.goo(2, 3))    --> 5    -1
```

Of course, we can also use constructors:

```
Lib = {
  foo = function (x,y) return x + y end,
  goo = function (x,y) return x - y end
}
```

Moreover, Lua offers yet another syntax to define such functions:

```
Lib = {}
function Lib.foo (x,y) return x + y end
function Lib.goo (x,y) return x - y end
```

When we store a function into a local variable, we get a *local function*, that is, a function that is restricted to a given scope. Such definitions are particularly useful for packages: because Lua handles each chunk as a function, a chunk can declare local functions, which are visible only inside the chunk. Lexical scoping ensures that other functions in the package can use these local functions:

```
local f = function (<params>)
  <body>
end

local g = function (<params>)
  <some code>
  f()                     -- 'f' is visible here
  <some code>
end
```

Lua supports such uses of local functions with a syntactic sugar for them:

```
local function f (<params>)
  <body>
end
```

A subtle point arises in the definition of recursive local functions. The naive approach does not work here. Consider the next definition:

```
local fact = function (n)
  if n == 0 then return 1
  else return n*fact(n-1)    -- buggy
  end
end
```

When Lua compiles the call fact(n-1) in the function body, the local fact is not yet defined. Therefore, this expression will try to call a global fact, not the local one. We can solve this problem by first defining the local variable and then the function:

```
local fact
fact = function (n)
  if n == 0 then return 1
  else return n*fact(n-1)
  end
end
```

Now the fact inside the function refers to the local variable. Its value when the function is defined does not matter; by the time the function executes, fact already has the right value.

When Lua expands its syntactic sugar for local functions, it does not use the naive definition. Instead, a definition like

```
local function foo (<params>)  <body>  end
```

expands to

```
local foo; foo = function (<params>)  <body>  end
```

So, we can use this syntax for recursive functions without worrying.

Of course, this trick does not work if you have indirect recursive functions. In such cases, you must use the equivalent of an explicit forward declaration:

```
local f, g     -- 'forward' declarations

function g ()
   <some code>  f()  <some code>
end

function f ()
   <some code>  g()  <some code>
end
```

Beware not to write `local function f` in the last definition. Otherwise, Lua would create a fresh local variable f, leaving the original f (the one that g is bound to) undefined.

6.3   Proper Tail Calls

Another interesting feature of functions in Lua is that Lua does tail-call elimination. (This means that Lua is *properly tail recursive*, although the concept does not involve recursion directly; see Exercise 6.3.)

A *tail call* is a goto dressed as a call. A tail call happens when a function calls another as its last action, so it has nothing else to do. For instance, in the following code, the call to g is a tail call:

```
function f (x)  return g(x)  end
```

After f calls g, it has nothing else to do. In such situations, the program does not need to return to the calling function when the called function ends. Therefore, after the tail call, the program does not need to keep any information about the calling function in the stack. When g returns, control can return directly to the point that called f. Some language implementations, such as the Lua interpreter, take advantage of this fact and actually do not use any extra stack space when doing a tail call. We say that these implementations do *tail-call elimination*.

Because tail calls use no stack space, the number of nested tail calls that a program can make is unlimited. For instance, we can call the following function passing any number as argument:

```
function foo (n)
   if n > 0 then return foo(n - 1) end
end
```

It will never overflow the stack.

A subtle point when we assume tail-call elimination is what a tail call is. Some apparently obvious candidates fail the criterion that the calling function has nothing else to do after the call. For instance, in the following code, the call to g is not a tail call:

```
function f (x)  g(x)  end
```

The problem in this example is that, after calling g, f still has to discard occasional results from g before returning. Similarly, all the following calls fail the criterion:

```
return g(x) + 1      -- must do the addition
return x or g(x)     -- must adjust to 1 result
return (g(x))        -- must adjust to 1 result
```

In Lua, only a call with the form return *func* (*args*) is a tail call. However, both *func* and its arguments can be complex expressions, because Lua evaluates them before the call. For instance, the next call is a tail call:

```
return x[i].foo(x[j] + a*b, i + j)
```

Exercises

Exercise 6.1: Write a function integral that receives a function f and returns an approximation of its integral.

Exercise 6.2: Exercise 3.3 asked you to write a function that receives a polynomial (represented as a table) and a value for its variable, and returns the polynomial value. Write the *curried* version of that function. Your function should receive a polynomial and returns a function that, when called with a value for x, returns the value of the polynomial for that x. See the example:

```
f = newpoly({3, 0, 1})
print(f(0))     --> 1
print(f(5))     --> 76
print(f(10))    --> 301
```

Exercise 6.3: Sometimes, a language with proper-tail calls is called *properly tail recursive*, with the argument that this property is relevant only when we have recursive calls. (Without recursive calls, the maximum call depth of a program would be statically fixed.)

Show that this argument does not hold in a dynamic language like Lua: write a program that performs an unbounded call chain without recursion. (Hint: see Section 8.1.)

Exercise 6.4: As we have seen, a tail call is a goto in disguise. Using this idea, reimplement the simple maze game from Section 4.4 using tail calls. Each block should become a new function, and each goto becomes a tail call.

7

Iterators and the Generic for

In this chapter, we cover how to write iterators for the generic **for**. Starting with simple iterators, we will learn how to use all the power of the generic **for** to write simpler and more efficient iterators.

7.1 Iterators and Closures

An *iterator* is any construction that allows you to iterate over the elements of a collection. In Lua, we typically represent iterators by functions: each time we call the function, it returns the "next" element from the collection.

Any iterator needs to keep some state between successive calls, so that it knows where it is and how to proceed from there. Closures provide an excellent mechanism for this task. Remember that a closure is a function that accesses one or more local variables from its enclosing environment. These variables keep their values across successive calls to the closure, allowing the closure to remember where it is along a traversal. Of course, to create a new closure we must also create its non-local variables. Therefore, a closure construction typically involves two functions: the closure itself and a *factory*, the function that creates the closure plus its enclosing variables.

As an example, let us write a simple iterator for a list. Unlike ipairs, this iterator does not return the index of each element, only its value:

```
function values (t)
  local i = 0
  return function ()  i = i + 1; return t[i]  end
end
```

In this example, `values` is the factory. Each time we call this factory, it creates a new closure (the iterator itself). This closure keeps its state in its external variables `t` and `i`. Each time we call the iterator, it returns a next value from the list `t`. After the last element the iterator returns nil, which signals the end of the iteration.

We can use this iterator in a **while** loop:

```
t = {10, 20, 30}
iter = values(t)          -- creates the iterator
while true do
  local element = iter()   -- calls the iterator
  if element == nil then break end
  print(element)
end
```

However, it is easier to use the generic **for**. After all, it was designed for this kind of iteration:

```
t = {10, 20, 30}
for element in values(t) do
  print(element)
end
```

The generic **for** does all the bookkeeping for an iteration loop: it keeps the iterator function internally, so we do not need the `iter` variable; it calls the iterator for each new iteration; and it stops the loop when the iterator returns nil. (In the next section, we will see that the generic **for** does even more than that.)

As a more advanced example, Listing 7.1 shows an iterator to traverse all the words from the current input file. To do this traversal, we keep two values: the contents of the current line (variable `line`), and where we are on this line (variable `pos`). With this data, we can always generate the next word. The main part of the iterator function is the call to `string.find`. This call searches for a word in the current line, starting at the current position. It describes a "word" using the pattern '%w+', which matches one or more alphanumeric characters. If it finds the word, the function updates the current position to the first character after the word and returns this word.[1] Otherwise, the iterator reads a new line and repeats the search. If there are no more lines, it returns nil to signal the end of the iteration.

Despite its complexity, the use of `allwords` is straightforward:

```
for word in allwords() do
  print(word)
end
```

This is a common situation with iterators: they may not be easy to write, but they are easy to use. This is not a big problem; more often than not, end users programming in Lua do not define iterators, but just use those provided by the application.

---

[1] The `string.sub` call extracts a substring from `line` between the given positions; we will see it in more detail in Section 21.2.

Listing 7.1. Iterator to traverse all words from the input file:

```
function allwords ()
  local line = io.read()   -- current line
  local pos = 1            -- current position in the line
  return function ()       -- iterator function
    while line do          -- repeat while there are lines
      local s, e = string.find(line, "%w+", pos)
      if s then            -- found a word?
        pos = e + 1        -- next position is after this word
        return string.sub(line, s, e)      -- return the word
      else
        line = io.read()   -- word not found; try next line
        pos = 1            -- restart from first position
      end
    end
    return nil             -- no more lines: end of traversal
  end
end
```

7.2 The Semantics of the Generic for

One drawback of those previous iterators is that we need to create a new closure to initialize each new loop. For most situations, this is not a real problem. For instance, in the allwords iterator, the cost of creating one single closure is negligible compared to the cost of reading a whole file. However, in some situations this overhead can be inconvenient. In such cases, we can use the generic **for** itself to keep the iteration state. In this section, we will see the facilities that the generic **for** offers to hold state.

We saw that the generic **for** keeps the iterator function internally, during the loop. Actually, it keeps three values: the iterator function, an *invariant state*, and a *control variable*. Let us see the details now.

The syntax for the generic **for** is as follows:

```
for <var-list> in <exp-list> do
  <body>
end
```

Here, *var-list* is a list of one or more variable names, separated by commas, and *exp-list* is a list of one or more expressions, also separated by commas. More often than not, the expression list has only one element, a call to an iterator factory. In the next code, for instance, the list of variables is k,v and the list of expressions has the single element pairs(t):

```
for k, v in pairs(t) do print(k, v) end
```

Often the list of variables has only one variable too, as in the next loop:

```
for line in io.lines() do
  io.write(line, "\n")
end
```

We call the first variable in the list the *control variable*. Its value is never nil during the loop, because when it becomes nil the loop ends.

The first thing the **for** does is to evaluate the expressions after the **in**. These expressions should result in the three values kept by the **for**: the iterator function, the invariant state, and the initial value for the control variable. Like in a multiple assignment, only the last (or the only) element of the list can result in more than one value; and the number of values is adjusted to three, extra values being discarded or nils added as needed. (When we use simple iterators, the factory returns only the iterator function, so the invariant state and the control variable get nil.)

After this initialization step, the **for** calls the iterator function with two arguments: the invariant state and the control variable. (From the standpoint of the **for** construct, the invariant state has no meaning at all. The **for** only passes the state value from the initialization step to the calls to the iterator function.) Then the **for** assigns the values returned by the iterator function to the variables declared by its variable list. If the first value returned (the one assigned to the control variable) is nil, the loop terminates. Otherwise, the **for** executes its body and calls the iteration function again, repeating the process.

More precisely, a construction like

```
for var_1, ..., var_n in <explist> do <block> end
```

is equivalent to the following code:

```
do
  local _f, _s, _var = <explist>
  while true do
    local var_1, ... , var_n = _f(_s, _var)
    _var = var_1
    if _var == nil then break end
    <block>
  end
end
```

So, if our iterator function is f, the invariant state is s, and the initial value for the control variable is a_0, the control variable will loop over the values $a_1 = f(s, a_0)$, $a_2 = f(s, a_1)$, and so on, until a_i is nil. If the **for** has other variables, they simply get the extra values returned by each call to f.

7.3   Stateless Iterators

As the name implies, a stateless iterator is an iterator that does not keep any state by itself. Therefore, we can use the same stateless iterator in multiple loops, avoiding the cost of creating new closures.

As we just saw, the **for** loop calls its iterator function with two arguments: the invariant state and the control variable. A stateless iterator generates the next element for the iteration using only these two values. A typical example of this kind of iterator is ipairs, which iterates over all elements of an array:

```
a = {"one", "two", "three"}
for i, v in ipairs(a) do
  print(i, v)
end
```

The state of the iteration is the table being traversed (that is the invariant state, which does not change during the loop), plus the current index (the control variable). Both ipairs (the factory) and the iterator are quite simple; we could write them in Lua as follows:

```
local function iter (a, i)
  i = i + 1
  local v = a[i]
  if v then
    return i, v
  end
end

function ipairs (a)
  return iter, a, 0
end
```

When Lua calls ipairs(a) in a **for** loop, it gets three values: the iter function as the iterator, a as the invariant state, and zero as the initial value for the control variable. Then, Lua calls iter(a, 0), which results in 1,a[1] (unless a[1] is already nil). In the second iteration, it calls iter(a, 1), which results in 2,a[2], and so on, until the first nil element.

The pairs function, which iterates over all elements of a table, is similar, except that the iterator function is the next function, which is a primitive function in Lua:

```
function pairs (t)
  return next, t, nil
end
```

The call next(t, k), where k is a key of the table t, returns a next key in the table, in an arbitrary order, plus the value associated with this key as a second return value. The call next(t, nil) returns a first pair. When there are no more pairs, next returns nil.

Some people prefer to use next directly, without calling pairs:

```
for k, v in next, t do
  <loop body>
end
```

Remember that the **for** loop adjusts its expression list to three results, so that it gets next, t, and nil; this is exactly what it gets when it calls pairs(t).

An iterator to traverse a linked list is another interesting example of a stateless iterator. (As we already mentioned, linked lists are not frequent in Lua, but sometimes we need them.)

```
local function getnext (list, node)
  if not node then
    return list
  else
    return node.next
  end
end

function traverse (list)
  return getnext, list, nil
end
```

The trick here is to use the list main node as the invariant state (the second value returned by traverse) and the current node as the control variable. The first time the iterator function getnext is called, node will be nil, and so the function will return list as the first node. In subsequent calls, node will not be nil, and so the iterator will return node.next, as expected. As usual, it is trivial to use the iterator:

```
list = nil
for line in io.lines() do
  list = {val = line, next = list}
end

for node in traverse(list) do
  print(node.val)
end
```

7.4 Iterators with Complex State

Frequently, an iterator needs to keep more state than fits into a single invariant state and a control variable. The simplest solution is to use closures. An alternative solution is to pack all that the iterator needs into a table and use this table as the invariant state for the iteration. Using a table, an iterator can keep as much data as it needs along the loop. Moreover, it can change this data as it goes. Although the state is always the same table (and therefore invariant), the table contents change along the loop. Because such iterators have all their data in the state, they typically ignore the second argument provided by the generic **for** (the iterator variable).

As an example of this technique, we will rewrite the iterator allwords, which traverses all the words from the current input file. This time, we will keep its state using a table with two fields: line and pos.

The function that starts the iteration is simple. It must return the iterator function and the initial state:

```
local iterator    -- to be defined later

function allwords ()
  local state = {line = io.read(), pos = 1}
  return iterator, state
end
```

The `iterator` function does the real work:

```
function iterator (state)
  while state.line do          -- repeat while there are lines
    -- search for next word
    local s, e = string.find(state.line, "%w+", state.pos)
    if s then                  -- found a word?
      -- update next position (after this word)
      state.pos = e + 1
      return string.sub(state.line, s, e)
    else                       -- word not found
      state.line = io.read() -- try next line...
      state.pos = 1            -- ... from first position
    end
  end
  return nil                   -- no more lines: end loop
end
```

Whenever possible, you should try to write stateless iterators, those that keep all their state in the **for** variables. With them, you do not create new objects when you start a loop. If you cannot fit your iteration into this model, then you should try closures. Besides being more elegant, typically a closure is more efficient than an iterator using tables: first, it is cheaper to create a closure than a table; second, access to non-local variables is faster than access to table fields. Later we will see yet another way to write iterators, with coroutines. This is the most powerful solution, but a little more expensive.

7.5   True Iterators

The name "iterator" is a little misleading, because our iterators do not iterate: what iterates is the **for** loop. Iterators only provide the successive values for the iteration. Maybe a better name would be "generator", but "iterator" is already well established in other languages, such as Java.

However, there is another way to build iterators wherein iterators actually do the iteration. When we use such iterators, we do not write a loop; instead, we simply call the iterator with an argument that describes what the iterator must do at each iteration. More specifically, the iterator receives as argument a function that it calls inside its loop.

As a concrete example, let us rewrite once more the allwords iterator using this style:

```
function allwords (f)
  for line in io.lines() do
    for word in string.gmatch(line, "%w+") do
      f(word)      -- call the function
    end
  end
end
```

To use this iterator, we must supply the loop body as a function. If we want only to print each word, we simply use `print`:

```
allwords(print)
```

Often, we use an anonymous function as the body. For instance, the next code fragment counts how many times the word "hello" appears in the input file:

```
local count = 0
allwords(function (w)
  if w == "hello" then count = count + 1 end
end)
print(count)
```

The same task, written with the previous iterator style, is not very different:

```
local count = 0
for w in allwords() do
  if w == "hello" then count = count + 1 end
end
print(count)
```

True iterators were popular in older versions of Lua, when the language did not have the **for** statement. How do they compare with generator-style iterators? Both styles have approximately the same overhead: one function call per iteration. On the one hand, it is easier to write the iterator with true iterators (although we can recover this easiness with coroutines). On the other hand, the generator style is more flexible. First, it allows two or more parallel iterations. (For instance, consider the problem of iterating over two files comparing them word by word.) Second, it allows the use of **break** and **return** inside the iterator body. With a true iterator, a **return** returns from the anonymous function, not from the function doing the iteration. Overall, I usually prefer generators.

Exercises

Exercise 7.1: Write an iterator `fromto` such that the next two loops become equivalent:

```
for i in fromto(n, m)
  <body>
end
```

```
for i = n, m
  <body>
end
```

Can you implement it as a stateless iterator?

Exercise 7.2: Add a step parameter to the iterator from the previous exercise. Can you still implement it as a stateless iterator?

Exercise 7.3: Write an iterator uniquewords that returns all words from a given file without repetitions. (Hint: start with the allwords code in Listing 7.1; use a table to keep all words already reported.)

Exercise 7.4: Write an iterator that returns all non-empty substrings of a given string. (You will need the string.sub function.)

8

Compilation, Execution, and Errors

Although we refer to Lua as an interpreted language, Lua always precompiles source code to an intermediate form before running it. (This is not a big deal: many interpreted languages do the same.) The presence of a compilation phase may sound out of place in an interpreted language like Lua. However, the distinguishing feature of interpreted languages is not that they are not compiled, but that it is possible (and easy) to execute code generated on the fly. We may say that the presence of a function like dofile is what allows Lua to be called an interpreted language.

8.1 Compilation

Previously, we introduced dofile as a kind of primitive operation to run chunks of Lua code, but dofile is actually an auxiliary function: loadfile does the hard work. Like dofile, loadfile loads a Lua chunk from a file, but it does not run the chunk. Instead, it only compiles the chunk and returns the compiled chunk as a function. Moreover, unlike dofile, loadfile does not raise errors, but instead returns error codes, so that we can handle the error. We could define dofile as follows:

```
function dofile (filename)
  local f = assert(loadfile(filename))
  return f()
end
```

Note the use of `assert` to raise an error if `loadfile` fails.

For simple tasks, `dofile` is handy, because it does the complete job in one call. However, `loadfile` is more flexible. In case of an error, `loadfile` returns nil plus the error message, which allows us to handle the error in customized ways. Moreover, if we need to run a file several times, we can call `loadfile` once and call its result several times. This approach is much cheaper than several calls to `dofile`, because it compiles the file only once.

The `load` function is similar to `loadfile`, except that it reads its chunk from a string, not from a file.[1] For instance, consider the next line:

```
f = load("i = i + 1")
```

After this code, `f` will be a function that executes `i = i + 1` when invoked:

```
i = 0
f(); print(i)    --> 1
f(); print(i)    --> 2
```

The `load` function is powerful; we should use it with care. It is also an expensive function (when compared to some alternatives) and can result in incomprehensible code. Before you use it, make sure that there is no simpler way to solve the problem at hand.

If you want to do a quick-and-dirty `dostring` (i.e., to load and run a chunk), you can call the result from `load` directly:

```
load(s)()
```

However, if there is any syntax error, `load` will return nil and the final error message will be something like *"attempt to call a nil value"*. For clearer error messages, use `assert`:

```
assert(load(s))()
```

Usually, it does not make sense to use `load` on a literal string. For instance, the next two lines are roughly equivalent:

```
f = load("i = i + 1")

f = function () i = i + 1 end
```

However, the second line is much faster, because Lua compiles the function together with its enclosing chunk. In the first line, the call to `load` involves a separate compilation.

Because `load` does not compile with lexical scoping, the two lines in the previous example may not be truly equivalent. To see the difference, let us change the example a little:

---

[1] In Lua 5.1, function `loadstring` did this role of `load`.

```
i = 32
local i = 0
f = load("i = i + 1; print(i)")
g = function () i = i + 1; print(i) end
f()               --> 33
g()               --> 1
```

Function g manipulates the local i, as expected, but f manipulates a global i, because load always compiles its chunks in the global environment.

The most typical use of load is to run external code, that is, pieces of code that come from outside your program. For instance, you may want to plot a function defined by the user; the user enters the function code and then you use load to evaluate it. Note that load expects a chunk, that is, statements. If you want to evaluate an expression, you can prefix the expression with **return**, so that you get a statement that returns the value of the given expression. See the example:

```
print "enter your expression:"
local l = io.read()
local func = assert(load("return " .. l))
print("the value of your expression is " .. func())
```

Because the function returned by load is a regular function, you can call it several times:

```
print "enter function to be plotted (with variable 'x'):"
local l = io.read()
local f = assert(load("return " .. l))
for i = 1, 20 do
  x = i    -- global 'x' (to be visible from the chunk)
  print(string.rep("*", f()))
end
```

(The string.rep function replicates a string a given number of times.)

We can call the load function also with a *reader function* as its first argument. A reader function can return the chunk in parts; load calls the reader successively until it returns nil, which signals the chunk's end. As an example, the next call is equivalent to loadfile:

```
f = load(io.lines(filename, "*L"))
```

As we will see in more detail in Chapter 22, the call io.lines(filename,"*L") returns a function that, each time it is called, returns a new line from the given file.[2] So, load will read the chunk from the file line by line. The following version is similar, but more efficient:

```
f = load(io.lines(filename, 1024))
```

---

[2]Options for io.lines are new in Lua 5.2.

Here, the iterator returned by `io.lines` reads the file in blocks of 1024 bytes.

Lua treats any independent chunk as the body of an anonymous function with a variable number of arguments. For instance, `load("a = 1")` returns the equivalent of the following expression:

```
function (...) a = 1 end
```

Like any other function, chunks can declare local variables:

```
f = load("local a = 10; print(a + 20)")
f()              --> 30
```

Using these features, we can rewrite our plot example to avoid the use of a global variable x:

```
print "enter function to be plotted (with variable 'x'):"
local l = io.read()
local f = assert(load("local x = ...; return " .. l))
for i = 1, 20 do
  print(string.rep("*", f(i)))
end
```

We append the declaration "`local x = ...`" at the beginning of the chunk to declare x as a local variable. We then call f with an argument i that becomes the value of the vararg expression (`...`).

The load functions never raise errors. In case of any kind of error, they return nil plus an error message:

```
print(load("i i"))
   --> nil     [string "i i"]:1: '=' expected near 'i'
```

Moreover, these functions never have any kind of side effect. They only compile the chunk to an internal representation and return the result as an anonymous function. A common mistake is to assume that loading a chunk defines functions. In Lua, function definitions are assignments; as such, they happen at runtime, not at compile time. For instance, suppose we have a file `foo.lua` like this:

```
-- file 'foo.lua'
function foo (x)
  print(x)
end
```

We then run the command

```
f = loadfile("foo.lua")
```

After this command, `foo` is compiled, but it is not defined yet. To define it, you must run the chunk:

```
print(foo)     --> nil
f()            -- defines 'foo'
foo("ok")      --> ok
```

In a production-quality program that needs to run external code, you should handle any errors reported when loading a chunk. Moreover, you may want to run the new chunk in a protected environment, to avoid unpleasant side effects. We will discuss environments in detail in Chapter 14.

8.2 Precompiled Code

As I mentioned in the beginning of this chapter, Lua precompiles source code before running it. Lua also allows us to distribute code in precompiled form.

The simplest way to produce a precompiled file — also called a *binary chunk* in Lua jargon — is with the luac program, which comes in the standard distribution. For instance, the next call creates a new file prog.lc with a precompiled version of a file prog.lua:

```
$ luac -o prog.lc prog.lua
```

The interpreter can execute this new file just like normal Lua code, performing exactly as with the original source:

```
$ lua prog.lc
```

Lua accepts precompiled code mostly anywhere it accepts source code. In particular, both loadfile and load accept precompiled code.

We can write a poor man's luac directly in Lua:

```
p = loadfile(arg[1])
f = io.open(arg[2], "wb")
f:write(string.dump(p))
f:close()
```

The key function here is string.dump: it receives a Lua function and returns its precompiled code as a string, properly formatted to be loaded back by Lua.

The luac program offers some other interesting options. In particular, option -l lists the opcodes that the compiler generates for a given chunk. As an example, Listing 8.1 shows the output of luac with option -l on the following one-line file:

```
a = x + y - z
```

(We will not discuss the internals of Lua in this book; if you are interested in more details about those opcodes, a web search for "lua opcode" should give you relevant material.)

Code in precompiled form is not always smaller than the original, but it loads faster. Another benefit is that it gives a protection against accidental changes in sources. Unlike source code, however, maliciously corrupted binary code can crash the Lua interpreter or even execute user-provided machine code. When running usual code, there is nothing to worry about. However, you should avoid running untrusted code in precompiled form. The load function has an option exactly for this task.

Listing 8.1. Example of output from `luac -l`:

```
main <stdin:0,0> (7 instructions, 28 bytes at 0x988cb30)
0+ params, 2 slots, 0 upvalues, 0 locals, 4 constants, 0 functions
    1 [1] GETGLOBAL 0 -2 ; x
    2 [1] GETGLOBAL 1 -3 ; y
    3 [1] ADD       0 0 1
    4 [1] GETGLOBAL 1 -4 ; z
    5 [1] SUB       0 0 1
    6 [1] SETGLOBAL 0 -1 ; a
    7 [1] RETURN    0 1
```

Besides its required first argument, `load` has three more arguments, all of them optional. The second is a name for the chunk, which is used only in error messages. The fourth argument is an environment, which we will discuss in Chapter 14. The third argument is the one we are interested here; it controls what kinds of chunks can be loaded. If present, this argument must be a string: the string "t" allows only textual (normal) chunks; "b" allows only binary (precompiled) chunks; "bt", the default, allows both formats.

8.3   C Code

Unlike code written in Lua, C code needs to be linked with an application before use. In several popular operating systems, the easiest way to do this link is with a dynamic linking facility. However, this facility is not part of the ANSI C specification; therefore, there is no portable way to implement it.

Normally, Lua does not include facilities that cannot be implemented in ANSI C. However, dynamic linking is different. We can view it as the mother of all other facilities: once we have it, we can dynamically load any other facility that is not in Lua. Therefore, in this particular case, Lua breaks its portability rules and implements a dynamic linking facility for several platforms. The standard implementation offers this support for Windows, Mac OS X, Linux, FreeBSD, Solaris, and most other UNIX implementations. It should not be difficult to extend this facility to other platforms; check your distribution. (To check it, run `print(package.loadlib("a","b"))` from the Lua prompt and see the result. If it complains about a non-existent file, then you have dynamic linking facility. Otherwise, the error message should indicate that this facility is not supported or not installed.)

Lua provides all the functionality of dynamic linking through a single function, called `package.loadlib`. It has two string arguments: the complete path of a library and the name of a function in that library. So, a typical call to it looks like the next fragment:

```
local path = "/usr/local/lib/lua/5.1/socket.so"
local f = package.loadlib(path, "luaopen_socket")
```

The `loadlib` function loads the given library and links Lua to it. However, it does not call the given function. Instead, it returns the C function as a Lua function. If there is any error loading the library or finding the initialization function, `loadlib` returns nil plus an error message.

The `loadlib` function is a very low-level function. We must provide the full path of the library and the correct name for the function (including occasional leading underscores included by the compiler). More often than not, we load C libraries using `require`. This function searches for the library and uses `loadlib` to load an initialization function for the library. When called, this initialization function builds and returns a table with the functions from that library, much as a typical Lua library does. We will discuss `require` in Section 15.1, and more details about C libraries in Section 27.3.

8.4 Errors

Errare humanum est. Therefore, we must handle errors the best way we can. Because Lua is an extension language, frequently embedded in an application, it cannot simply crash or exit when an error happens. Instead, whenever an error occurs, Lua ends the current chunk and returns to the application.

Any unexpected condition that Lua encounters raises an error. Errors occur when you (that is, your program) try to add values that are not numbers, call values that are not functions, index values that are not tables, and so on. (You can modify this behavior using *metatables*, as we will see later.) You can also explicitly raise an error calling the `error` function with an error message as an argument. Usually, this function is the appropriate way to signal errors in your code:

```
print "enter a number:"
n = io.read("*n")
if not n then error("invalid input") end
```

This construction of calling error subject to some condition is so common that Lua has a built-in function just for this job, called assert:

```
print "enter a number:"
n = assert(io.read("*n"), "invalid input")
```

The `assert` function checks whether its first argument is not false and simply returns this argument; if the argument is false, `assert` raises an error. Its second argument, the message, is optional. Beware, however, that assert is a regular function. As such, Lua always evaluates its arguments before calling the function. Therefore, if you have something like

```
n = io.read()
assert(tonumber(n), "invalid input: " .. n .. " is not a number")
```

Lua will always do the concatenation, even when n is a number. It may be wiser to use an explicit test in such cases.

When a function finds an unexpected situation (an *exception*), it can assume two basic behaviors: it can return an error code (typically nil) or it can raise an error, calling function error. There are no fixed rules for choosing between these two options, but we can provide a general guideline: an exception that is easily avoided should raise an error; otherwise, it should return an error code.

For instance, let us consider the sin function. How should it behave when called on a table? Suppose it returns an error code. If we need to check for errors, we would have to write something like

```
local res = math.sin(x)
if not res then       -- error?
  <error-handling code>
```

However, we could as easily check this exception *before* calling the function:

```
if not tonumber(x) then       -- x is not a number?
  <error-handling code>
```

Frequently we check neither the argument nor the result of a call to sin; if the argument is not a number, it means that probably there is something wrong in our program. In such situations, to stop the computation and to issue an error message is the simplest and most practical way to handle the exception.

On the other hand, let us consider the io.open function, which opens a file. How should it behave when asked to read a file that does not exist? In this case, there is no simple way to check for the exception before calling the function. In many systems, the only way of knowing whether a file exists is by trying to open it. Therefore, if io.open cannot open a file because of an external reason (such as "file does not exist" or "permission denied"), it returns nil, plus a string with the error message. In this way, you have a chance to handle the situation in an appropriate way, for instance by asking the user for another file name:

```
local file, msg
repeat
  print "enter a file name:"
  local name = io.read()
  if not name then return end   -- no input
  file, msg = io.open(name, "r")
  if not file then print(msg) end
until file
```

If you do not want to handle such situations, but still want to play safe, you simply use assert to guard the operation:

```
file = assert(io.open(name, "r"))
```

This is a typical Lua idiom: if io.open fails, assert will raise an error.

```
file = assert(io.open("no-file", "r"))
  --> stdin:1: no-file: No such file or directory
```

Notice how the error message, which is the second result from io.open, goes as the second argument to assert.

8.5 Error Handling and Exceptions

For many applications, you do not need to do any error handling in Lua; the application program does this handling. All Lua activities start from a call by the application, usually asking Lua to run a chunk. If there is any error, this call returns an error code, so that the application can take appropriate actions. In the case of the stand-alone interpreter, its main loop just prints the error message and continues showing the prompt and running the commands.

However, if you need to handle errors in Lua, you must use the pcall (*protected call*) function to encapsulate your code.

Suppose you want to run a piece of Lua code and to catch any error raised while running that code. Your first step is to encapsulate that piece of code in a function; more often than not, you will use an anonymous function for that. Then, you call that function with pcall:

```
local ok, msg = pcall(function ()
    <some code>
    if unexpected_condition then error() end
    <some code>
    print(a[i])     -- potential error: 'a' may not be a table
    <some code>
  end)

if ok then     -- no errors while running protected code
  <regular code>
else    -- protected code raised an error: take appropriate action
  <error-handling code>
end
```

The pcall function calls its first argument in *protected mode*, so that it catches any errors while the function is running. If there are no errors, pcall returns **true**, plus any values returned by the call. Otherwise, it returns **false**, plus the error message.

Despite its name, the error message does not have to be a string: pcall will return any Lua value that you pass to error.

```
local status, err = pcall(function () error({code=121}) end)
print(err.code)   --> 121
```

These mechanisms provide all we need to do exception handling in Lua. We throw an exception with error and catch it with pcall. The error message identifies the kind of error.

8.6 Error Messages and Tracebacks

Although you can use a value of any type as an error message, usually error messages are strings describing what went wrong. When there is an internal error (such as an attempt to index a non-table value), Lua generates the error message; otherwise, the error message is the value passed to the `error` function. Whenever the message is a string, Lua tries to add some information about the location where the error happened:

```
local status, err = pcall(function () a = "a"+1 end)
print(err)
   --> stdin:1: attempt to perform arithmetic on a string value

local status, err = pcall(function () error("my error") end)
print(err)
   --> stdin:1: my error
```

The location information gives the file name (`stdin`, in the example) plus the line number (1, in the example).

The error function has an additional second parameter, which gives the *level* where it should report the error; you use this parameter to blame someone else for the error. For instance, suppose you write a function whose first task is to check whether it was called correctly:

```
function foo (str)
  if type(str) ~= "string" then
    error("string expected")
  end
  <regular code>
end
```

Then, someone calls your function with a wrong argument:

```
foo({x=1})
```

As it is, Lua points its finger to your function — after all, it was `foo` that called `error` — and not to the real culprit, the caller. To correct this problem, you inform `error` that the error you are reporting occurred on level 2 in the calling hierarchy (level 1 is your own function):

```
function foo (str)
  if type(str) ~= "string" then
    error("string expected", 2)
  end
  <regular code>
end
```

Frequently, when an error happens, we want more debug information than only the location where the error occurred. At least, we want a traceback, showing the complete stack of calls leading to the error. When `pcall` returns its error message, it destroys part of the stack (the part that goes from it to the error point). Consequently, if we want a traceback, we must build it before `pcall` returns. To do this, Lua provides the `xpcall` function. Besides the function to be called, it receives a second argument, a *message handler function*. In case of an error, Lua calls this message handler before the stack unwinds, so that it can use the debug library to gather any extra information it wants about the error. Two common message handlers are debug.debug, which gives you a Lua prompt so that you can inspect by yourself what was going on when the error happened; and debug.traceback, which builds an extended error message with a traceback.[3] The latter is the function that the stand-alone interpreter uses to build its error messages.

Exercises

Exercise 8.1: Frequently, it is useful to add some prefix to a chunk of code when loading it. (We saw an example previously in this chapter, where we prefixed a **return** to an expression being loaded.) Write a function loadwithprefix that works like load, except that it adds its extra first argument (a string) as a prefix to the chunk being loaded.

Like the original load, loadwithprefix should accept chunks represented both as strings and as reader functions. Even in the case that the original chunk is a string, loadwithprefix should not actually concatenate the prefix with the chunk. Instead, it should call load with a proper reader function that first returns the prefix and then returns the original chunk.

Exercise 8.2: Write a function multiload that generalizes loadwithprefix by receiving a list of readers, as in the following example:

```
f = multiload("local x = 10;",
              io.lines("temp", "*L"),
              " print(x)")
```

For the above example, multiload should load a chunk equivalent to the concatenation of the string "local..." with the contents of the temp file with the string "print(x)". Again, like function loadwithprefix from the previous exercise, multiload should not actually concatenate anything.

Exercise 8.3: Function stringrep, in Listing 8.2, uses a binary multiplication algorithm to concatenate n copies of a given string s. For any fixed n, we can create a specialized version of stringrep by unrolling the loop into a sequence of instructions r=r..s and s=s..s. As an example, for n=5 the unrolling gives us the following function:

```
function stringrep_5 (s)
  local r = ""
  r = r .. s
  s = s .. s
  s = s .. s
  r = r .. s
  return r
end
```

---

[3]In Chapter 24 we will see more about these functions, when we discuss the debug library.

Listing 8.2. String repetition:

```
function stringrep (s, n)
  local r = ""
  if n > 0 then
    while n > 1 do
      if n % 2 ~= 0 then  r = r .. s   end
      s = s .. s
      n = math.floor(n / 2)
    end
    r = r .. s
  end
  return r
end
```

Write a function that, given n, returns a specialized function stringrep_*n*. Instead of using a closure, your function should build the text of a Lua function with the proper sequence of instructions (r=r .. s and s=s .. s) and then use load to produce the final function. Compare the performance of the generic function stringrep (or of a closure using it) with your tailor-made functions.

Exercise 8.4: Can you find any value for f such that the call pcall(pcall,f) returns **false** as its first result?

9

Coroutines

A *coroutine* is similar to a thread (in the sense of multithreading): it is a line of execution, with its own stack, its own local variables, and its own instruction pointer; but it shares global variables and mostly anything else with other coroutines. The main difference between threads and coroutines is that, conceptually (or literally, in a multiprocessor machine), a program with threads runs several threads in parallel. Coroutines, on the other hand, are collaborative: at any given time, a program with coroutines is running only one of its coroutines, and this running coroutine suspends its execution only when it explicitly requests to be suspended.

Coroutine is a powerful concept. As such, several of its main uses are complex. Do not worry if you do not understand some of the examples in this chapter on your first reading. You can read the rest of the book and come back here later. But please come back; it will be time well spent.

9.1 Coroutine Basics

Lua packs all its coroutine-related functions in the `coroutine` table. The `create` function creates new coroutines. It has a single argument, a function with the code that the coroutine will run. It returns a value of type `thread`, which represents the new coroutine. Often, the argument to create is an anonymous function, like here:

```
co = coroutine.create(function () print("hi") end)

print(co)    --> thread: 0x8071d98
```

A coroutine can be in one of four states: suspended, running, dead, and normal. We can check the state of a coroutine with the `status` function:

```
print(coroutine.status(co))    --> suspended
```

When we create a coroutine, it starts in the suspended state; a coroutine does not run its body automatically when we create it. Function `coroutine.resume` (re)starts the execution of a coroutine, changing its state from suspended to running:

```
coroutine.resume(co)    --> hi
```

In this first example, the coroutine body simply prints "hi" and terminates, leaving the coroutine in the dead state, from which it does not return:

```
print(coroutine.status(co))    --> dead
```

Until now, coroutines look like nothing more than a complicated way to call functions. The real power of coroutines stems from the `yield` function, which allows a running coroutine to suspend its own execution so that it can be resumed later. Let us see a simple example:

```
co = coroutine.create(function ()
       for i = 1, 10 do
         print("co", i)
         coroutine.yield()
       end
     end)
```

Now, when we resume this coroutine, it starts its execution and runs until the first `yield`:

```
coroutine.resume(co)    --> co    1
```

If we check its status, we can see that the coroutine is suspended and therefore can be resumed again:

```
print(coroutine.status(co))    --> suspended
```

From the coroutine's point of view, all activity that happens while it is suspended is happening inside its call to `yield`. When we resume the coroutine, this call to `yield` finally returns and the coroutine continues its execution until the next yield or until its end:

```
coroutine.resume(co)    --> co    2
coroutine.resume(co)    --> co    3
   ...
coroutine.resume(co)    --> co    10
coroutine.resume(co)    -- prints nothing
```

During the last call to `resume`, the coroutine body finishes the loop and then returns, without printing anything. If we try to resume it again, `resume` returns **false** plus an error message:

```
print(coroutine.resume(co))
   --> false    cannot resume dead coroutine
```

Note that `resume` runs in protected mode. Therefore, if there is any error inside a coroutine, Lua will not show the error message, but instead will return it to the `resume` call.

When a coroutine resumes another, it is not suspended; after all, we cannot resume it. However, it is not running either, because the running coroutine is the other one. So, its own status is what we call the *normal* state.

A useful facility in Lua is that a pair resume–yield can exchange data. The first resume, which has no corresponding `yield` waiting for it, passes its extra arguments as arguments to the coroutine main function:

```
co = coroutine.create(function (a, b, c)
        print("co", a, b, c + 2)
     end)
coroutine.resume(co, 1, 2, 3)    --> co  1  2  5
```

A call to resume returns, after the **true** that signals no errors, any arguments passed to the corresponding `yield`:

```
co = coroutine.create(function (a,b)
        coroutine.yield(a + b, a - b)
     end)
print(coroutine.resume(co, 20, 10))   --> true   30   10
```

Symmetrically, `yield` returns any extra arguments passed to the corresponding resume:

```
co = coroutine.create (function (x)
        print("co1", x)
        print("co2", coroutine.yield())
     end)
coroutine.resume(co, "hi")      --> co1  hi
coroutine.resume(co, 4, 5)      --> co2  4  5
```

Finally, when a coroutine ends, any values returned by its main function go to the corresponding resume:

```
co = coroutine.create(function ()
        return 6, 7
     end)
print(coroutine.resume(co))    --> true  6  7
```

We seldom use all these facilities in the same coroutine, but all of them have their uses.

For those that already know something about coroutines, it is important to clarify some concepts before we go on. Lua offers what we call *asymmetric coroutines*. This means that it has a function to suspend the execution of a coroutine and a different function to resume a suspended coroutine. Some other languages offer *symmetric coroutines*, where there is only one function to transfer control from any coroutine to another.

Some people call asymmetric coroutine *semi-coroutines* (being not symmetrical, they are not really *co*). However, other people use the same term *semi-coroutine* to denote a restricted implementation of coroutines, where a coroutine can suspend its execution only when it is not calling any function, that is, when it has no pending calls in its control stack. In other words, only the main body of such semi-coroutines can yield. A *generator* in Python is an example of this meaning of semi-coroutines.

Unlike the difference between symmetric and asymmetric coroutines, the difference between coroutines and generators (as presented in Python) is a deep one; generators are simply not powerful enough to implement several interesting constructions that we can write with full coroutines. Lua offers full, asymmetric coroutines. Those that prefer symmetric coroutines can implement them on top of the asymmetric facilities of Lua. It is not a difficult task. (Basically, each transfer does a yield followed by a resume.)

9.2 Pipes and Filters

One of the most paradigmatic examples of coroutines is the producer–consumer problem. Let us suppose that we have a function that continually produces values (e.g., reading them from a file) and another function that continually consumes these values (e.g., writing them to another file). Typically, these two functions look like this:

```
function producer ()
  while true do
    local x = io.read()       -- produce new value
    send(x)                   -- send it to consumer
  end
end

function consumer ()
  while true do
    local x = receive()          -- receive value from producer
    io.write(x, "\n")            -- consume it
  end
end
```

(In this implementation, both the producer and the consumer run forever. It is easy to change them to stop when there are no more data to handle.) The problem here is how to match send with receive. It is a typical instance of the "who-has-the-main-loop" problem. Both the producer and the consumer are active, both have their own main loops, and both assume that the other is a callable service. For this particular example, it is easy to change the structure of one of the functions, unrolling its loop and making it a passive agent. However, this change of structure may be far from easy in other real scenarios.

Coroutines provide an ideal tool to match producers and consumers, because a resume–yield pair turns upside-down the typical relationship between caller and callee. When a coroutine calls `yield`, it does not enter into a new function; instead, it returns a pending call (to resume). Similarly, a call to `resume` does not start a new function, but returns a call to `yield`. This property is exactly what we need to match a send with a `receive` in such a way that each one acts as if it were the master and the other the slave. So, `receive` resumes the producer, so that it can produce a new value; and send yields the new value back to the consumer:

```
function receive ()
  local status, value = coroutine.resume(producer)
  return value
end

function send (x)
  coroutine.yield(x)
end
```

Of course, the producer must now be a coroutine:

```
producer = coroutine.create(
  function ()
    while true do
    local x = io.read()      -- produce new value
      send(x)
    end
  end)
```

In this design, the program starts by calling the consumer. When the consumer needs an item, it resumes the producer, which runs until it has an item to give to the consumer, and then stops until the consumer resumes it again. Therefore, we have what we call a *consumer-driven* design. Another way to write the program is to use a *producer-driven* design, where the consumer is the coroutine.

We can extend this design with filters, which are tasks that sit between the producer and the consumer doing some kind of transformation in the data. A *filter* is a consumer and a producer at the same time, so it resumes a producer to get new values and yields the transformed values to a consumer. As a trivial example, we can add to our previous code a filter that inserts a line number at the beginning of each line. The code is in Listing 9.1. The final bit simply creates the components it needs, connects them, and starts the final consumer:

```
p = producer()
f = filter(p)
consumer(f)
```

Or better yet:

```
consumer(filter(producer()))
```

Listing 9.1. Producer–consumer with filters:

```lua
function receive (prod)
  local status, value = coroutine.resume(prod)
  return value
end

function send (x)
  coroutine.yield(x)
end

function producer ()
  return coroutine.create(function ()
    while true do
      local x = io.read()      -- produce new value
      send(x)
    end
  end)
end

function filter (prod)
  return coroutine.create(function ()
    for line = 1, math.huge do
      local x = receive(prod)   -- get new value
      x = string.format("%5d %s", line, x)
      send(x)        -- send it to consumer
    end
  end)
end

function consumer (prod)
  while true do
    local x = receive(prod)     -- get new value
    io.write(x, "\n")           -- consume new value
  end
end
```

Listing 9.2. Function to generate all permutations of the first n elements of a:

```
function permgen (a, n)
  n = n or #a          -- default for 'n' is size of 'a'
  if n <= 1 then       -- nothing to change?
    printResult(a)
  else
    for i = 1, n do
      -- put i-th element as the last one
      a[n], a[i] = a[i], a[n]
      -- generate all permutations of the other elements
      permgen(a, n - 1)
      -- restore i-th element
      a[n], a[i] = a[i], a[n]
    end
  end
end
```

If you thought about UNIX pipes after reading the previous example, you are not alone. After all, coroutines are a kind of (non-preemptive) multithreading. With pipes, each task runs in a separate process; with coroutines, each task runs in a separate coroutine. Pipes provide a buffer between the writer (producer) and the reader (consumer) so there is some freedom in their relative speeds. This is important in the context of pipes, because the cost of switching between processes is high. With coroutines, the cost of switching between tasks is much smaller (roughly equivalent to a function call), so the writer and the reader can run hand in hand.

9.3 Coroutines as Iterators

We can see loop iterators as a particular example of the producer–consumer pattern: an iterator produces items to be consumed by the loop body. Therefore, it seems appropriate to use coroutines to write iterators. Indeed, coroutines provide a powerful tool for this task. Again, the key feature is their ability to turn inside out the relationship between caller and callee. With this feature, we can write iterators without worrying about how to keep state between successive calls to the iterator.

To illustrate this kind of use, let us write an iterator to traverse all permutations of a given array. It is not an easy task to write directly such an iterator, but it is not so difficult to write a recursive function that generates all these permutations. The idea is simple: put each array element in the last position, in turn, and recursively generate all permutations of the remaining elements. The code is in Listing 9.2. To put it to work, we must define an appropriate printResult function and call permgen with proper arguments:

```
function printResult (a)
  for i = 1, #a do
    io.write(a[i], " ")
  end
  io.write("\n")
end

permgen ({1,2,3,4})
  --> 2 3 4 1
  --> 3 2 4 1
  --> 3 4 2 1
      . . .
  --> 2 1 3 4
  --> 1 2 3 4
```

After we have the generator ready, it is an automatic task to convert it to an iterator. First, we change printResult to yield:

```
function permgen (a, n)
  n = n or #a
  if n <= 1 then
    coroutine.yield(a)
  else
    <as before>
```

Then, we define a factory that arranges for the generator to run inside a coroutine, and then create the iterator function. The iterator simply resumes the coroutine to produce the next permutation:

```
function permutations (a)
  local co = coroutine.create(function () permgen(a) end)
  return function ()    -- iterator
    local code, res = coroutine.resume(co)
    return res
  end
end
```

With this machinery in place, it is trivial to iterate over all permutations of an array with a **for** statement:

```
for p in permutations{"a", "b", "c"} do
  printResult(p)
end
  --> b c a
  --> c b a
  --> c a b
  --> a c b
  --> b a c
  --> a b c
```

The permutations function uses a common pattern in Lua, which packs a call to resume with its corresponding coroutine inside a function. This pattern is so common that Lua provides a special function for it: coroutine.wrap. Like create, wrap creates a new coroutine. Unlike create, wrap does not return the coroutine itself; instead, it returns a function that, when called, resumes the coroutine. Unlike the original resume, that function does not return an error code as its first result; instead, it raises the error in case of error. Using wrap, we can write permutations as follows:

```
function permutations (a)
  return coroutine.wrap(function () permgen(a) end)
end
```

Usually, coroutine.wrap is simpler to use than coroutine.create. It gives us exactly what we need from a coroutine: a function to resume it. However, it is also less flexible. There is no way to check the status of a coroutine created with wrap. Moreover, we cannot check for runtime errors.

9.4 Non-Preemptive Multithreading

As we saw earlier, coroutines allow a kind of collaborative multithreading. Each coroutine is equivalent to a thread. A pair yield–resume switches control from one thread to another. However, unlike regular multithreading, coroutines are non-preemptive. While a coroutine is running, it cannot be stopped from the outside. It suspends execution only when it explicitly requests so (through a call to yield). For several applications, this is not a problem, quite the opposite. Programming is much easier in the absence of preemption. You do not need to be paranoid about synchronization bugs, because all synchronization among threads is explicit in the program. You just need to ensure that a coroutine yields only when it is outside a critical region.

However, with non-preemptive multithreading, whenever any thread calls a blocking operation, the whole program blocks until the operation completes. For most applications, this is an unacceptable behavior, which leads many programmers to disregard coroutines as a real alternative to conventional multithreading. As we will see here, this problem has an interesting (and obvious, with hindsight) solution.

Let us assume a typical multithreading situation: we want to download several remote files through HTTP. To download several remote files, first we must learn how to download one remote file. In this example, we will use the *LuaSocket* library, developed by Diego Nehab. To download a file, we must open a connection to its site, send a request to the file, receive the file (in blocks), and close the connection. In Lua, we can write this task as follows. First, we load the LuaSocket library:

```
local socket = require "socket"
```

Then, we define the host and the file we want to download. In this example, we will download the HTML 3.2 Reference Specification from the World Wide Web Consortium site:

```
host = "www.w3.org"
file = "/TR/REC-html32.html"
```

Then, we open a TCP connection to port 80 (the standard port for HTTP connections) of that site:

```
c = assert(socket.connect(host, 80))
```

This operation returns a connection object, which we use to send the file request:

```
c:send("GET " .. file .. " HTTP/1.0\r\n\r\n")
```

Next, we read the file in blocks of 1 kB, writing each block to the standard output:

```
while true do
  local s, status, partial = c:receive(2^10)
  io.write(s or partial)
  if status == "closed" then break end
end
```

The receive function returns either a string with what it read or nil in case of error; in the later case it also returns an error code (status) and what it read until the error (partial). When the host closes the connection we print that remaining input and break the receive loop.

After downloading the file, we close the connection:

```
c:close()
```

Now that we know how to download one file, let us return to the problem of downloading several files. The trivial approach is to download one at a time. However, this sequential approach, where we start reading a file only after finishing the previous one, is too slow. When reading a remote file, a program spends most of its time waiting for data to arrive. More specifically, it spends most of its time blocked in the call to receive. So, the program could run much faster if it downloaded all files concurrently. Then, while a connection has no data available, the program can read from another connection. Clearly, coroutines offer a convenient way to structure these simultaneous downloads. We create a new thread for each download task. When a thread has no data available, it yields control to a simple dispatcher, which invokes another thread.

To rewrite the program with coroutines, we first rewrite the previous download code as a function. The result is in Listing 9.3. Because we are not interested in the remote file contents, this function counts and prints the file size, instead of writing the file to the standard output. (With several threads reading several files, the output would shuffle all files.)

In this new code, we use an auxiliary function (receive) to receive data from the connection. In the sequential approach, its code would be like this:

Listing 9.3. Function to download a Web page:

```
function download (host, file)
  local c = assert(socket.connect(host, 80))
  local count = 0     -- counts number of bytes read
  c:send("GET " .. file .. " HTTP/1.0\r\n\r\n")
  while true do
    local s, status = receive(c)
    count = count + #s
    if status == "closed" then break end
  end
  c:close()
  print(file, count)
end
```

```
function receive (connection)
  local s, status, partial = connection:receive(2^10)
  return s or partial, status
end
```

For the concurrent implementation, this function must receive data without blocking. Instead, if there is not enough data available, it yields. The new code is like this:

```
function receive (connection)
  connection:settimeout(0)        -- do not block
  local s, status, partial = connection:receive(2^10)
  if status == "timeout" then
    coroutine.yield(connection)
  end
  return s or partial, status
end
```

The call to settimeout(0) makes any operation over the connection a non-blocking operation. When the operation status is "timeout", it means that the operation returned without completion. In this case, the thread yields. The non-false argument passed to yield signals to the dispatcher that the thread is still performing its task. Note that, even in case of a timeout, the connection returns what it read until the timeout, which is in the partial variable.

Listing 9.4 shows the dispatcher plus some auxiliary code. Table threads keeps a list of all live threads for the dispatcher. Function get ensures that each download runs in an individual thread. The dispatcher itself is mainly a loop that goes through all threads, resuming them one by one. It must also remove from the list the threads that have finished their tasks. It stops the loop when there are no more threads to run.

Finally, the main program creates the threads it needs and calls the dispatcher. For instance, to download four documents from the W3C site, the main

Listing 9.4. The dispatcher:

```lua
threads = {}      -- list of all live threads

function get (host, file)
  -- create coroutine
  local co = coroutine.create(function ()
    download(host, file)
  end)
  -- insert it in the list
  table.insert(threads, co)
end

function dispatch ()
  local i = 1
  while true do
    if threads[i] == nil then    -- no more threads?
      if threads[1] == nil then break end   -- list is empty?
      i = 1                       -- restart the loop
    end
    local status, res = coroutine.resume(threads[i])
    if not res then       -- thread finished its task?
      table.remove(threads, i)
    else
      i = i + 1   -- go to next thread
    end
  end
end
```

program could be like this:

```lua
host = "www.w3.org"

get(host, "/TR/html401/html40.txt")
get(host, "/TR/2002/REC-xhtml1-20020801/xhtml1.pdf")
get(host, "/TR/REC-html32.html")
get(host, "/TR/2000/REC-DOM-Level-2-Core-20001113/DOM2-Core.txt")

dispatch()   -- main loop
```

My machine takes six seconds to download these four files using coroutines. With the sequential implementation, it takes more than twice this time (15 seconds).

Despite the speedup, this last implementation is far from optimal. Everything goes fine while at least one thread has something to read. However, when no thread has data to read, the dispatcher does a busy wait, going from thread

Listing 9.5. Dispatcher using `select`:

```
function dispatch ()
  local i = 1
  local timedout = {}
  while true do
    if threads[i] == nil then    -- no more threads?
      if threads[1] == nil then break end
      i = 1                       -- restart the loop
      timedout = {}
    end
    local status, res = coroutine.resume(threads[i])
    if not res then     -- thread finished its task?
      table.remove(threads, i)
    else                     -- time out
      i = i + 1
      timedout[#timedout + 1] = res
      if #timedout == #threads then    -- all threads blocked?
        socket.select(timedout)
      end
    end
  end
end
```

to thread only to check that they still have no data. As a result, this coroutine implementation uses almost 30 times more CPU than the sequential solution.

To avoid this behavior, we can use the `select` function from LuaSocket: it allows a program to block while waiting for a status change in a group of sockets. The changes in our implementation are small: we have to change only the dispatcher, as shown in Listing 9.5. Along the loop, this new dispatcher collects the timed-out connections in table `timedout`. (Remember that `receive` passes such connections to `yield`, thus `resume` returns them.) If all connections time out, the dispatcher calls `select` to wait for any of these connections to change status. This final implementation runs as fast as the previous implementation, with coroutines. Moreover, as it does not do busy waits, it uses just a little more CPU than the sequential implementation.

Exercises

Exercise 9.1: Use coroutines to transform the function in Exercise 5.4 into a generator for combinations, to be used like here:

```
for c in combinations({"a", "b", "c"}, 2) do
  printResult(c)
end
```

Exercise 9.2:   Implement and run the code of the previous section (non-preemptive multitasking).

Exercise 9.3:   Implement a `transfer` function in Lua. If you think about resume–yield as similar to call–return, a transfer would be like a goto: it suspends the running coroutine and resumes any other coroutine, given as an argument. (Hint: use a kind of dispatch to control your coroutines. Then, a transfer would yield to the dispatch signaling the next coroutine to run, and the dispatch would resume that next coroutine.)

10

Complete Examples

To end this introduction about the language, we show three simple but complete programs. The first example is the eight-queen problem. The second is a word-frequency program, which prints the most frequent words in a text. The last example is an implementation of the Markov chain algorithm, described by Kernighan & Pike in their book *The Practice of Programming* (Addison-Wesley, 1999).

10.1 The Eight-Queen Puzzle

Our first example is a very simple program that solves the *eight-queen puzzle*: the goal is to put eight queens in a chessboard in such a way that no queen can attack another one.

The first step to solve this problem is to note that any valid solution must have exactly one queen in each row. Therefore, we can represent solutions with a simple array of eight numbers, one for each row; each number tells at which column is the queen at that row. For instance, the array $\{3, 7, 2, 1, 8, 6, 5, 4\}$ means that there is one queen at row 1–column 3, another at row 2–column 7, etc. (By the way, this is not a valid solution; for instance, the queen at row 3–column 2 can attack the one at row 4–column 1.) Note that any valid solution must be a permutation of the integers 1 to 8, as a valid solution also must have exactly one queen in each column.

The complete program is in Listing 10.1. The first function is isplaceok, which checks whether a given position on a board is free from attacks from previously placed queens. Remember that, by representation, two queens cannot be on the same row, so function isplaceok checks whether there are no queens on the same column or on the same diagonals of the new position.

Listing 10.1. The eight-queen program:

```
local N = 8      -- board size

-- check whether position (n,c) is free from attacks
local function isplaceok (a, n, c)
  for i = 1, n - 1 do    -- for each queen already placed
    if (a[i] == c) or                 -- same column?
       (a[i] - i == c - n) or         -- same diagonal?
       (a[i] + i == c + n) then       -- same diagonal?
      return false              -- place can be attacked
    end
  end
  return true    -- no attacks; place is OK
end

-- print a board
local function printsolution (a)
  for i = 1, N do
    for j = 1, N do
      io.write(a[i] == j and "X" or "-", " ")
    end
    io.write("\n")
  end
  io.write("\n")
end

-- add to board 'a' all queens from 'n' to 'N'
local function addqueen (a, n)
  if n > N then    -- all queens have been placed?
    printsolution(a)
  else  -- try to place n-th queen
    for c = 1, N do
      if isplaceok(a, n, c) then
        a[n] = c    -- place n-th queen at column 'c'
        addqueen(a, n + 1)
      end
    end
  end
end

-- run the program
addqueen({}, 1)
```

Next we have function `printsolution`, which prints a board. It simply traverses the entire board, printing an 'X' at positions with a queen and a '-' at other positions. Each result looks like this:

```
X - - - - - - -
- - - - X - - -
- - - - - - - X
- - - - - X - -
- - X - - - - -
- - - - - - X -
- X - - - - - -
- - - X - - - -
```

The last function, `addqueen`, is the core of the program. It uses backtracking to search for valid solutions. First, it checks whether the solution is complete and, if so, prints that solution. Otherwise, it loops through all columns; for each column that is free from attacks, the program places the queen there and recursively tries to place the other queens.

Finally, the main body simply calls `addqueen` on an empty solution.

10.2 Most Frequent Words

Our next example is a simple program that reads a text and prints the most frequent words in that text.

The main data structure of this program is a simple table that associates each word in the text with its frequency counter. With this data structure, the program has three main tasks:

- Read the text, counting the number of occurrences of each word.

- Sort the list of word in descending order of frequencies.

- Print the first n entries in the sorted list.

To read the text, we can use the iterator `allwords` that we developed in Section 7.1. For each word we read, we increment its respective counter:

```
local counter = {}
for w in allwords do
  counter[w] = (counter[w] or 0) + 1
end
```

Note the **or** trick to handle non-initialized counters.

The next step is to sort the list of words. However, as the attentive reader may have noticed already, we do not have a list of words to sort! Nevertheless, it is easy to create one, using the words that appear as keys in table `counter`:

```
local words = {}
for w in pairs(counter) do
  words[#words + 1] = w
end
```

Listing 10.2. Word-frequency program:

```
local function allwords ()
  local auxwords = function ()
    for line in io.lines() do
      for word in string.gmatch(line, "%w+") do
        coroutine.yield(word)
      end
    end
  end
  return coroutine.wrap(auxwords)
end

local counter = {}
for w in allwords() do
  counter[w] = (counter[w] or 0) + 1
end

local words = {}
for w in pairs(counter) do
  words[#words + 1] = w
end

table.sort(words, function (w1, w2)
  return counter[w1] > counter[w2] or
         counter[w1] == counter[w2] and w1 < w2
end)

for i = 1, (tonumber(arg[1]) or 10) do
  print(words[i], counter[words[i]])
end
```

Once we have the list, we can sort it using the predefined function `table.sort`, which we discussed briefly in Chapter 6:

```
table.sort(words, function (w1, w2)
  return counter[w1] > counter[w2] or
         counter[w1] == counter[w2] and w1 < w2
end)
```

Words with larger counters come first; words with equal counts come in alphabetical order.

Listing 10.2 presents the complete program. Note the use of a coroutine to turn inside out the `auxwords` iterator, which is used in the following loop. In the last loop, which prints the results, the program assumes that its first argument is the number of words to be printed and uses a default of 10 words if no argument is given.

10.3   Markov Chain Algorithm

Our last example is an implementation of the *Markov chain algorithm*. The program generates pseudo-random text based on what words can follow a sequence of n previous words in a base text. For this implementation, we will assume that n is two.

The first part of the program reads the base text and builds a table that, for each prefix of two words, gives a list of the words that follow that prefix in the text. After building the table, the program uses it to generate random text, wherein each word follows two previous words with the same probability as in the base text. As a result, we have text that is very, but not quite, random. For instance, when applied to this book, the output of the program has pieces like *"Constructors can also traverse a table constructor, then the parentheses in the following line does the whole file in a field n to store the contents of each function, but to show its only argument. If you want to find the maximum element in an array can return both the maximum value and continues showing the prompt and running the code. The following words are reserved and cannot be used to convert between degrees and radians."*

We will code each prefix by its two words concatenated with a space in between:

```
function prefix (w1, w2)
    return w1 .. " " .. w2
end
```

We use the string NOWORD (a newline) to initialize the prefix words and to mark the end of the text. For instance, for the text "the more we try the more we do" the table of following words would be like this:

```
{ ["\n \n"] = {"the"},
  ["\n the"] = {"more"},
  ["the more"] = {"we", "we"},
  ["more we"] = {"try", "do"},
  ["we try"] = {"the"},
  ["try the"] = {"more"},
  ["we do"] = {"\n"},
}
```

The program keeps its table in variable statetab. To insert a new word in a prefix list of this table, we use the following function:

```
function insert (index, value)
    local list = statetab[index]
    if list == nil then
        statetab[index] = {value}
    else
        list[#list + 1] = value
    end
end
```

It first checks whether that prefix already has a list; if not, it creates a new one with the new value. Otherwise, it inserts the new value at the end of the existing list.

To build the statetab table, we keep two variables, w1 and w2, with the last two words read. For each new word read, we add it to the list associated with w1–w2 and then update w1 and w2.

After building the table, the program starts to generate a text with MAXGEN words. First, it re-initializes variables w1 and w2. Then, for each prefix, it chooses a next word randomly from the list of valid next words, prints this word, and updates w1 and w2. Listing 10.3 and Listing 10.4 show the complete program. Unlike our previous example, for most frequent words, here we use an implementation of allwords based on closures.

Exercises

Exercise 10.1: Modify the eight-queen program so that it stops after printing the first solution.

Exercise 10.2: An alternative implementation for the eight-queen problem would be to generate all possible permutations of 1 to 8 and, for each permutation, to check whether it is valid. Change the program to use this approach. How does the performance of the new program compare with the old one? (Hint: compare the total number of permutations with the number of times that the original program calls function isplaceok.)

Exercise 10.3: When we apply the word-frequency program to a text, usually the most frequent words are uninteresting small words like articles and prepositions. Change the program so that it ignores words with less than four letters.

Exercise 10.4: Generalize the Markov-chain algorithm so that it can use any size for the sequence of previous words used in the choice of the next word.

Listing 10.3. Auxiliary definitions for the Markov program:

```lua
function allwords ()
  local line = io.read()      -- current line
  local pos = 1               -- current position in the line
  return function ()          -- iterator function
    while line do             -- repeat while there are lines
      local s, e = string.find(line, "%w+", pos)
      if s then                             -- found a word?
        pos = e + 1                         -- update next position
        return string.sub(line, s, e)   -- return the word
      else
        line = io.read()          -- word not found; try next line
        pos = 1                   -- restart from first position
      end
    end
    return nil                -- no more lines: end of traversal
  end
end

function prefix (w1, w2)
  return w1 .. " " .. w2
end

local statetab = {}

function insert (index, value)
  local list = statetab[index]
  if list == nil then
    statetab[index] = {value}
  else
    list[#list + 1] = value
  end
end
```

Listing 10.4. The Markov program:

```
local N  = 2
local MAXGEN = 10000
local NOWORD = "\n"

-- build table
local w1, w2 = NOWORD, NOWORD
for w in allwords() do
  insert(prefix(w1, w2), w)
  w1 = w2; w2 = w;
end
insert(prefix(w1, w2), NOWORD)

-- generate text
w1 = NOWORD; w2 = NOWORD     -- reinitialize
for i = 1, MAXGEN do
  local list = statetab[prefix(w1, w2)]
  -- choose a random item from list
  local r = math.random(#list)
  local nextword = list[r]
  if nextword == NOWORD then return end
  io.write(nextword, " ")
  w1 = w2; w2 = nextword
end
```

Part II

Tables and Objects

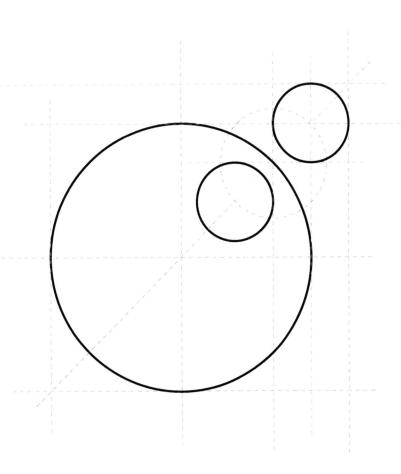

11

Data Structures

Tables in Lua are not a data structure; they are *the* data structure. All structures that other languages offer — arrays, records, lists, queues, sets — can be represented with tables in Lua. More to the point, Lua tables implement all these structures efficiently.

In traditional languages, such as C and Pascal, we implement most data structures with arrays and lists (where lists = records + pointers). Although we can implement arrays and lists using Lua tables (and sometimes we do this), tables are more powerful than arrays and lists; many algorithms are simplified to the point of triviality with the use of tables. For instance, we seldom write a search in Lua, because tables offer direct access to any type.

It takes a while to learn how to use tables efficiently. Here, I will show how to implement typical data structures with tables and will provide some examples of their use. We will start with arrays and lists, not because we need them for the other structures, but because most programmers are already familiar with them. We have already seen the basics of this material in the chapters about the language, but I will repeat it here for completeness.

11.1 Arrays

We implement arrays in Lua simply by indexing tables with integers. Therefore, arrays do not have a fixed size, but grow as needed. Usually, when we initialize the array we define its size indirectly. For instance, after the following code, any attempt to access a field outside the range 1–1000 will return nil, instead of zero:

```
a = {}      -- new array
for i = 1, 1000 do
  a[i] = 0
end
```

The length operator ('#') uses this fact to find the size of an array:

```
print(#a)          --> 1000
```

You can start an array at index 0, 1, or any other value:

```
-- creates an array with indices from -5 to 5
a = {}
for i = -5, 5 do
  a[i] = 0
end
```

However, it is customary in Lua to start arrays with index 1. The Lua libraries adhere to this convention; so does the length operator. If your arrays do not start with 1, you will not be able to use these facilities.

We can use a constructor to create and initialize arrays in a single expression:

```
squares = {1, 4, 9, 16, 25, 36, 49, 64, 81}
```

Such constructors can be as large as you need (well, up to a few million elements).

11.2   Matrices and Multi-Dimensional Arrays

There are two main ways to represent matrices in Lua. The first one is to use an array of arrays, that is, a table wherein each element is another table. For instance, you can create a matrix of zeros with dimensions N by M with the following code:

```
mt = {}            -- create the matrix
for i = 1, N do
  mt[i] = {}       -- create a new row
  for j = 1, M do
    mt[i][j] = 0
  end
end
```

Because tables are objects in Lua, you have to create each row explicitly to create a matrix. On the one hand, this is certainly more verbose than simply declaring a matrix, as you do in C or Pascal. On the other hand, it gives you more flexibility. For instance, you can create a triangular matrix changing the loop for j=1,M do... end in the previous example to for j=1,i do... end. With this code, the triangular matrix uses only half the memory of the original one.

The second way to represent a matrix in Lua is by composing the two indices into a single one. If the two indices are integers, you can multiply the first one by a suitable constant and then add the second index. With this approach, the following code would create our matrix of zeros with dimensions N by M:

```
mt = {}              -- create the matrix
for i = 1, N do
  for j = 1, M do
    mt[(i - 1)*M + j] = 0
  end
end
```

If the indices are strings, you can create a single index concatenating both indices with a character in between to separate them. For instance, you can index a matrix m with string indices s and t using the code m[s.."".."":".."..t], provided that both s and t do not contain colons; otherwise, pairs like ("a:", "b") and ("a", ":b") would collapse into a single index, "a::b". When in doubt, you can use a control character like '\0' to separate the indices.

Quite often, applications use a *sparse matrix*, a matrix wherein most elements are zero or nil. For instance, you can represent a graph by its adjacency matrix, which has the value x in position m,n when there is a connection with cost x between nodes m and n. When these nodes are not connected, the value in position m,n is nil. To represent a graph with ten thousand nodes, where each node has about five neighbors, you will need a matrix with a hundred million entries (a square matrix with 10000 columns and 10000 rows), but approximately only fifty thousand of them will not be nil (five non-nil columns for each row, corresponding to the five neighbors of each node). Many books on data structures discuss at length how to implement such sparse matrices without wasting 400 MB of memory, but you seldom need these techniques when programming in Lua. Because arrays are represented by tables, they are naturally sparse. With our first representation (tables of tables), you will need ten thousand tables, each one with about five elements, with a grand total of fifty thousand entries. With the second representation, you will have a single table, with fifty thousand entries in it. Whatever the representation, you need space only for the non-nil elements.

We cannot use the length operator over sparse matrices, because of the holes (nil values) between active entries. This is not a big loss; even if we could use it, we should not. For most operations, it would be quite inefficient to traverse all these empty entries. Instead, we can use pairs to traverse only the non-nil elements. For instance, to multiply a row by a constant, we can use the following code:

```
function mult (a, rowindex, k)
  local row = a[rowindex]
  for i, v in pairs(row) do
    row[i] = v * k
  end
end
```

Be aware, however, that keys have no intrinsic order in a table, so the iteration with pairs does not ensure that we visit the columns in increasing order. For some tasks (like our previous example), this is not a problem. For other tasks, you may need an alternative approach, such as linked lists.

11.3   Linked Lists

Because tables are dynamic entities, it is easy to implement linked lists in Lua. Each node is represented by a table and links are simply table fields that contain references to other tables. For instance, let us implement a basic list, where each node has two fields, next and value. A simple variable is the list root:

```
list = nil
```

To insert an element at the beginning of the list, with a value v, we do:

```
list = {next = list, value = v}
```

To traverse the list, we write:

```
local l = list
while l do
  <visit l.value>
  l = l.next
end
```

Other kinds of lists, such as double-linked lists or circular lists, are also implemented easily. However, you seldom need those structures in Lua, because usually there is a simpler way to represent your data without using linked lists. For instance, we can represent a stack with an (unbounded) array.

11.4   Queues and Double Queues

A simple way to implement queues in Lua is with functions insert and remove from the table library. These functions insert and remove elements in any position of an array, moving other elements to accommodate the operation. However, these moves can be expensive for large structures. A more efficient implementation uses two indices, one for the first element and another for the last:

```
function ListNew ()
  return {first = 0, last = -1}
end
```

To avoid polluting the global space, we will define all list operations inside a table, properly called List (that is, we will create a *module*). Therefore, we rewrite our last example like this:

```
List = {}
function List.new ()
  return {first = 0, last = -1}
end
```

Now, we can insert or remove an element at both ends in constant time:

```
function List.pushfirst (list, value)
  local first = list.first - 1
  list.first = first
  list[first] = value
end

function List.pushlast (list, value)
  local last = list.last + 1
  list.last = last
  list[last] = value
end

function List.popfirst (list)
  local first = list.first
  if first > list.last then error("list is empty") end
  local value = list[first]
  list[first] = nil        -- to allow garbage collection
  list.first = first + 1
  return value
end

function List.poplast (list)
  local last = list.last
  if list.first > last then error("list is empty") end
  local value = list[last]
  list[last] = nil         -- to allow garbage collection
  list.last = last - 1
  return value
end
```

If you use this structure in a strict queue discipline, calling only pushlast and popfirst, both first and last will increase continually. However, because we represent arrays in Lua with tables, you can index them either from 1 to 20 or from 16777216 to 16777236. Because Lua uses double precision to represent numbers, your program can run for two hundred years, doing one million insertions per second, before it has problems with overflows.

11.5   Sets and Bags

Suppose you want to list all identifiers used in a program source; somehow you need to filter the reserved words out of your listing. Some C programmers could be tempted to represent the set of reserved words as an array of strings, and then to search this array to know whether a given word is in the set. To speed up the search, they could even use a binary tree to represent the set.

In Lua, an efficient and simple way to represent such sets is to put the set elements as *indices* in a table. Then, instead of searching the table for a given element, you just index the table and test whether the result is nil or not. In our example, we could write the next code:

```
reserved = {
  ["while"] = true,      ["end"] = true,
  ["function"] = true,   ["local"] = true,
}

for w in allwords() do
  if not reserved[w] then
    <do something with 'w'>    -- 'w' is not a reserved word
  end
end
```

(Because these words are reserved in Lua, we cannot use them as identifiers; for instance, we cannot write while=true. Instead, we use the ["while"]=true notation.)

You can have a clearer initialization using an auxiliary function to build the set:

```
function Set (list)
  local set = {}
  for _, l in ipairs(list) do set[l] = true end
  return set
end

reserved = Set{"while", "end", "function", "local", }
```

Bags, also called *multisets*, differ from regular sets in that each element can appear multiple times. An easy representation for bags in Lua is similar to the previous representation for sets, but with a counter associated to each key. To insert an element we increment its counter:

```
function insert (bag, element)
  bag[element] = (bag[element] or 0) + 1
end
```

To remove an element we decrement its counter:

```
function remove (bag, element)
  local count = bag[element]
  bag[element] = (count and count > 1) and count - 1 or nil
end
```

We only keep the counter if it already exists and it is still greater than zero.

ers

a string piecemeal, for instance reading a file line by
ld look like this:

```
es() do
ne .. "\n"
```

is code in Lua can cause a huge performance penalty
it takes 1.5 minutes to read a 1 MB file on my old

Why is that? To understand what happens, let us assume that we are
in the middle of the read loop; each line has 20 bytes and we have already
read some 2500 lines, so buff is a string with 50 kB. When Lua concatenates
buff..line.."\n", it allocates a new string with 50 020 bytes and copies the
50 000 bytes from buff into this new string. That is, for each new line, Lua
moves around 50 kB of memory, and growing. More specifically, the algorithm
is quadratic. After reading 100 new lines (only 2 kB), Lua has already moved
more than 5 MB of memory. When Lua finishes reading 350 kB, it has moved
around more than 50 GB. (This problem is not peculiar to Lua: other languages
wherein strings are immutable values present a similar behavior, Java being
the most famous example.)

Before we continue, we should remark that, despite all I said, this situation
is not a common problem. For small strings, the above loop is fine. To read
an entire file, Lua provides the io.read("*a") option, which reads the file at
once. However, sometimes we must face this problem. Java offers the structure
StringBuffer to ameliorate the problem. In Lua, we can use a table as the string
buffer. The key to this approach is the table.concat function, which returns the
concatenation of all the strings of a given list. Using concat, we can write our
previous loop as follows:

```
local t = {}
for line in io.lines() do
  t[#t + 1] = line .. "\n"
end
local s = table.concat(t)
```

This algorithm takes less than 0.5 seconds to read the same file that took almost
a minute to read with the original code. (Nevertheless, for reading a whole file
it is still better to use io.read with the "*a" option.)

We can do even better. The concat function accepts an optional second
argument, which is a separator to be inserted between the strings. Using this
separator, we do not need to insert a newline after each line:

---

[1]My "old Pentium machine" is a single-core 32-bit Pentium 3GHz. I measured all performance
data in this book on that machine.

```
local t = {}
for line in io.lines() do
  t[#t + 1] = line
end
s = table.concat(t, "\n") .. "\n"
```

Function `concat` inserts the separator between the strings, but we still have to add the last newline. This last concatenation duplicates the resulting string, which can be quite long. There is no option to make `concat` insert this extra separator, but we can deceive it, inserting an extra empty string in t:

```
t[#t + 1] = ""
s = table.concat(t, "\n")
```

The extra newline that `concat` adds before this empty string is at the end of the resulting string, as we wanted.

11.7   Graphs

Like any reasonable language, Lua allows multiple implementations for graphs, each one better adapted to some particular algorithms. Here we will see a simple object-oriented implementation, where we represent nodes as objects (actually tables, of course) and arcs as references between nodes.

We will represent each node as a table with two fields: `name`, with the node's name; and `adj`, the set of nodes adjacent to this one. Because we will read the graph from a text file, we need a way to find a node given its name. So, we will use an extra table mapping names to nodes. Given a name, function `name2node` returns the corresponding node:

```
local function name2node (graph, name)
  local node = graph[name]
  if not node then
    -- node does not exist; create a new one
    node = {name = name, adj = {}}
    graph[name] = node
  end
  return node
end
```

Listing 11.1 shows the function that builds a graph. It reads a file where each line has two node names, meaning that there is an arc from the first node to the second. For each line, it uses `string.match` to split the line in two names, finds the nodes corresponding to these names (creating the nodes if needed), and connects the nodes.

Listing 11.2 illustrates an algorithm using such graphs. Function `findpath` searches for a path between two nodes using a depth-first traversal. Its first parameter is the current node; the second is its goal; the third parameter keeps the path from the origin to the current node; the last parameter is a set with all

Listing 11.1. Reading a graph from a file:

```lua
function readgraph ()
  local graph = {}
  for line in io.lines() do
    -- split line in two names
    local namefrom, nameto = string.match(line, "(%S+)%s+(%S+)")
    -- find corresponding nodes
    local from = name2node(graph, namefrom)
    local to = name2node(graph, nameto)
    -- adds 'to' to the adjacent set of 'from'
    from.adj[to] = true
  end
  return graph
end
```

Listing 11.2. Finding a path between two nodes:

```lua
function findpath (curr, to, path, visited)
  path = path or {}
  visited = visited or {}
  if visited[curr] then      -- node already visited?
    return nil               -- no path here
  end
  visited[curr] = true       -- mark node as visited
  path[#path + 1] = curr     -- add it to path
  if curr == to then         -- final node?
    return path
  end
  -- try all adjacent nodes
  for node in pairs(curr.adj) do
    local p = findpath(node, to, path, visited)
    if p then return p end
  end
  path[#path] = nil          -- remove node from path
end
```

the nodes already visited (to avoid loops). Note how the algorithm manipulates nodes directly, without using their names. For instance, `visited` is a set of nodes, not of node names. Similarly, `path` is a list of nodes.

To test this code, we add a function to print a path and some code to put it all to work:

```
function printpath (path)
  for i = 1, #path do
    print(path[i].name)
  end
end

g = readgraph()
a = name2node(g, "a")
b = name2node(g, "b")
p = findpath(a, b)
if p then printpath(p) end
```

Exercises

Exercise 11.1: Modify the queue implementation so that both indices return to zero when the queue is empty.

Exercise 11.2: Repeat Exercise 10.3 but, instead of using length as the criteria for ignoring a word, the program should read from a text file a list of words to be ignored.

Exercise 11.3: Modify the graph structure so that it can keep a label for each arc. The structure should represent each arc by an object, too, with two fields: its label and the node it points to. Instead of an adjacent set, each node keeps an incident set that contains the arcs that originate at that node.

Adapt the `readgraph` function to read two node names plus a label from each line in the input file. (Assume that the label is a number.)

Exercise 11.4: Assume the graph representation of the previous exercise, where the label of each arc represents the distance between its end nodes. Write a function to find the shortest path between two given nodes. (Hint: use Dijkstra's algorithm.)

12

Data Files and Persistence

When dealing with data files, it is usually much easier to write the data than to read it back. When we write a file, we have full control of what is going on. When we read a file, on the other hand, we do not know what to expect. Besides all the kinds of data that a correct file can contain, a robust program should also handle bad files gracefully. Therefore, coding robust input routines is always difficult.

In this chapter, we will see how we can use Lua to eliminate all code for reading data from our programs, simply by writing the data in an appropriate format.

12.1 Data Files

Table constructors provide an interesting alternative for file formats. With a little extra work when writing data, reading becomes trivial. The technique is to write our data file as Lua code that, when run, builds the data into the program. With table constructors, these chunks can look remarkably like a plain data file.

As usual, let us see an example to make things clear. If our data file is in a predefined format, such as CSV (Comma-Separated Values) or XML, we have little choice. However, if we are going to create the file for our own use, we can use Lua constructors as our format. In this format, we represent each data record as a Lua constructor. Instead of writing in our data file something like

```
Donald E. Knuth,Literate Programming,CSLI,1992
Jon Bentley,More Programming Pearls,Addison-Wesley,1990
```

we write

```
Entry{"Donald E. Knuth",
      "Literate Programming",
      "CSLI",
      1992}

Entry{"Jon Bentley",
      "More Programming Pearls",
      "Addison-Wesley",
      1990}
```

Remember that Entry{*code*} is the same as Entry({*code*}), that is, a call to some function Entry with a table as its single argument. So, that previous piece of data is a Lua program. To read that file, we only need to run it, with a sensible definition for Entry. For instance, the following program counts the number of entries in a data file:

```
local count = 0
function Entry () count = count + 1 end
dofile("data")
print("number of entries: " .. count)
```

The next program collects in a set the names of all authors found in the file, and then prints them (not necessarily in the same order as in the file):

```
local authors = {}       -- a set to collect authors
function Entry (b) authors[b[1]] = true end
dofile("data")
for name in pairs(authors) do print(name) end
```

Notice the event-driven approach in these program fragments: the Entry function acts as a callback function, which is called during the dofile for each entry in the data file.

When file size is not a big concern, we can use name-value pairs for our representation:[1]

```
Entry{
  author = "Donald E. Knuth",
  title = "Literate Programming",
  publisher = "CSLI",
  year = 1992
}

Entry{
  author = "Jon Bentley",
  title = "More Programming Pearls",
  year = 1990,
  publisher = "Addison-Wesley",
}
```

---

[1]If this format reminds you of BibTeX, it is not a coincidence. BibTeX was one of the inspirations for the constructor syntax in Lua.

This format is what we call a *self-describing data* format, because each piece of data has attached to it a short description of its meaning. Self-describing data are more readable (by humans, at least) than CSV or other compact notations; they are easy to edit by hand, when necessary; and they allow us to make small modifications in the basic format without having to change the data file. For instance, if we add a new field we need only a small change in the reading program, so that it supplies a default value when the field is absent.

With the name-value format, our program to collect authors becomes this:

```
local authors = {}       -- a set to collect authors
function Entry (b) authors[b.author] = true end
dofile("data")
for name in pairs(authors) do print(name) end
```

Now the order of fields is irrelevant. Even if some entries do not have an author, we have to adapt only the Entry function:

```
function Entry (b)
    if b.author then authors[b.author] = true end
end
```

Lua not only runs fast, but it also compiles fast. For instance, the above program for listing authors processes 1 MB of data in a tenth of a second.[2] This is not by chance. Data description has been one of the main applications of Lua since its creation and we took great care to make its compiler fast for large programs.

12.2 Serialization

Frequently we need to serialize some data, that is, to convert the data into a stream of bytes or characters, so that we can save it into a file or send it through a network connection. We can represent serialized data as Lua code in such a way that, when we run the code, it reconstructs the saved values into the reading program.

Usually, if we want to restore the value of a global variable, our chunk will be something like varname=*exp*, where *exp* is the Lua code to create the value. The varname is the easy part, so let us see how to write the code that creates a value. For a numeric value, the task is easy:

```
function serialize (o)
    if type(o) == "number" then
        io.write(o)
    else <other cases>
    end
end
```

By writing a number in decimal format, however, you risk losing some precision. In Lua 5.2, you can use a hexadecimal format to avoid this problem:

---

[2]This is on my old Pentium machine.

```
        if type(o) == "number" then
          io.write(string.format("%a", o))
```

With this format ("%a"), the read number will have exactly the same bits of the original one.

For a string value, a naive approach would be something like this:

```
        if type(o) == "string" then
          io.write("'", o, "'")
```

However, if the string contains special characters (such as quotes or newlines) the resulting code will not be a valid Lua program.

You may be tempted to solve this problem changing quotes:

```
        if type(o) == "string" then
          io.write("[[", o, "]]")
```

Beware! If a malicious user manages to direct your program to save something like "]]..os.execute('rm *')..[[" (for instance, she can supply this string as her address), your final chunk will be

```
        varname = [[ ]]..os.execute('rm *')..[[ ]]
```

You will have a bad surprise trying to load this "data".

A simple way to quote a string in a secure way is with the option "%q" from the string.format function. It surrounds the string with double quotes and properly escapes double quotes, newlines, and some other characters inside the string:

```
        a = 'a "problematic" \\string'
        print(string.format("%q", a))     --> "a \"problematic\" \\string"
```

Using this feature, our serialize function now looks like this:

```
        function serialize (o)
          if type(o) == "number" then
            io.write(o)
          elseif type(o) == "string" then
            io.write(string.format("%q", o))
          else <other cases>
          end
        end
```

Since version 5.1 Lua offers another option to quote arbitrary strings in a secure way, with the notation [=[...]=] for long strings. However, this new notation is mainly intended for hand-written code, where we do not want to change a literal string in any way. In automatically generated code, it is easier to escape problematic characters, as the option "%q" from string.format does.

If you nevertheless want to use the long-string notation for automatically generated code, you must take care of some details. The first one is that you must choose a proper number of equal signs. A good proper number is one more than the maximum that appears in the original string. Because strings

Listing 12.1. Quoting arbitrary literal strings:

```
function quote (s)
  -- find maximum length of sequences of equal signs
  local n = -1
  for w in string.gmatch(s, "]=*]") do
    n = math.max(n, #w - 2)    -- -2 to remove the ']'s
  end

  -- produce a string with 'n' plus one equal signs
  local eq = string.rep("=", n + 1)

  -- build quoted string
  return string.format(" [%s[\n%s]%s] ", eq, s, eq)
end
```

containing long sequences of equal signs are not uncommon (e.g., comments delimiting parts of a source code), we can limit our attention to sequences of equal signs enclosed by closing square brackets; other sequences cannot produce an erroneous end-of-string mark. The second detail is that Lua always ignores a newline at the beginning of a long string; a simple way to avoid this problem is to add a newline to be ignored.

The quote function in Listing 12.1 is the result of our previous remarks. It receives an arbitrary string and returns it formatted as a long string. The call to string.gmatch creates an iterator to traverse all occurrences of the pattern ']=*]' (that is, a closing square bracket followed by a sequence of zero or more equal signs followed by another closing square bracket) in the string s.[3] For each occurrence, the loop updates n with the maximum number of equal signs so far. After the loop, we use string.rep to replicate an equal sign n+1 times, which is one more than the maximum occurring in the string. Finally, string.format encloses s with pairs of brackets with the correct number of equal signs in between and adds extra spaces around the quoted string plus a newline at the beginning of the enclosed string.

Saving tables without cycles

Our next (and harder) task is to save tables. There are several ways to save them, according to what restrictions we assume about the table structure. No single algorithm is appropriate for all cases. Simple tables not only need simpler algorithms, but also the resulting files can be more aesthetic.

Our first attempt is in Listing 12.2. Despite its simplicity, that function does a reasonable job. It even handles nested tables (that is, tables within other tables), as long as the table structure is a tree (that is, there are no shared

---

[3]We will discuss pattern matching in Chapter 21.

Listing 12.2. Serializing tables without cycles:

```
function serialize (o)
  if type(o) == "number" then
    io.write(o)
  elseif type(o) == "string" then
    io.write(string.format("%q", o))
  elseif type(o) == "table" then
    io.write("{\n")
    for k,v in pairs(o) do
      io.write("  ", k, " = ")
      serialize(v)
      io.write(",\n")
    end
    io.write("}\n")
  else
    error("cannot serialize a " .. type(o))
  end
end
```

subtables and no cycles). A small aesthetic improvement would be to indent occasional nested tables; see Exercise 12.1.

The previous function assumes that all keys in a table are valid identifiers. If a table has numeric keys, or string keys that are not syntactic valid Lua identifiers, we are in trouble. A simple way to solve this difficulty is to use the following code to write each key:

```
io.write("  ["); serialize(k); io.write("] = ")
```

With this change, we improve the robustness of our function, at the cost of the aesthetics of the resulting file. Consider the next call:

```
serialize{a=12, b='Lua', key='another "one"'}
```

The result of this call using the first version of serialize is this:

```
{
  a = 12,
  b = "Lua",
  key = "another \"one\"",
}
```

Compare it with the result using the second version:

```
{
  ["a"] = 12,
  ["b"] = "Lua",
  ["key"] = "another \"one\"",
}
```

We can have both robustness and aesthetics by testing for each case whether it needs the square brackets; again, we will leave this improvement as an exercise.

Saving tables with cycles

To handle tables with generic topology (i.e., with cycles and shared subtables) we need a different approach. Constructors cannot represent such tables, so we will not use them. To represent cycles we need names, so our next function will get as arguments the value to be saved plus its name. Moreover, we must keep track of the names of the tables already saved, to reuse them when we detect a cycle. We will use an extra table for this tracking. This table will have tables as indices and their names as the associated values.

The resulting code is in Listing 12.3. We keep the restriction that the tables we want to save have only strings and numbers as keys. The basicSerialize function serializes these basic types, returning the result. The next function, save, does the hard work. The saved parameter is the table that keeps track of tables already saved. As an example, if we build a table like

```
a = {x=1, y=2; {3,4,5}}
a[2] = a      -- cycle
a.z = a[1]    -- shared subtable
```

then the call save("a",a) will save it as follows:

```
a = {}
a[1] = {}
a[1][1] = 3
a[1][2] = 4
a[1][3] = 5

a[2] = a
a["y"] = 2
a["x"] = 1
a["z"] = a[1]
```

The actual order of these assignments can vary, as it depends on a table traversal. Nevertheless, the algorithm ensures that any previous node needed in a new definition is already defined.

If we want to save several values with shared parts, we can make the calls to save using the same saved table. For instance, assume the following two tables:

```
a = {{"one", "two"}, 3}
b = {k = a[1]}
```

Listing 12.3. Saving tables with cycles:

```
function basicSerialize (o)
  if type(o) == "number" then
    return tostring(o)
  else    -- assume it is a string
    return string.format("%q", o)
  end
end

function save (name, value, saved)
  saved = saved or {}                     -- initial value
  io.write(name, " = ")
  if type(value) == "number" or type(value) == "string" then
    io.write(basicSerialize(value), "\n")
  elseif type(value) == "table" then
    if saved[value] then                  -- value already saved?
      io.write(saved[value], "\n")        -- use its previous name
    else
      saved[value] = name                 -- save name for next time
      io.write("{}\n")                    -- create a new table
      for k,v in pairs(value) do          -- save its fields
        k = basicSerialize(k)
        local fname = string.format("%s[%s]", name, k)
        save(fname, v, saved)
      end
    end
  else
    error("cannot save a " .. type(value))
  end
end
```

If we save them independently, the result will not have common parts:

```
save("a", a)
save("b", b)

  --> a = {}
  --> a[1] = {}
  --> a[1][1] = "one"
  --> a[1][2] = "two"
  --> a[2] = 3
  --> b = {}
  --> b["k"] = {}
  --> b["k"][1] = "one"
  --> b["k"][2] = "two"
```

However, if we use the same saved table for both calls to save, then the result will share common parts:

```
local t = {}
save("a", a, t)
save("b", b, t)

    --> a = {}
    --> a[1] = {}
    --> a[1][1] = "one"
    --> a[1][2] = "two"
    --> a[2] = 3
    --> b = {}
    --> b["k"] = a[1]
```

As is usual in Lua, there are several other alternatives. Among them, we can save a value without giving it a global name (instead, the chunk builds a local value and returns it), we can handle functions (by building an auxiliary table that associates each function to its name), and so on. Lua gives you the power; you build the mechanisms.

Exercises

Exercise 12.1: Modify the code in Listing 12.2 so that it indents nested tables. (Hint: add an extra parameter to serialize with the indentation string.)

Exercise 12.2: Modify the code in Listing 12.2 so that it uses the syntax ["*key*"]=*value*, as suggested in Section 12.2.

Exercise 12.3: Modify the code of the previous exercise so that it uses the syntax ["*key*"]=*value* only when necessary (that is, when the key is a string but not a valid identifier).

Exercise 12.4: Modify the code of the previous exercise so that it uses the constructor syntax for lists whenever possible. For instance, it should serialize the table {14, 15, 19} as {14, 15, 19}, not as {[1]=14, [2]=15, [3]=19}. (Hint: start by saving the values of keys 1,2,..., as long as they are not nil. Take care not to save them again when traversing the rest of the table.)

Exercise 12.5: The approach of avoiding constructors when saving tables with cycles is too radical. It is possible to save the table in a more pleasant format using constructors for the general case, and to use assignments later only to fix sharing and loops.

Reimplement function save using this approach. Add to it all the goodies that you have implemented in the previous exercises (indentation, record syntax, and list syntax).

13

Metatables and Metamethods

Usually, each value in Lua has a quite predictable set of operations. We can add numbers, we can concatenate strings, we can insert key–value pairs into tables, and so on. However, we cannot add tables, we cannot compare functions, and we cannot call a string. Unless we use metatables.

Metatables allow us to change the behavior of a value when confronted with an undefined operation. For instance, using metatables, we can define how Lua computes the expression a+b, where a and b are tables. Whenever Lua tries to add two tables, it checks whether either of them has a *metatable* and whether this metatable has an __add field. If Lua finds this field, it calls the corresponding value — the so-called *metamethod*, which should be a function — to compute the sum.

Each value in Lua can have an associated metatable. Tables and userdata have individual metatables; values of other types share one single metatable for all values of that type. Lua always creates new tables without metatables:

```
t = {}
print(getmetatable(t))   --> nil
```

We can use setmetatable to set or change the metatable of any table:

```
t1 = {}
setmetatable(t, t1)
print(getmetatable(t) == t1)   --> true
```

From Lua we can set the metatables only of tables; to manipulate the metatables of values of other types we must use C code.[1] As we will see later, in

---

[1]The main reason for this restriction is to curb excessive use of type-wide metatables. Experience with older versions of Lua has shown that those global settings frequently lead to non-reusable code.

Chapter 21, the string library sets a metatable for strings. All other types by
default have no metatable:

```
print(getmetatable("hi"))          --> table: 0x80772e0
print(getmetatable("xuxu"))        --> table: 0x80772e0
print(getmetatable(10))            --> nil
print(getmetatable(print))         --> nil
```

Any table can be the metatable of any value; a group of related tables can
share a common metatable, which describes their common behavior; a table
can be its own metatable, so that it describes its own individual behavior. Any
configuration is valid.

13.1   Arithmetic Metamethods

In this section, we will introduce a simple example to explain how to use metatables. Suppose we are using tables to represent sets, with functions to compute
set union, intersection, and the like, as shown in Listing 13.1. To keep our
namespace clean, we store these functions inside a table called Set.

Now, we want to use the addition operator ('+') to compute the union of
two sets. For that, we will arrange for all tables representing sets to share a
metatable. This metatable will define how they react to the addition operator.
Our first step is to create a regular table, which we will use as the metatable for
sets:

```
local mt = {}      -- metatable for sets
```

The next step is to modify the Set.new function, which creates sets. The new
version has only one extra line, which sets mt as the metatable for the tables
that it creates:

```
function Set.new (l)     -- 2nd version
  local set = {}
  setmetatable(set, mt)
  for _, v in ipairs(l) do set[v] = true end
  return set
end
```

After that, every set we create with Set.new will have that same table as its
metatable:

```
s1 = Set.new{10, 20, 30, 50}
s2 = Set.new{30, 1}
print(getmetatable(s1))          --> table: 00672B60
print(getmetatable(s2))          --> table: 00672B60
```

Finally, we add to the metatable the metamethod, a field __add that describes
how to perform the addition:

```
mt.__add = Set.union
```

Listing 13.1. A simple implementation for sets:

```lua
Set = {}
-- create a new set with the values of a given list
function Set.new (l)
  local set = {}
  for _, v in ipairs(l) do set[v] = true end
  return set
end

function Set.union (a, b)
  local res = Set.new{}
  for k in pairs(a) do res[k] = true end
  for k in pairs(b) do res[k] = true end
  return res
end

function Set.intersection (a, b)
  local res = Set.new{}
  for k in pairs(a) do
    res[k] = b[k]
  end
  return res
end

-- presents a set as a string
function Set.tostring (set)
  local l = {}      -- list to put all elements from the set
  for e in pairs(set) do
    l[#l + 1] = e
  end
  return "{" .. table.concat(l, ", ") .. "}"
end

-- print a set
function Set.print (s)
  print(Set.tostring(s))
end
```

After that, whenever Lua tries to add two sets it will call the Set.union function, with the two operands as arguments.

With the metamethod in place, we can use the addition operator to do set unions:

```
s3 = s1 + s2
Set.print(s3)   --> {1, 10, 20, 30, 50}
```

Similarly, we may set the multiplication operator to perform set intersection:

```
mt.__mul = Set.intersection
```

```
Set.print((s1 + s2)*s1)      --> {10, 20, 30, 50}
```

For each arithmetic operator there is a corresponding field name in a metatable. Besides __add and __mul, there are __sub (for subtraction), __div (for division), __unm (for negation), __mod (for modulo), and __pow (for exponentiation). We may define also the field __concat, to describe a behavior for the concatenation operator.

When we add two sets, there is no question about what metatable to use. However, we may write an expression that mixes two values with different metatables, for instance like this:

```
s = Set.new{1,2,3}
s = s + 8
```

When looking for a metamethod, Lua does the following steps: if the first value has a metatable with an __add field, Lua uses this field as the metamethod, independently of the second value; otherwise, if the second value has a metatable with an __add field, Lua uses this field as the metamethod; otherwise, Lua raises an error. Therefore, the last example will call Set.union, as will the expressions 10+s and "hello"+s.

Lua does not care about these mixed types, but our implementation does. If we run the s=s+8 example, the error we get will be inside Set.union:

```
bad argument #1 to 'pairs' (table expected, got number)
```

If we want more lucid error messages, we must check the type of the operands explicitly before attempting to perform the operation:

```
function Set.union (a, b)
  if getmetatable(a) ~= mt or getmetatable(b) ~= mt then
    error("attempt to 'add' a set with a non-set value", 2)
  end
  <as before>
```

Remember that the second argument to error (2, in this example) directs the error message to where the operation was called.

13.2 Relational Metamethods

Metatables also allow us to give meaning to the relational operators, through the metamethods __eq (*equal to*), __lt (*less than*), and __le (*less than or equal to*). There are no separate metamethods for the other three relational operators: Lua translates a~=b to not (a==b), a>b to b<a, and a>=b to b<=a.

Until version 4.0, Lua translated all order operators to a single one, by translating a<=b to not (b<a). However, this translation is incorrect when we have a *partial order*, that is, when not all elements in our type are properly ordered. For instance, floating-point numbers are not totally ordered in most machines, because of the value *Not a Number* (*NaN*). According to the IEEE 754 standard, NaN represents undefined values, such as the result of $0/0$. The standard specifies that any comparison that involves NaN should result in false. This means that NaN<=x is always false, but x<NaN is also false. It also implies that the translation from a<=b to not (b<a) is not valid in this case.

In our example with sets, we have a similar problem. An obvious (and useful) meaning for <= in sets is set containment: a<=b means that a is a subset of b. With this meaning, again it is possible that both a<=b and b<a are false; therefore, we need separate implementations for __le (*less or equal*) and __lt (*less than*):

```
mt.__le = function (a, b)     -- set containment
  for k in pairs(a) do
    if not b[k] then return false end
  end
  return true
end

mt.__lt = function (a, b)
  return a <= b and not (b <= a)
end
```

Finally, we can define set equality through set containment:

```
mt.__eq = function (a, b)
  return a <= b and b <= a
end
```

After these definitions, we are ready to compare sets:

```
s1 = Set.new{2, 4}
s2 = Set.new{4, 10, 2}
print(s1 <= s2)        --> true
print(s1 < s2)         --> true
print(s1 >= s1)        --> true
print(s1 > s1)         --> false
print(s1 == s2 * s1)   --> true
```

For types that have a complete order, we do not need to define a __leq metamethod. In its absence, Lua will use the __lt entry.

The equality comparison has some restrictions. If two objects have different basic types or different metamethods, the equality operation results in **false**, without even calling any metamethod. So, a set will always be different from a number, no matter what its metamethod says.

13.3 Library-Defined Metamethods

So far, all the metamethods we have seen are for the Lua core. It is the virtual machine that detects that the values involved in an operation have metatables with metamethods for that particular operation. However, because metatables are regular tables, anyone can use them. So, it is a common practice for libraries to define their own fields in metatables.

Function `tostring` provides a typical example. As we saw earlier, `tostring` represents tables in a rather simple format:

```
print({})      --> table: 0x8062ac0
```

Function `print` always calls `tostring` to format its output. However, when formatting any value, `tostring` first checks whether the value has a `__tostring` metamethod. In this case, `tostring` calls the metamethod to do its job, passing the object as an argument. Whatever this metamethod returns is the result of `tostring`.

In our example with sets, we have already defined a function to present a set as a string. So, we need only to set the `__tostring` field in the metatable:

```
mt.__tostring = Set.tostring
```

After that, whenever we call `print` with a set as its argument, `print` calls `tostring` that calls `Set.tostring`:

```
s1 = Set.new{10, 4, 5}
print(s1)     --> {4, 5, 10}
```

Functions `setmetatable` and `getmetatable` also use a metafield, in this case to protect metatables. Suppose you want to protect your sets, so that users can neither see nor change their metatables. If you set a `__metatable` field in the metatable, `getmetatable` will return the value of this field, whereas `setmetatable` will raise an error:

```
mt.__metatable = "not your business"

s1 = Set.new{}
print(getmetatable(s1))     --> not your business
setmetatable(s1, {})
   stdin:1: cannot change protected metatable
```

In Lua 5.2, `pairs` and `ipairs` also got metatables, so that a table can modify the way it is traversed (and non-table objects can be traversed).

13.4 Table-Access Metamethods

The metamethods for arithmetic and relational operators all define behavior for otherwise erroneous situations. They do not change the normal behavior of the language. But Lua also offers a way to change the behavior of tables for two normal situations, the query and modification of absent fields in a table.

The __index metamethod

I said earlier that, when we access an absent field in a table, the result is nil. This is true, but it is not the whole truth. Actually, such accesses trigger the interpreter to look for an __index metamethod: if there is no such method, as usually happens, then the access results in nil; otherwise, the metamethod will provide the result.

The archetypal example here is inheritance. Suppose we want to create several tables describing windows. Each table must describe several window parameters, such as position, size, color scheme, and the like. All these parameters have default values and so we want to build window objects giving only the non-default parameters. A first alternative is to provide a constructor that fills in the absent fields. A second alternative is to arrange for the new windows to *inherit* any absent field from a prototype window. First, we declare the prototype and a constructor function, which creates new windows sharing a metatable:

```
-- create the prototype with default values
prototype = {x = 0, y = 0, width = 100, height = 100}
mt = {}    -- create a metatable
-- declare the constructor function
function new (o)
  setmetatable(o, mt)
  return o
end
```

Now, we define the __index metamethod:

```
mt.__index = function (_, key)
  return prototype[key]
end
```

After this code, we create a new window and query it for an absent field:

```
w = new{x=10, y=20}
print(w.width)    --> 100
```

Lua detects that w does not have the requested field, but has a metatable with an __index field. So, Lua calls this __index metamethod, with arguments w (the table) and "width" (the absent key). The metamethod then indexes the prototype with the given key and returns the result.

The use of the __index metamethod for inheritance is so common that Lua provides a shortcut. Despite being called a *method*, the __index metamethod does not need to be a function: it can be a table, instead. When it is a function, Lua calls it with the table and the absent key as its arguments, as we have just seen. When it is a table, Lua redoes the access in this table. Therefore, in our previous example, we could declare `__index` simply like this:

```
mt.__index = prototype
```

Now, when Lua looks for the metatable's `__index` field, it finds the value of prototype, which is a table. Consequently, Lua repeats the access in this table, that is, it executes the equivalent of `prototype["width"]`. This access then gives the desired result.

The use of a table as an `__index` metamethod provides a fast and simple way of implementing single inheritance. A function, although more expensive, provides more flexibility: we can implement multiple inheritance, caching, and several other variations. We will discuss these forms of inheritance in Chapter 16.

When we want to access a table without invoking its `__index` metamethod, we use the rawget function. The call `rawget(t,i)` does a *raw* access to table t, that is, a primitive access without considering metatables. Doing a raw access will not speed up your code (the overhead of a function call kills any gain you could have), but sometimes you need it, as we will see later.

The `__newindex` **metamethod**

The `__newindex` metamethod does for table updates what `__index` does for table accesses. When you assign a value to an absent index in a table, the interpreter looks for a `__newindex` metamethod: if there is one, the interpreter calls it instead of making the assignment. Like `__index`, if the metamethod is a table, the interpreter does the assignment in this table, instead of in the original one. Moreover, there is a raw function that allows you to bypass the metamethod: the call `rawset(t,k,v)` sets the value v associated with key k in table t without invoking any metamethod.

The combined use of `__index` and `__newindex` metamethods allows several powerful constructs in Lua, such as read-only tables, tables with default values, and inheritance for object-oriented programming. In this chapter, we will see some of these uses. Object-oriented programming has its own chapter.

Tables with default values

The default value of any field in a regular table is nil. It is easy to change this default value with metatables:

```
function setDefault (t, d)
  local mt = {__index = function () return d end}
  setmetatable(t, mt)
end
```

```
tab = {x=10, y=20}
print(tab.x, tab.z)      --> 10    nil
setDefault(tab, 0)
print(tab.x, tab.z)      --> 10    0
```

After the call to setDefault, any access to an absent field in tab calls its __index metamethod, which returns zero (the value of d for this metamethod).

The setDefault function creates a new closure plus a new metatable for each table that needs a default value. This can be expensive if we have many tables that need default values. However, the metatable has the default value d wired into its metamethod, so the function cannot use a single metatable for all tables. To allow the use of a single metatable for tables with different default values, we can store the default value of each table in the table itself, using an exclusive field. If we are not worried about name clashes, we can use a key like "___" for our exclusive field:

```
local mt = {__index = function (t) return t.___ end}
function setDefault (t, d)
  t.___ = d
  setmetatable(t, mt)
end
```

Note that now we create the table mt only once, outside the SetDefault function.

If we are worried about name clashes, it is easy to ensure the uniqueness of the special key. All we need is to create a new table and use it as the key:

```
local key = {}    -- unique key
local mt = {__index = function (t) return t[key] end}
function setDefault (t, d)
  t[key] = d
  setmetatable(t, mt)
end
```

An alternative approach for associating each table with its default value is to use a separate table, where the indices are the tables and the values are their default values. However, for the correct implementation of this approach, we need a special breed of table called *weak tables*, and so we will not use it here; we will return to the subject in Chapter 17.

Another alternative is to *memorize* metatables in order to reuse the same metatable for tables with the same default. However, that needs weak tables too, so that again we will have to wait until Chapter 17.

Tracking table accesses

Both __index and __newindex are relevant only when the index does not exist in the table. The only way to catch all accesses to a table is to keep it empty. So, if we want to monitor all accesses to a table, we should create a *proxy* for the real table. This proxy is an empty table, with proper __index and __newindex metamethods that track all accesses and redirect them to the original table.

Suppose that t is the original table we want to track. We can write something like this:

```
t = {}    -- original table (created somewhere)

-- keep a private access to the original table
local _t = t

-- create proxy
t = {}

-- create metatable
local mt = {
  __index = function (t, k)
    print("*access to element " .. tostring(k))
    return _t[k]    -- access the original table
  end,

  __newindex = function (t, k, v)
    print("*update of element " .. tostring(k) ..
          " to " .. tostring(v))
    _t[k] = v    -- update original table
  end
}
setmetatable(t, mt)
```

This code tracks every access to t:

```
> t[2] = "hello"
*update of element 2 to hello
> print(t[2])
*access to element 2
hello
```

If we want to traverse the table, we need to define a __pairs entry in the proxy:

```
mt.__pairs = function ()
  return function (_, k)
            return next(_t, k)
         end
end
```

We may want something similar for __ipairs.

If we want to monitor several tables, we do not need a different metatable for each one. Instead, we can somehow associate each proxy to its original table and share a common metatable for all proxies. This problem is similar to the problem of associating tables to their default values, which we discussed in the previous section. For instance, we can keep the original table in a proxy's field, using an exclusive key. The result is the following code:

```
local index = {}                    -- create private index
```

```
local mt = {                         -- create metatable
  __index = function (t, k)
    print("*access to element " .. tostring(k))
    return t[index][k]    -- access the original table
  end,

  __newindex = function (t, k, v)
    print("*update of element " .. tostring(k) ..
                        " to " .. tostring(v))
    t[index][k] = v   -- update original table
  end,

  __pairs = function (t)
            return function (t, k)
              return next(t[index], k)
            end, t
          end
}
function track (t)
  local proxy = {}
  proxy[index] = t
  setmetatable(proxy, mt)
  return proxy
end
```

Now, whenever we want to monitor a table t, all we have to do is to execute
t=track(t).

Read-only tables

It is easy to adapt the concept of proxies to implement read-only tables. All
we have to do is to raise an error whenever we track any attempt to update
the table. For the __index metamethod, we can use a table—the original table
itself—instead of a function, as we do not need to track queries; it is simpler
and rather more efficient to redirect all queries to the original table. This
use, however, demands a new metatable for each read-only proxy, with __index
pointing to the original table:

```
function readOnly (t)
  local proxy = {}
  local mt = {          -- create metatable
    __index = t,
    __newindex = function (t, k, v)
      error("attempt to update a read-only table", 2)
    end
  }
  setmetatable(proxy, mt)
  return proxy
end
```

As an example of use, we can create a read-only table for weekdays:

```
days = readOnly{"Sunday", "Monday", "Tuesday", "Wednesday",
        "Thursday", "Friday", "Saturday"}

print(days[1])      --> Sunday
days[2] = "Noday"
stdin:1: attempt to update a read-only table
```

Exercises

Exercise 13.1: Define a metamethod __sub for sets that returns the difference of two sets. (The set $a - b$ is the set of elements from a that are not in b.)

Exercise 13.2: Define a metamethod __len for sets so that #s returns the number of elements in set s.

Exercise 13.3: Complete the implementation of proxies in Section 13.4 with an __ipairs metamethod.

Exercise 13.4: An alternative way to implement read-only tables might use a function as the __index metamethod. This alternative makes accesses more expensive, but the creation of read-only tables is cheaper, as all read-only tables can share a single metatable. Rewrite function readOnly using this approach.

14

The Environment

Lua keeps all its global variables in a regular table, called the *global environment*. (To be more precise, Lua keeps its "global" variables in several environments, but we will ignore this multiplicity for a while.) One advantage of this structure is that it simplifies the internal implementation of Lua, because there is no need for a different data structure for global variables. The other advantage is that we can manipulate this table like any other table. To facilitate such manipulations, Lua stores the environment itself in a global variable _G. (Yes, _G._G is equal to _G.) For instance, the following code prints the names of all global variables defined in the global environment:

```
for n in pairs(_G) do print(n) end
```

In this chapter, we will see several useful techniques for manipulating the environment.

14.1 Global Variables with Dynamic Names

Usually, assignment is enough for accessing and setting global variables. However, often we need some form of meta-programming, such as when we need to manipulate a global variable whose name is stored in another variable, or somehow computed at run time. To get the value of this variable, many programmers are tempted to write something like this:

```
value = loadstring("return " .. varname)()
```

If varname is x, for example, the concatenation will result in "return x", which when run achieves the desired result. However, this code involves the creation and compilation of a new chunk, which is somewhat expensive. You can accomplish the same effect with the following code, which is more than an order of magnitude more efficient than the previous one:

```
value = _G[varname]
```

Because the environment is a regular table, you can simply index it with the desired key (the variable name).

In a similar way, you can assign a value to a global variable whose name is computed dynamically, by writing _G[varname]=value. Beware, however: some programmers get a little excited with these facilities and end up writing code like _G["a"]=_G["var1"], which is just a complicated way to write a=var1.

A generalization of the previous problem is to allow fields in the dynamic name, such as "io.read" or "a.b.c.d". If we write _G["io.read"], clearly we do not get the read field from the io table. But we can write a function getfield such that getfield("io.read") returns the expected result. This function is mainly a loop, which starts at _G and evolves field by field:

```
function getfield (f)
  local v = _G      -- start with the table of globals
  for w in string.gmatch(f, "[%w_]+") do
    v = v[w]
  end
  return v
end
```

We rely on gmatch, from the string library, to iterate over all words in f (where "word" is a sequence of one or more alphanumeric characters and underscores).

The corresponding function to set fields is a little more complex. An assignment like a.b.c.d=v is equivalent to the following code:

```
local temp = a.b.c
temp.d = v
```

That is, we must retrieve up to the last name and then handle this last name separately. The next setfield function does the task and also creates intermediate tables in a path when they do not exist:

```
function setfield (f, v)
  local t = _G                 -- start with the table of globals
  for w, d in string.gmatch(f, "([%w_]+)(%.?)") do
    if d == "." then          -- not last name?
      t[w] = t[w] or {}       -- create table if absent
      t = t[w]                -- get the table
    else                      -- last name
      t[w] = v                -- do the assignment
    end
  end
end
```

This new pattern captures the field name in variable w and an optional following dot in variable d.[1] If a field name is not followed by a dot then it is the last name.

With the previous functions in place, the next call creates a global table t, another table t.x, and assigns 10 to t.x.y:

```
setfield("t.x.y", 10)

print(t.x.y)      --> 10
print(getfield("t.x.y"))   --> 10
```

14.2 Global-Variable Declarations

Global variables in Lua do not need declarations. Although this is handy for small programs, in larger programs a simple typo can cause bugs that are difficult to find. However, we can change this behavior if we like. Because Lua keeps its global variables in a regular table, we can use metatables to change its behavior when accessing global variables.

A first approach simply detects any access to absent keys in the global table:

```
setmetatable(_G, {
  __newindex = function (_, n)
    error("attempt to write to undeclared variable " .. n, 2)
  end,
  __index = function (_, n)
    error("attempt to read undeclared variable " .. n, 2)
  end,
})
```

After this code, any attempt to access a non-existent global variable will trigger an error:

```
> print(a)
stdin:1: attempt to read undeclared variable a
```

But how do we declare new variables? One option is to use rawset, which bypasses the metamethod:

```
function declare (name, initval)
  rawset(_G, name, initval or false)
end
```

(The **or** with **false** ensures that the new global always gets a value different from nil.)

A simpler option is to restrict assignments to new global variables only inside functions, allowing free assignments in the outer level of a chunk.

To check whether the assignment is in the main chunk, we must use the debug library. The call debug.getinfo(2, "S") returns a table whose field what

---

[1]We will discuss pattern matching at great length in Chapter 21.

tells whether the function that called the metamethod is a main chunk, a regular Lua function, or a C function. (We will see debug.getinfo in more detail in Chapter 24.) Using this function, we can rewrite the __newindex metamethod like this:

```
__newindex = function (t, n, v)
  local w = debug.getinfo(2, "S").what
  if w ~= "main" and w ~= "C" then
    error("attempt to write to undeclared variable " .. n, 2)
  end
  rawset(t, n, v)
end
```

This new version also accepts assignments from C code, as this kind of code usually knows what it is doing.

To test whether a variable exists, we cannot simply compare it to nil because, if it is nil, the access will throw an error. Instead, we use rawget, which avoids the metamethod:

```
if rawget(_G, var) == nil then
  -- 'var' is undeclared
  ...
end
```

As it is, our scheme does not allow global variables with nil values, as they would be automatically considered undeclared. But it is not difficult to correct this problem. All we need is an auxiliary table that keeps the names of declared variables. Whenever a metamethod is called, it checks in this table whether the variable is undeclared or not. The code can be like in Listing 14.1. Now even an assignment like x=nil is enough to declare a global variable.

The overhead for both solutions is negligible. With the first solution, the metamethods are never called during normal operation. In the second, they can be called, but only when the program accesses a variable holding a nil.

The Lua distribution comes with a module strict.lua that implements a global-variable check that uses essentially the code we just reviewed. It is a good habit to use it when developing Lua code.

14.3   Non-Global Environments

One of the problems with the environment is that it is global. Any modification you do on it affects all parts of your program. For instance, when you install a metatable to control global access, your whole program must follow the guidelines. If you want to use a library that uses global variables without declaring them, you are in bad luck.

In Lua, global variables do not need to be truly global. We can even say that Lua does not have global variables. That may sound strange at first, as we have been using global variables all along this text. Clearly, Lua goes to great lengths

Listing 14.1. Checking global-variable declaration:

```
local declaredNames = {}

setmetatable(_G, {
  __newindex = function (t, n, v)
    if not declaredNames[n] then
      local w = debug.getinfo(2, "S").what
      if w ~= "main" and w ~= "C" then
        error("attempt to write to undeclared variable "..n, 2)
      end
      declaredNames[n] = true
    end
    rawset(t, n, v)    -- do the actual set
  end,

  __index = function (_, n)
    if not declaredNames[n] then
      error("attempt to read undeclared variable "..n, 2)
    else
      return nil
    end
  end,
})
```

to give the programmer an illusion of global variables. Let us see how Lua builds this illusion.[2]

Let us start with the concept of free names. A *free name* is a name that is not bound to an explicit declaration, that is, it does not occur inside the scope of a local variable (or a **for** variable or a parameter) with that name. For instance, both var1 and var2 are free names in the following chunk:

```
var1 = var2 + 3
```

Unlike what we said earlier, a free name does not refer to a global variable (at least not in a direct way). Instead, the Lua compiler translates any free name var to _ENV.var. So, the previous chunk is equivalent to this one:

```
_ENV.var1 = _ENV.var2 + 3
```

But what is this new _ENV variable? It cannot be a global variable; otherwise, we would be back to the original problem. Again, the compiler does the trick. I already mentioned that Lua treats any chunk as an anonymous function. Actually, Lua compiles our original chunk as the following code:

---

[2]Note that this mechanism was one of the parts of Lua that changed most from version 5.1 to 5.2. The following discussion refers to Lua 5.2 and very little of it applies to previous versions.

```
local _ENV = <some value>
return function (...)
  _ENV.var1 = _ENV.var2 + 3
end
```

That is, Lua compiles any chunk in the presence of a predefined upvalue called _ENV.

Usually, when we load a chunk, the load function initializes this predefined upvalue with the global environment. So, our original chunk becomes equivalent to this one:

```
local _ENV = <the global environment>
return function (...)
  _ENV.var1 = _ENV.var2 + 3
end
```

The result of all these arrangements is that the var1 field of the global environment gets the value of the var2 field plus 3.

At first sight, this may seem a rather convoluted way to manipulate global variables. I will not argue that it is the simplest way, but it offers a flexibility that is difficult to achieve with a simpler implementation.

Before we go on, let us summarize the handling of global variables in Lua 5.2:

- Lua compiles any chunk in the scope of an upvalue called _ENV.

- The compiler translates any free name var to _ENV.var.

- The load (or loadfile) function initializes the first upvalue of a chunk with the global environment.

After all, it is not that complicated.

Some people get confused because they try to infer extra magic from these rules. There is no extra magic. In particular, the first two rules are done entirely by the compiler. Except for being predefined by the compiler, _ENV is a plain regular variable. Outside compilation, the name _ENV has no special meaning at all to Lua.[3] Similarly, the translation from var to _ENV.var is a plain syntactic translation, with no hidden meanings. In particular, after the translation, _ENV will refer to whatever _ENV variable is visible at that point in the code, following the standard visibility rules.

14.4 Using _ENV

In this section, we will see some ways to explore the flexibility brought by _ENV. Keep in mind that most examples in this section must be run as a single chunk. If you enter code line by line in interactive mode, each line becomes a different chunk and therefore each has a distinct _ENV variable. To run a piece of code as

---

[3]To be completely honest, Lua uses that name for error messages, so that it reports an error involving a variable _ENV.x as being about global x.

a single chunk, you can either run it from a file or enclose it with a pair **do–end** in interactive mode.

Because _ENV is a regular variable, we can assign to and access it as any other variable. The assignment _ENV=nil will invalidate any direct access to global variables in the rest of the chunk. This can be useful to control what variables your code uses:

```
local print, sin = print, math.sin
_ENV = nil
print(13)                    --> 13
print(sin(13))               --> 0.42016703682664
print(math.cos(13))          -- error!
```

Any assignment to a free name will raise a similar error.

We can write the _ENV explicitly to bypass a local declaration:

```
a = 13              -- global
local a = 12
print(a)           --> 12  (local)
print(_ENV.a)      --> 13  (global)
```

Of course, a main use for _ENV is to change the environment used by a piece of code. Once you change your environment, all global accesses will use the new table:

```
-- change current environment to a new empty table
_ENV = {}
a = 1          -- create a field in _ENV
print(a)
   --> stdin:4: attempt to call global 'print' (a nil value)
```

If the new environment is empty, you have lost all your global variables, including print. So, you should first populate it with some useful values, such as the old environment:

```
a = 15                    -- create a global variable
_ENV = {g = _G}           -- change current environment
a = 1                     -- create a field in _ENV
g.print(a)                --> 1
g.print(g.a)              --> 15
```

Now, when you access the "global" g you get the old environment, wherein you will find the print function.

We can rewrite the previous example using the name _G instead of g:

```
a = 15                    -- create a global variable
_ENV = {_G = _G}          -- change current environment
a = 1                     -- create a field in _ENV
_G.print(a)               --> 1
_G.print(_G.a)            --> 15
```

For Lua, _G is a name like any other. Its only special status happens when Lua creates the initial global table and assigns this table to the global variable _G. Lua does not care about the current value of this variable. But it is customary to use this same name whenever we have a reference to the global environment, as we did in the rewritten example.

Another way to populate your new environment is with inheritance:

```
a = 1
local newgt = {}          -- create new environment
setmetatable(newgt, {__index = _G})
_ENV = newgt              -- set it
print(a)                  --> 1
```

In this code, the new environment inherits both print and a from the old one. Nevertheless, any assignment goes to the new table. There is no danger of changing a variable in the global environment by mistake, although you still can change them through _G:

```
-- continuing previous code
a = 10
print(a)                  --> 10
print(_G.a)               --> 1
_G.a = 20
print(_G.a)               --> 20
```

Being a regular variable, _ENV follows the usual scoping rules. In particular, functions defined inside a chunk access _ENV as they access any other external variable:

```
_ENV = {_G = _G}
local function foo ()
   _G.print(a)       -- compiled as '_ENV._G.print(_ENV.a)'
end
a = 10               -- _ENV.a
foo()                --> 10
_ENV = {_G = _G, a = 20}
foo()                --> 20
```

If we define a new local variable called _ENV, references to free names will bind with that new variable:

```
a = 2
do
   local _ENV = {print = print, a = 14}
   print(a)     --> 14
end
print(a)        --> 2   (back to the original _ENV)
```

Therefore, it is not difficult to define a function with a private environment:

```
function factory (_ENV)
   return function ()
             return a          -- "global" a
          end
end

f1 = factory{a = 6}
f2 = factory{a = 7}
print(f1())        --> 6
print(f2())        --> 7
```

The factory function creates simple closures that return the value of their global a. When the closure is created, the visible _ENV variable is the parameter _ENV of the enclosing factory function; therefore, the closure will use this external variable (as an upvalue) to access its free names.

Using the usual scoping rules, we can manipulate the environments in several other ways. For instance, we may have several functions sharing a common environment, or a function that changes the environment shared by other functions.

14.5   _ENV **and** load

As I mentioned earlier, load usually initializes the _ENV upvalue of a loaded chunk with the global environment. However, load has an optional fourth parameter that gives the value for _ENV. (Function loadfile has a similar parameter.)

For an initial example, consider that we have a typical configuration file, defining several constants and functions to be used by a program; it can be something like this:

```
-- file 'config.lua'
width = 200
height = 300

...
```

We can load it whit the following code:

```
env = {}
f = loadfile("config.lua", "t", env)
f()
```

The whole code in the configuration file will run in the empty environment env. More importantly, all its definitions will go into this environment. The configuration file has no way to affect anything else, even by mistake. Even malicious code cannot do much damage. It can do a DoS (denial of service) attack, by wasting CPU time and memory, but nothing else.

Sometimes, you may want to run a chunk several times, each time with a different environment table. In that case, the extra argument to load is not useful. Instead, we have two other options.

The first option is to use the `debug.setupvalue` function from the debug library. As its name implies, `setupvalue` allows us to change any upvalue of a given function. The next fragment illustrates its use:

```
f = loadfile(filename)
...
env = {}
debug.setupvalue(f, 1, env)
```

The first argument in the call to `setupvalue` is the function, the second is the upvalue index, and the third is the new value for the upvalue. For that kind of use, the second argument is always one: when the function is the result of `load` or `loadfile`, Lua ensures that it has only one upvalue and that this upvalue is `_ENV`.

A small drawback of this option is its dependence on the debug library. This library breaks some usual assumptions about programs. For instance, `debug.setupvalue` breaks Lua's visibility rules, which ensures that a local variable cannot be accessed from outside its lexical scope.

Another option to run a chunk with several different environments is to twist the chunk a little when loading it. Imagine that we add the following line just before the chunk being loaded:

```
_ENV = ...;
```

Remember from Section 8.1 that Lua compiles any chunk as a variadic function. So, that extra line of code will assign to the `_ENV` variable the first argument to the chunk, thereby setting that argument as the environment. After loading the chunk, we call the resulting function passing the target environment as a first argument. The following code snippet illustrates the idea, using the `loadwithprefix` function from Exercise 8.1:

```
f = loadwithprefix("local _ENV = ...;", io.lines(filename, "*L"))
...
env = {}
f(env)
```

Exercises

Exercise 14.1: The `getfield` function that we defined in the beginning of this chapter is too forgiving, as it accepts "fields" like `math?sin` or `string!!!gsub`. Rewrite it so that it accepts only single dots as name separators. (You may need some knowledge from Chapter 21 to do this exercise.)

Exercise 14.2: Explain in detail what happens in the following program and what its output is.

```
local foo
do
  local _ENV = _ENV
  function foo ()  print(X) end
end
X = 13
_ENV = nil
foo()
X = 0
```

Exercise 14.3: Explain in detail what happens in the following program and what its output is.

```
local print = print
function foo (_ENV, a)
  print(a + b)
end

foo({b = 14}, 12)
foo({b = 10}, 1)
```

15

Modules and Packages

Usually, Lua does not set policies. Instead, Lua provides mechanisms that are powerful enough for groups of developers to implement the policies that best suit them. However, this approach does not work well for modules. One of the main goals of a module system is to allow different groups to share code. The lack of a common policy impedes this sharing.

Starting in version 5.1, Lua has defined a set of policies for modules and packages (a package being a collection of modules). These policies do not demand any extra facility from the language; programmers can implement them using what we have seen so far: tables, functions, metatables, and environments. Programmers are free to use different policies. Of course, alternative implementations may lead to programs that cannot use foreign modules and modules that cannot be used by foreign programs.

From the point of view of the user, a *module* is some code (either in Lua or in C) that can be loaded through require and that creates and returns a table. Everything that the module exports, such as functions and constants, it defines inside this table, which works as a namespace.

As an example, all standard libraries are modules. You can use the mathematical library like this:

```
local m = require "math"
print(m.sin(3.14))
```

However, the stand-alone interpreter preloads all standard libraries with code equivalent to this:

```
math = require "math"
string = require "string"
...
```

This preloading allows us to write the usual notation `math.sin`.

An obvious benefit of using tables to implement modules is that we can manipulate modules like any other table and use the whole power of Lua to create extra facilities. In most languages, modules are not first-class values (that is, they cannot be stored in variables, passed as arguments to functions, etc.), so those languages need special mechanisms for each extra facility they want to offer for modules. In Lua, you get extra facilities for free.

For instance, there are several ways for a user to call a function from a module. The usual way is this:

```
local mod = require "mod"
mod.foo()
```

The user can set any local name for the module:

```
local m = require "mod"
m.foo()
```

She can also provide alternative names for individual functions:

```
local m = require "mod"
local f = mod.foo
f()
```

The nice thing about these facilities is that they involve no special support from the language. They use what the language already offers.

A common complaint against `require` is that it cannot pass arguments to the module being loaded. For instance, the mathematical module might have an option for choosing between degrees and radians:

```
-- bad code
local math = require("math", "degree")
```

The problem here is that one of the main goals of `require` is to avoid loading a module multiple times. Once a module is loaded, it will be reused by whatever part of the program that requires it again. There would be a conflict if the same module were required with different parameters:

```
-- bad code
local math = require("math", "degree")

-- somewhere else in the same program
local math = require("math", "radians")
```

In case you really want your module to have parameters, it is better to create an explicit function to set them, like here:

```
local mod = require"mod"
mod.init(0, 0)
```

If the initialization function returns the module itself, we can write that code like this:

```
local mod = require"mod".init(0, 0)
```

Another option is to make the module returns its initialization function, and only that function returns the module table:

```
local mod = require"mod"(0, 0)
```

In any way, remember that the module itself is loaded only once; it is up to the module to handle conflicting initializations.

15.1 The require **Function**

The require function tries to keep to a minimum its assumptions about what a module is. For require, a module is just any code that defines some values (such as functions or tables containing functions). Typically, that code returns a table comprising the module functions. However, because this action is done by the module code, not by require, some modules may choose to return other values or even to have side effects.

To load a module, we simply call require "*modname*". The first step of require is to check in table package.loaded whether the module is already loaded. If so, require returns its corresponding value. Therefore, once a module is loaded, other calls requiring the same module simply return the same value, without running any code again.

If the module is not loaded yet, require searches for a Lua file with the module name. If it finds a Lua file, it loads it with loadfile. The result of that is a function that we call a *loader*. (The loader is a function that, when called, loads the module.)

If require cannot find a Lua file with the module name, it searches for a C library with the module name. If it finds a C library, it loads it with package.loadlib (which we discussed in Section 8.3), looking for a function called luaopen_*modname*.[1] The loader in this case is the result of loadlib, that is, the function luaopen_*modname* represented as a Lua function.

No matter whether the module was found in a Lua file or a C library, require now has a loader for it. To finally load the module, require calls the loader with two arguments: the module name and the name of the file where it got the loader. (Most modules just ignore these arguments.) If the loader returns any value, require returns this value and stores it in the package.loaded table to return the same value in future calls for this same module. If the loader returns no value, require behaves as if the module returned **true**. Without this correction, a subsequent call to require would run the module again.

To force require into loading the same module twice, we simply erase the library entry from package.loaded:

```
package.loaded.<modname> = nil
```

The next time the module is required, require will do all its work again.

---

[1]In Section 27.3, we will discuss how to write C libraries.

Renaming a module

Usually, we use modules with their original names, but sometimes we must rename a module to avoid name clashes. A typical situation is when we need to load different versions of the same module, for instance for testing. Lua modules do not have their names fixed internally, so usually it is enough to rename the .lua file. However, we cannot edit a binary library to correct the name of its luaopen_* function. To allow for such renamings, require uses a small trick: if the module name contains a hyphen, require strips from the name its prefix up to the hyphen when creating the luaopen_* function name. For instance, if a module is named a-b, require expects its open function to be named luaopen_b, instead of luaopen_a-b (which would not be a valid C name anyway). So, if we need to use two modules named mod, we can rename one of them to v1-mod, for instance. When we call m1=require "v1-mod", require will find the renamed file v1-mod and, inside this file, the function with the original name luaopen_mod.

Path searching

When searching for a Lua file, require uses a path that is a little different from typical paths. The typical path is a list of directories wherein to search for a given file. However, ANSI C (the abstract platform where Lua runs) does not have the concept of directories. Therefore, the path used by require is a list of *templates*, each of them specifying an alternative way to transform a module name (the argument to require) into a file name. More specifically, each template in the path is a file name containing optional question marks. For each template, require replaces the module name for each '?' and checks whether there is a file with the resulting name; if not, it goes to the next template. The templates in a path are separated by semicolons (a character seldom used for file names in most operating systems). For instance, if the path is

```
?;?.lua;c:\windows\?;/usr/local/lua/?/?.lua
```

then the call require "sql" will try to open the following Lua files:

```
sql
sql.lua
c:\windows\sql
/usr/local/lua/sql/sql.lua
```

The require function assumes only the semicolon (as the component separator) and the question mark; everything else, including directory separators and file extensions, is defined by the path itself.

The path that require uses to search for Lua files is always the current value of variable package.path. When Lua starts, it initializes this variable with the value of the environment variable LUA_PATH_5_2. If this environment variable is not defined, Lua tries the environment variable LUA_PATH. If both are not defined, Lua uses a compiled-defined default path.[2] When using the value of an

---

[2]In Lua 5.2, the command-line option -E prevents the use of those environment variables and forces the default.

environment variable, Lua substitutes the default path for any substring ";;".
For instance, if you set LUA_PATH_5_2 to "mydir/?.lua;;", the final path will be
the template "mydir/?.lua" followed by the default path.

The path used to search for a C library works exactly in the same way,
but its value comes from variable package.cpath (instead of package.path).
Similarly, this variable gets its initial value from the environment variables
LUA_CPATH_5_2 or LUA_CPATH. A typical value for this path in UNIX is like this:

```
./?.so;/usr/local/lib/lua/5.2/?.so
```

Note that the path defines the file extension. The previous example uses .so for
all templates; in Windows, a typical path would be more like this one:

```
.\?.dll;C:\Program Files\Lua502\dll\?.dll
```

Function package.searchpath encodes all those rules for searching libraries.
It receives a module name and a path, and looks for a file following the rules
described here. It returns either the name of the first file that exists or nil plus
an error message describing all files it unsuccessfully tried to open, as in the
next example:

```
> path = ".\\?.dll;C:\\Program Files\\Lua502\\dll\\?.dll"
> print(package.searchpath("X", path))
nil
  no file '.\X.dll'
  no file 'C:\Program Files\Lua502\dll\X.dll'
```

Searchers

In reality, require is a little more complex than we have described. The search
for a Lua file and the search for a C library are just two instances of a more
general concept of *searchers*. A searcher is simply a function that receives the
module name and returns either a loader for that module or nil if it cannot find
one.

The array package.searchers lists the searchers that require uses. When
looking for a module, require calls each searcher in the list passing the module
name, until one of them finds a loader for the module. If the list ends without a
positive response, require raises an error.

The use of a list to drive the search for a module allows great flexibility to
require. For instance, if you want to store modules compressed in zip files, you
only need to provide a proper searcher function for that and add it to the list.
However, more often than not, programs do not change the default contents of
package.searchers. In this default configuration, the searcher for Lua files and
the searcher for C libraries that we described earlier are respectively the second
and the third elements in the list. Before them, there is the preload searcher.

The *preload* searcher allows the definition of an arbitrary function to load a
module. It uses a table, called package.preload, to map module names to loader
functions. When searching for a module name, this searcher simply looks for the

given name in the table. If it finds a function there, it returns this function as the module loader. Otherwise, it returns nil. This searcher provides a generic method to handle some non-conventional situations. For instance, a C library statically linked to Lua can register its luaopen_ function into the preload table, so that it will be called only when (and if) the user requires that module. In this way, the program does not waste time opening the module if it is not used.

The default content of package.searchers includes a fourth function that is relevant only for submodules. We will discuss it at Section 15.4.

15.2   The Basic Approach for Writing Modules in Lua

The simplest way to create a module in Lua is really simple: we create a table, put all functions we want to export inside it, and return this table. Listing 15.1 illustrates this approach. Note how we define inv as a private function simply by declaring it local to the chunk.

Some people do not like the final return statement. One way of eliminating it is to assign the module table directly into package.loaded:

```
local M = {}
package.loaded[...] = M
    <as before>
```

Remember that require calls the loader passing the module name as the first argument. So, the vararg expression ... in the index results in that name. After this assignment, we do not need to return M at the end of the module: if a module does not return a value, require will return the current value of package.loaded[modname] (if it is not nil). Anyway, I still prefer to write the final return, because it looks clearer.

Another variant for writing a module is to define all functions as locals and build the returning table at the end, as in Listing 15.2. What are the advantages of this approach? You do not need to prefix each name with M. or something similar; there is an explicit export list; and you define and use exported and internal functions in the same way inside the module. What are the disadvantages? The export list is at the end of the module instead of at the beginning, where it would be more useful as a quick documentation; and the export list is somewhat redundant, as you must write each name twice. (This last disadvantage may become an advantage, as it allows functions to have different names inside and outside the module, but I think programmers seldom do this.) I particularly like this style, but tastes may differ.

Anyway, remember that no matter how a module is defined, users should be able to use it in a standard way:

```
local cpx = require "complex"
print(cpx.tostring(cpx.add(cpx.new(3,4), cpx.i)))
    --> (3,5)
```

Listing 15.1. A simple module for complex numbers:

```lua
local M = {}

function M.new (r, i) return {r=r, i=i} end

-- defines constant 'i'
M.i = M.new(0, 1)

function M.add (c1, c2)
  return M.new(c1.r + c2.r, c1.i + c2.i)
end

function M.sub (c1, c2)
  return M.new(c1.r - c2.r, c1.i - c2.i)
end

function M.mul (c1, c2)
  return M.new(c1.r*c2.r - c1.i*c2.i, c1.r*c2.i + c1.i*c2.r)
end

local function inv (c)
  local n = c.r^2 + c.i^2
  return M.new(c.r/n, -c.i/n)
end

function M.div (c1, c2)
  return M.mul(c1, inv(c2))
end

function M.tostring (c)
  return "(" .. c.r .. "," .. c.i .. ")"
end

return M
```

Listing 15.2. Module with export list:

```
local function new (r, i) return {r=r, i=i} end

-- defines constant 'i'
local i = complex.new(0, 1)

   <other functions follow the same pattern>

return {
   new      = new,
   i        = i,
   add      = add,
   sub      = sub,
   mul      = mul,
   div      = div,
   tostring = tostring,
}
```

15.3   Using Environments

One drawback of those basic methods for creating modules is that it is all too easy to pollute the global space, for instance by forgetting a **local** in a private declaration.

Environments offer an interesting technique for creating modules that solves this problem. Once the module main chunk has an exclusive environment, not only all its functions share this table, but also all its global variables go to this table. Therefore, we can declare all public functions as global variables and they will go to a separate table automatically. All the module has to do is to assign this table to the _ENV variable. After that, when we declare function add, it goes to M.add:

```
local M = {}
_ENV = M
function add (c1, c2)
   return new(c1.r + c2.r, c1.i + c2.i)
end
```

Moreover, we can call other functions from the same module without any prefix. In the previous code, add gets new from its environment, that is, it calls M.new.

This method offers a good support for modules, with little extra work for the programmer. It needs no prefixes at all. There is no difference between calling an exported and a private function. If the programmer forgets a **local**, he does not pollute the global namespace; instead, a private function simply becomes public.

Nevertheless, currently I still prefer one of the two methods that we discussed in the previous section. They may need more work, but the resulting code states clearly what it does. To avoid creating a global by mistake, I use the simple method of assigning nil to _ENV. After that, any assignment to a global name will raise an error.

What is missing, of course, is access to other modules. Once we change the value of _ENV, we lose access to all previous global variables. There are several ways to recover this access, each with its pros and cons.

One solution is inheritance:

```
local M = {}
setmetatable(M, {__index = _G})
_ENV = M
```

(You must call setmetatable before assigning to _ENV; why?) With this construction, the module has direct access to any global identifier, paying a small overhead for each access. A funny consequence of this solution is that, conceptually, your module now contains all global variables. For instance, someone using your module can call the standard sine function by writing complex.math.sin(x). (Perl's package system has this peculiarity, too.)

Another quick method of accessing other modules is to declare a local variable that holds the original environment:

```
local M = {}
local _G = _G
_ENV = M           -- or _ENV = nil
```

Now you must prefix any global name with _G., but the access is a little faster, because there is no metamethod involved.

A more disciplined approach is to declare as locals only the functions you need or, at most, the modules you need:

```
-- module setup
local M = {}

-- Import Section:
-- declare everything this module needs from outside
local sqrt = math.sqrt
local io = io

-- no more external access after this point
_ENV = nil     -- or _ENV = M
```

This technique demands more work, but it documents your module dependencies better. It also results in code that runs a little faster than code with the previous schemes, because of its usage of local variables.

15.4 Submodules and Packages

Lua allows module names to be hierarchical, using a dot to separate name levels. For instance, a module named mod.sub is a *submodule* of mod. A *package* is a complete tree of modules; it is the unit of distribution in Lua.

When you require a module called mod.sub, require queries first the table package.loaded and then the table package.preload using the original module name "mod.sub" as the key; here, the dot is just a character like any other in the module name.

However, when searching for a file that defines that submodule, require translates the dot into another character, usually the system's directory separator (e.g., '/' for UNIX or '\' for Windows). After the translation, require searches for the resulting name like any other name. For instance, assume '/' as the directory separator and the following path:

```
./?.lua;/usr/local/lua/?.lua;/usr/local/lua/?/init.lua
```

The call require "a.b" will try to open the following files:

```
./a/b.lua
/usr/local/lua/a/b.lua
/usr/local/lua/a/b/init.lua
```

This behavior allows all modules of a package to live in a single directory. For instance, if a package has modules p, p.a, and p.b, their respective files can be p/init.lua, p/a.lua, and p/b.lua, with the directory p within some appropriate directory.

The directory separator used by Lua is configured at compile time and can be any string (remember, Lua knows nothing about directories). For instance, systems without hierarchical directories can use a '_' as the "directory" separator, so that require "a.b" will search for a file a_b.lua.

Names in C cannot contain dots, so a C library for submodule a.b cannot export a function luaopen_a.b. Here require translates the dot into another character, an underscore. So, a C library named a.b should name its initialization function luaopen_a_b. We can use the hyphen trick here too, with some subtle results. For instance, if we have a C library a and we want to make it a submodule of mod, we can rename the file to mod/v-a. When we write require "mod.v-a", require correctly finds the new file mod/v-a as well as the function luaopen_a inside it.

As an extra facility, require has one more searcher for loading C submodules. When it cannot find either a Lua file or a C file for a submodule, this last searcher searches again the C path, but this time looking for the package name. For example, if the program requires a submodule a.b.c this searcher will look for a. If it finds a C library for this name, then require looks into this library for an appropriate open function, luaopen_a_b_c in this example. This facility allows a distribution to put several submodules together into a single C library, each with its own open function.

From the point of view of Lua, submodules in the same package have no explicit relationship. Requiring a module a does not automatically load any of its submodules; similarly, requiring a.b does not automatically load a. Of course, the package implementer is free to create these links if she wants. For instance, a particular module a may start by explicitly requiring one or all of its submodules.

Exercises

Exercise 15.1: Rewrite the code in Listing 13.1 as a proper module.

Exercise 15.2: What happens in the search for a library if the path has some fixed component (that is, a component without a question mark)? Can this behavior be useful?

Exercise 15.3: Write a searcher that searches for Lua files and C libraries at the same time. For instance, the path used for this searcher could be something like this:

```
./?.lua;./?.so;/usr/lib/lua5.2/?.so;/usr/share/lua5.2/?.lua
```

(Hint: use `package.searchpath` to find a proper file and then try to load it, first with `loadfile` and next with `package.loadlib`.)

Exercise 15.4: What happens if you set a metatable for table `package.preload` with an `__index` metamethod? Can this behavior be useful?

16

Object-Oriented Programming

A table in Lua is an object in more than one sense. Like objects, tables have a state. Like objects, tables have an identity (a *self*) that is independent of their values; specifically, two objects (tables) with the same value are different objects, whereas an object can have different values at different times. Like objects, tables have a life cycle that is independent of who created them or where they were created.

Objects have their own operations. Tables also can have operations, as in the following fragment:

```
Account = {balance = 0}
function Account.withdraw (v)
  Account.balance = Account.balance - v
end
```

This definition creates a new function and stores it in field `withdraw` of the Account object. Then, we can call it as

```
Account.withdraw(100.00)
```

This kind of function is almost what we call a *method*. However, the use of the global name `Account` inside the function is a bad programming practice. First, this function will work only for this particular object. Second, even for this particular object, the function will work only as long as the object is stored in that particular global variable. If we change the object's name, `withdraw` does not work any more:

```
a, Account = Account, nil
a.withdraw(100.00)       -- ERROR!
```

Such behavior violates the principle that objects have independent life cycles.

A more flexible approach is to operate on the *receiver* of the operation. For that, our method would need an extra parameter with the value of the receiver. This parameter usually has the name *self* or *this*:

```
function Account.withdraw (self, v)
  self.balance = self.balance - v
end
```

Now, when we call the method we have to specify the object it has to operate on:

```
a1 = Account; Account = nil
...
a1.withdraw(a1, 100.00)    -- OK
```

With the use of a *self* parameter, we can use the same method for many objects:

```
a2 = {balance=0, withdraw = Account.withdraw}
...
a2.withdraw(a2, 260.00)
```

This use of a *self* parameter is a central point in any object-oriented language. Most OO languages have this mechanism partly hidden from the programmer, so that she does not have to declare this parameter (although she still can use the name *self* or *this* inside a method). Lua also can hide this parameter, using the *colon operator*. We can rewrite the previous method definition as

```
function Account:withdraw (v)
  self.balance = self.balance - v
end
```

and the method call as

```
a:withdraw(100.00)
```

The effect of the colon is to add an extra hidden parameter in a method definition and to add an extra argument in a method call. The colon is only a syntactic facility, although a convenient one; there is nothing really new here. We can define a function with the dot syntax and call it with the colon syntax, or vice-versa, as long as we handle the extra parameter correctly:

```
Account = { balance=0,
            withdraw = function (self, v)
                         self.balance = self.balance - v
                       end
          }

function Account:deposit (v)
  self.balance = self.balance + v
end
```

```
Account.deposit(Account, 200.00)
Account:withdraw(100.00)
```

Until now, our objects have an identity, a state, and operations over this state. They still lack a class system, inheritance, and privacy. Let us tackle the first problem: how can we create several objects with similar behavior? Specifically, how can we create several accounts?

16.1 Classes

A class works as a mold for the creation of objects. Most object-oriented languages offer the concept of class. In such languages, each object is an instance of a specific class. Lua does not have the concept of class; each object defines its own behavior and has a shape of its own. Nevertheless, it is not difficult to emulate classes in Lua, following the lead from prototype-based languages like Self and NewtonScript. In these languages, objects have no classes. Instead, each object may have a prototype, which is a regular object where the first object looks up any operation that it does not know about. To represent a class in such languages, we simply create an object to be used exclusively as a prototype for other objects (its instances). Both classes and prototypes work as a place to put behavior to be shared by several objects.

In Lua, we can implement prototypes using the idea of inheritance that we saw in Section 13.4. More specifically, if we have two objects a and b, all we have to do to make b a prototype for a is this:

```
setmetatable(a, {__index = b})
```

After that, a looks up in b for any operation that it does not have. To see b as the class of object a is not much more than a change in terminology.

Let us go back to our example of a bank account. To create other accounts with behavior similar to Account, we arrange for these new objects to inherit their operations from Account, using the __index metamethod. A small optimization is that we do not need to create an extra table to be the metatable of the account objects; instead, we use the Account table itself for this purpose:

```
function Account:new (o)
  o = o or {}     -- create table if user does not provide one
  setmetatable(o, self)
  self.__index = self
  return o
end
```

(When we call Account:new, self is equal to Account; so, we could have used Account directly, instead of self. However, the use of self will fit nicely when we introduce class inheritance, in the next section.) After this code, what happens when we create a new account and call a method on it, like this?

```
a = Account:new{balance = 0}
a:deposit(100.00)
```

When we create the new account, a will have `Account` (the *self* in the call to `Account:new`) as its metatable. Then, when we call a:deposit(100.00), we are actually calling a.deposit(a, 100.00); the colon is only syntactic sugar. However, Lua cannot find a "deposit" entry in table a; so, Lua looks into the `__index` entry of the metatable. The situation now is more or less like this:

```
getmetatable(a).__index.deposit(a, 100.00)
```

The metatable of a is `Account` and `Account.__index` is also `Account` (because the new method did `self.__index=self`). Therefore, the previous expression reduces to

```
Account.deposit(a, 100.00)
```

That is, Lua calls the original `deposit` function, but passing a as the *self* parameter. So, the new account a inherited the `deposit` function from `Account`. By the same mechanism, it inherits all fields from `Account`.

The inheritance works not only for methods, but also for other fields that are absent in the new account. Therefore, a class can provide not only methods, but also default values for its instance fields. Remember that, in our first definition of `Account`, we provided a field `balance` with value 0. So, if we create a new account without an initial balance, it will inherit this default value:

```
b = Account:new()
print(b.balance)     --> 0
```

When we call the `deposit` method on b, it runs the equivalent of the following code (because self is b):

```
b.balance = b.balance + v
```

The expression b.balance evaluates to zero and the method assigns an initial deposit to b.balance. Subsequent accesses to b.balance will not invoke the index metamethod, because now b has its own balance field.

16.2   Inheritance

Because classes are objects, they can get methods from other classes, too. This behavior makes inheritance (in the usual object-oriented meaning) quite easy to implement in Lua.

Let us assume we have a base class like `Account`:

```
Account = {balance = 0}

function Account:new (o)
  o = o or {}
  setmetatable(o, self)
  self.__index = self
  return o
end
```

```
function Account:deposit (v)
  self.balance = self.balance + v
end

function Account:withdraw (v)
  if v > self.balance then error"insufficient funds" end
  self.balance = self.balance - v
end
```

From this class, we want to derive a subclass SpecialAccount that allows the customer to withdraw more than his balance. We start with an empty class that simply inherits all its operations from its base class:

```
SpecialAccount = Account:new()
```

Up to now, SpecialAccount is just an instance of Account. The nice thing happens now:

```
s = SpecialAccount:new{limit=1000.00}
```

SpecialAccount inherits new from Account, like any other method. This time, however, when new executes, its self parameter will refer to SpecialAccount. Therefore, the metatable of s will be SpecialAccount, whose value at field __index is also SpecialAccount. So, s inherits from SpecialAccount, which inherits from Account. When we evaluate

```
s:deposit(100.00)
```

Lua cannot find a deposit field in s, so it looks into SpecialAccount; it cannot find a deposit field there, too, so it looks into Account; there it finds the original implementation for a deposit.

What makes a SpecialAccount special is that we can redefine any method inherited from its superclass. All we have to do is to write the new method:

```
function SpecialAccount:withdraw (v)
  if v - self.balance >= self:getLimit() then
    error"insufficient funds"
  end
  self.balance = self.balance - v
end

function SpecialAccount:getLimit ()
  return self.limit or 0
end
```

Now, when we call s:withdraw(200.00), Lua does not go to Account, because it finds the new withdraw method in SpecialAccount first. As s.limit is 1000.00 (remember that we set this field when we created s), the program does the withdrawal, leaving s with a negative balance.

An interesting aspect of objects in Lua is that you do not need to create a new class to specify a new behavior. If only a single object needs a specific behavior, you can implement that behavior directly in the object. For instance, if the account s represents some special client whose limit is always 10% of her balance, you can modify only this single account:

```
function s:getLimit ()
  return self.balance * 0.10
end
```

After this declaration, the call s:withdraw(200.00) runs the withdraw method from SpecialAccount, but when withdraw calls self:getLimit, it is this last definition that it invokes.

16.3   Multiple Inheritance

Because objects are not primitive in Lua, there are several ways to do object-oriented programming in Lua. The approach that we have seen, using the index metamethod, is probably the best combination of simplicity, performance, and flexibility. Nevertheless, there are other implementations, which may be more appropriate for some particular cases. Here we will see an alternative implementation that allows multiple inheritance in Lua.

The key to this implementation is the use of a function for the metafield __index. Remember that, when a table's metatable has a function in the __index field, Lua will call this function whenever it cannot find a key in the original table. Then, __index can look up for the missing key in how many parents it wants.

Multiple inheritance means that a class can have more than one superclass. Therefore, we cannot use a class method to create subclasses. Instead, we will define a specific function for this purpose, createClass, which has as arguments the superclasses of the new class; see Listing 16.1. This function creates a table to represent the new class, and sets its metatable with an __index metamethod that does the multiple inheritance. Despite the multiple inheritance, each object instance still belongs to one single class, where it looks for all its methods. Therefore, the relationship between classes and superclasses is different from the relationship between classes and instances. Particularly, a class cannot be the metatable for its instances and for its subclasses at the same time. In Listing 16.1, we keep the class as the metatable for its instances, and create another table to be the metatable of the class.

Let us illustrate the use of createClass with a small example. Assume our previous class Account and another class, Named, with only two methods: setname and getname.

```
Named = {}
function Named:getname ()
  return self.name
end
function Named:setname (n)
  self.name = n
end
```

Listing 16.1. An implementation of multiple inheritance:

```
-- look up for 'k' in list of tables 'plist'
local function search (k, plist)
  for i = 1, #plist do
    local v = plist[i][k]      -- try 'i'-th superclass
    if v then return v end
  end
end

function createClass (...)
  local c = {}          -- new class
  local parents = {...}

  -- class will search for each method in the list of its parents
  setmetatable(c, {__index = function (t, k)
    return search(k, parents)
  end})

  -- prepare 'c' to be the metatable of its instances
  c.__index = c

  -- define a new constructor for this new class
  function c:new (o)
    o = o or {}
    setmetatable(o, c)
    return o
  end

  return c              -- return new class
end
```

To create a new class `NamedAccount` that is a subclass of both `Account` and `Named`, we simply call `createClass`:

```
NamedAccount = createClass(Account, Named)
```

To create and to use instances, we do as usual:

```
account = NamedAccount:new{name = "Paul"}
print(account:getname())      --> Paul
```

Now let us follow how this last statement works. Lua cannot find the field "getname" in account; so, it looks for the field __index of account's metatable, which is NamedAccount. But NamedAccount also cannot provide a "getname" field, so Lua looks for the field __index of NamedAccount's metatable. Because this field contains a function, Lua calls it. This function then looks for "getname" first in Account, without success, and then in Named, where it finds a non-nil value, which is the final result of the search.

Of course, due to the underlying complexity of this search, the performance of multiple inheritance is not the same as single inheritance. A simple way to improve this performance is to copy inherited methods into the subclasses. Using this technique, the index metamethod for classes would be like this:

```
setmetatable(c, {__index = function (t, k)
   local v = search(k, parents)
   t[k] = v         -- save for next access
   return v
end})
```

With this trick, accesses to inherited methods are as fast as to local methods (except for the first access). The drawback is that it is difficult to change method definitions after the system is running, because these changes do not propagate down the hierarchy chain.

16.4 Privacy

Many people consider privacy to be an integral part of an object-oriented language; the state of each object should be its own internal affair. In some object-oriented languages, such as C++ and Java, you can control whether an object field (also called an *instance variable*) or a method is visible outside the object. Smalltalk, which popularizes object-oriented languages, makes all variables private and all methods public. Simula, the first ever object-oriented language, did not offer any kind of protection.

The main design for objects in Lua, which we have shown previously, does not offer privacy mechanisms. Partly, this is a consequence of our use of a general structure (tables) to represent objects. Moreover, Lua avoids too much redundancy and artificial restrictions. If you do not want to access something inside an object, just *do not do it*.

Nevertheless, another aim of Lua is to be flexible, offering to the programmer meta-mechanisms that enable her to emulate many different mechanisms. Although the basic design for objects in Lua does not offer privacy mechanisms, we can implement objects in a different way, so as to have access control. Although programmers do not use this implementation frequently, it is instructive to know about it, both because it explores some interesting aspects of Lua and because it can be a good solution for other problems.

The basic idea of this alternative design is to represent each object through two tables: one for its state and another for its operations, or its interface. The object itself is accessed through the second table, that is, through the operations that compose its interface. To avoid unauthorized access, the table that represents the state of an object is not kept in a field of the other table; instead, it is kept only in the closure of the methods. For instance, to represent our bank account with this design, we could create new objects running the following factory function:

```
function newAccount (initialBalance)
   local self = {balance = initialBalance}
```

```
      local withdraw = function (v)
                        self.balance = self.balance - v
                      end
      local deposit = function (v)
                        self.balance = self.balance + v
                      end
      local getBalance = function () return self.balance end
      return {
        withdraw = withdraw,
        deposit = deposit,
        getBalance = getBalance
      }
    end
```

First, the function creates a table to keep the internal object state and stores it in the local variable `self`. Then, the function creates the methods of the object. Finally, the function creates and returns the external object, which maps method names to the actual method implementations. The key point here is that these methods do not get `self` as an extra parameter; instead, they access `self` directly. Because there is no extra argument, we do not use the colon syntax to manipulate such objects. We call their methods just like regular functions:

```
    acc1 = newAccount(100.00)
    acc1.withdraw(40.00)
    print(acc1.getBalance())     --> 60
```

This design gives full privacy to anything stored in the `self` table. After `newAccount` returns, there is no way to gain direct access to this table. We can access it only through the functions created inside `newAccount`. Although our example puts only one instance variable into the private table, we can store all private parts of an object in this table. We can also define private methods: they are like public methods, but we do not put them in the interface. For instance, our accounts may give an extra credit of 10% for users with balances above a certain limit, but we do not want the users to have access to the details of that computation. We can implement this functionality as follows:

```
    function newAccount (initialBalance)
      local self = {
        balance = initialBalance,
        LIM = 10000.00,
      }
      local extra = function ()
        if self.balance > self.LIM then
          return self.balance*0.10
        else
          return 0
        end
      end
```

```
local getBalance = function ()
  return self.balance + extra()
end
```

<as before>

Again, there is no way for any user to access the extra function directly.

16.5   The Single-Method Approach

A particular case of the previous approach for object-oriented programming occurs when an object has a single method. In such cases, we do not need to create an interface table; instead, we can return this single method as the object representation. If this sounds a little weird, it is worth remembering Section 7.1, where we saw how to construct iterator functions that keep state as closures. An iterator that keeps state is nothing more than a single-method object.

Another interesting case of single-method objects occurs when this single-method is actually a dispatch method that performs different tasks based on a distinguished argument. A possible implementation for such an object is as follows:

```
function newObject (value)
  return function (action, v)
    if action == "get" then return value
    elseif action == "set" then value = v
    else error("invalid action")
    end
  end
end
```

Its use is straightforward:

```
d = newObject(0)
print(d("get"))     --> 0
d("set", 10)
print(d("get"))     --> 10
```

This unconventional implementation for objects is quite effective. The syntax d("set",10), although peculiar, is only two characters longer than the more conventional d:set(10). Each object uses one single closure, which is cheaper than one table. There is no inheritance, but we have full privacy: the only way to access an object state is through its sole method.

Tcl/Tk uses a similar approach for its widgets. The name of a widget in Tk denotes a function (a *widget command*) that can perform all kinds of operations over the widget.

Exercises

Exercise 16.1: Implement a class Stack, with methods push, pop, top, and isempty.

Exercise 16.2: Implement a class StackQueue as a subclass of Stack. Besides the inherited methods, add to this class a method insertbottom, which inserts an element at the bottom of the stack. (This method allows us to use objects of this class as queues.)

Exercise 16.3: Another way to provide privacy for objects is to implement them using proxies (Section 13.4). Each object is represented by an empty proxy table. An internal table maps proxies to tables that carry the object state. This internal table is not accessible from the outside, but methods use it to translate their self parameters to the real tables where they operate. Implement the Account example using this approach and discuss its pros and cons.

(There is a small problem with this approach. Try to figure it out or see Section 17.3, which also presents a solution.)

17

Weak Tables and Finalizers

Lua does automatic memory management. Programs create objects (tables, threads, etc.), but there is no function to delete objects. Lua automatically deletes objects that become garbage, using *garbage collection*. This frees you from most of the burden of memory management and, more importantly, frees you from most of the bugs related to this activity, such as dangling pointers and memory leaks.

The use of a real garbage collector means that Lua has no problems with cycles. You do not need to take any special action when using cyclic data structures; they are collected like any other data. Nevertheless, sometimes even the smarter collector needs your help. No garbage collector allows you to forget all worries about resource management, such as hoarding memory and external resources.

Weak tables and finalizers are the mechanisms that you can use in Lua to help the garbage collector. Weak tables allow the collection of Lua objects that are still accessible to the program, while finalizers allow the collection of external objects that are not directly under control of the garbage collector. In this chapter, we will discuss both mechanisms.

17.1 Weak Tables

A garbage collector can collect only what it can be sure is garbage; it cannot guess what you consider garbage. A typical example is a stack, implemented with an array and an index to the top. You know that the valid part of the array goes only up to the top, but Lua does not. If you pop an element by simply decrementing the top, the object left in the array is not garbage to Lua.

Similarly, any object stored in a global variable is not garbage to Lua, even if
your program will never use it again. In both cases, it is up to you (i.e., your
program) to assign nil to these positions so that they do not lock an otherwise
disposable object.

However, simply cleaning your references is not always enough. Some constructions need extra collaboration between the program and the collector. A
typical example happens when you want to keep a collection of all live objects
of some kind (e.g., files) in your program. This task seems simple: all you have
to do is to insert each new object into the collection. However, once the object is
part of the collection, it will never be collected! Even if no one else points to it,
the collection does. Lua cannot know that this reference should not prevent the
reclamation of the object, unless you tell Lua about this fact.

Weak tables are the mechanism that you use to tell Lua that a reference
should not prevent the reclamation of an object. A *weak reference* is a reference
to an object that is not considered by the garbage collector. If all references
pointing to an object are weak, the object is collected and somehow these weak
references are deleted. Lua implements weak references as weak tables: a *weak
table* is a table whose entries are weak. This means that, if an object is held only
inside weak tables, Lua will eventually collect the object.

Tables have keys and values, and both can contain any kind of object. Under
normal circumstances, the garbage collector does not collect objects that appear
as keys or as values of an accessible table. That is, both keys and values are
strong references, as they prevent the reclamation of objects they refer to. In a
weak table, both keys and values can be weak. This means that there are three
kinds of weak tables: tables with weak keys, tables with weak values, and fully
weak tables, where both keys and values are weak. Irrespective of the table
kind, when a key or a value is collected the whole entry disappears from the
table.

The weakness of a table is given by the field __mode of its metatable. The
value of this field, when present, should be a string: if this string is "k", the keys
in the table are weak; if this string is "v", the values in the table are weak; if this
string is "kv", both keys and values are weak. The following example, although
artificial, illustrates the basic behavior of weak tables:

```
a = {}
b = {__mode = "k"}
setmetatable(a, b)      -- now 'a' has weak keys
key = {}                -- creates first key
a[key] = 1
key = {}                -- creates second key
a[key] = 2
collectgarbage()        -- forces a garbage collection cycle
for k, v in pairs(a) do print(v) end
   --> 2
```

In this example, the second assignment key={} overwrites the reference to the
first key. The call to collectgarbage forces the garbage collector to do a full

collection. As there is no other reference to the first key, this key is collected and the corresponding entry in the table is removed. The second key, however, is still anchored in variable key, so it is not collected.

Notice that only objects can be collected from a weak table. Values, such as numbers and booleans, are not collectible. For instance, if we insert a numeric key in table a (from our previous example), the collector will never remove it. Of course, if the value corresponding to a numeric key is collected in a table with weak values, then the whole entry is removed from the table.

Strings present a subtlety here: although strings are collectible, from an implementation point of view, they are not like other collectible objects. Other objects, such as tables and threads, are created explicitly. For instance, whenever Lua evaluates the expression {}, it creates a new table. However, does Lua create a new string when it evaluates "a".."b"? What if there is already a string "ab" in the system? Does Lua create a new one? Can the compiler create this string before running the program? It does not matter: these are implementation details. From the programmer's point of view, strings are values, not objects. Therefore, like a number or a boolean, a string is not removed from weak tables (unless its associated value is collected).

17.2 Memoize Functions

A common programming technique is to trade space for time. You can speed up a function by *memorizing* its results so that, later, when you call the function with the same argument, the function can reuse that result.

Imagine a generic server that receives requests containing strings with Lua code. Each time it gets a request, it runs load on the string, and then calls the resulting function. However, load is an expensive function, and some commands to the server may be quite frequent. Instead of calling load repeatedly each time it receives a common command like "closeconnection()", the server can *memorize* the results from load using an auxiliary table. Before calling load, the server checks in the table whether the given string already has a translation. If it cannot find the string, then (and only then) the server calls load and stores the result into the table. We can pack this behavior in a new function:

```lua
local results = {}
function mem_loadstring (s)
  local res = results[s]
  if res == nil then                -- result not available?
    res = assert(load(s))           -- compute new result
    results[s] = res                -- save for later reuse
  end
  return res
end
```

The savings with this scheme can be huge. However, it may also cause unsuspected waste. Although some commands repeat over and over, many other commands happen only once. Gradually, the table `results` accumulates all commands the server has ever received plus their respective codes; after enough time, this behavior will exhaust the server's memory. A weak table provides a simple solution to this problem. If the `results` table has weak values, each garbage-collection cycle will remove all translations not in use at that moment (which means virtually all of them):

```
local results = {}
setmetatable(results, {__mode = "v"})   -- make values weak
function mem_loadstring (s)
  <as before>
```

Actually, because the indices are always strings, we can make this table fully weak, if we want:

```
setmetatable(results, {__mode = "kv"})
```

The net result is the same.

The memorize technique is useful also to ensure the uniqueness of some kind of object. For instance, assume a system that represents colors as tables, with fields red, green, and blue in some range. A naive color factory generates a new color for each new request:

```
function createRGB (r, g, b)
  return {red = r, green = g, blue = b}
end
```

Using the memorize technique, we can reuse the same table for the same color. To create a unique key for each color, we simply concatenate the color indices with a separator in between:

```
local results = {}
setmetatable(results, {__mode = "v"})   -- make values weak
function createRGB (r, g, b)
  local key = r .. "-" .. g .. "-" .. b
  local color = results[key]
  if color == nil then
    color = {red = r, green = g, blue = b}
    results[key] = color
  end
  return color
end
```

An interesting consequence of this implementation is that the user can compare colors using the primitive equality operator, because two coexistent equal colors are always represented by the same table. Note that a given color can be represented by different tables at different times, because from time to time a garbage-collector cycle clears the `results` table. However, as long as a given color is in use, it is not removed from `results`. So, whenever a color survives long enough to be compared with a new one, its representation also survives long enough to be reused by the new color.

17.3   Object Attributes

Another important use of weak tables is to associate attributes with objects. There are endless situations where we need to attach some attribute to an object: names to functions, default values to tables, sizes to arrays, and so on.

When the object is a table, we can store the attribute in the table itself, with an appropriate unique key. As we saw before, a simple and error-proof way to create a unique key is to create a new object (typically a table) and use it as the key. However, if the object is not a table, it cannot keep its own attributes. Even for tables, sometimes we may not want to store the attribute in the original object. For instance, we may want to keep the attribute private, or we do not want the attribute to disturb a table traversal. In all these cases, we need an alternative way to associate attributes to objects.

Of course, an external table provides an ideal way to associate attributes to objects (it is not by chance that tables are sometimes called *associative arrays*). We use the objects as keys, and their attributes as values. An external table can keep attributes of any type of object, as Lua allows us to use any type of object as a key. Moreover, attributes kept in an external table do not interfere with other objects, and can be as private as the table itself.

However, this seemingly perfect solution has a huge drawback: once we use an object as a key in a table, we lock the object into existence. Lua cannot collect an object that is being used as a key. If we use a regular table to associate functions to its names, none of these functions will ever be collected. As you might expect, we can avoid this drawback by using a weak table. This time, however, we need weak keys. The use of weak keys does not prevent any key from being collected, once there are no other references to it. On the other hand, the table cannot have weak values; otherwise, attributes of live objects could be collected.

17.4   Revisiting Tables with Default Values

In Section 13.4, we discussed how to implement tables with non-nil default values. We saw one particular technique and commented that two other techniques needed weak tables so we postponed them. Now it is time to revisit the subject. As we will see, these two techniques for default values are actually particular applications of the two general techniques that we have just discussed: object attributes and memorizing.

In the first solution, we use a weak table to associate to each table its default value:

```
local defaults = {}
setmetatable(defaults, {__mode = "k"})
local mt = {__index = function (t) return defaults[t] end}
function setDefault (t, d)
  defaults[t] = d
  setmetatable(t, mt)
end
```

If `defaults` did not have weak keys, it would anchor all tables with default values into permanent existence.

In the second solution, we use distinct metatables for distinct default values, but we reuse the same metatable whenever we repeat a default value. This is a typical use of memorizing:

```
local metas = {}
setmetatable(metas, {__mode = "v"})
function setDefault (t, d)
  local mt = metas[d]
  if mt == nil then
    mt = {__index = function () return d end}
    metas[d] = mt      -- memorize
  end
  setmetatable(t, mt)
end
```

We use weak values, in this case, to allow the collection of metatables that are not being used anymore.

Given these two implementations for default values, which is best? As usual, it depends. Both have similar complexity and similar performance. The first implementation needs a few memory words for each table with a default value (an entry in `defaults`). The second implementation needs a few dozen memory words for each distinct default value (a new table, a new closure, plus an entry in `metas`). So, if your application has thousands of tables with a few distinct default values, the second implementation is clearly superior. On the other hand, if few tables share common defaults, then you should favor the first implementation.

17.5   Ephemeron Tables

A tricky situation occurs when, in a table with weak keys, a value refers to its own key.

This scenario is more common than it may seem. As a typical example, consider a constant-function factory. Such factory receives an object and returns a function that, whenever called, returns that object:

```
function factory (o)
  return function () return o end
end
```

This factory is a good candidate to memorization, to avoid the creation of a new closure when there is one already available:

```
do
  local mem = {}
  setmetatable(mem, {__mode = "k"})
  function factory (o)
    local res = mem[o]
    if not res then
      res = function () return o end
      mem[o] = res
    end
    return res
  end
end
```

There is a catch, however. Note that the value (the constant function) associated with an object in mem refers back to its own key (the object itself). Although the keys in that table are weak, the values are not. From a standard interpretation of weak tables, nothing would ever be removed from that memorizing table. Because values are not weak, there is always a strong reference to each function. Each function refers to its corresponding object, so there is always a strong reference to each object. Therefore, these objects will not be collected, despite the weak keys.

This strict interpretation, however, it is not very useful. Most people expect that a value in a table is only accessible through its respective key. So, we can think of the above scenario as a kind of cycle, where the closure refers to the object that (through the memorizing table) refers back to the closure.

Lua 5.2 solves the above problem with the concept of ephemeron tables. In Lua 5.2, a table with weak keys and strong values is an *ephemeron table*. In an ephemeron table, the accessibility of a key controls the accessibility of its corresponding value. More specifically, consider an entry (k, v) in an ephemeron table. The reference to v is only strong if there is some strong reference to k. Otherwise, the entry is eventually removed from the table, even if v refers (directly or indirectly) to k.

17.6 Finalizers

Although the goal of the garbage collector is to collect Lua objects, it can also help programs to release external resources. For that purpose, several programming languages offer a mechanism for finalizers. A *finalizer* is a function associated with an object that is called when that object is about to be collected.

Lua implements finalizers through the metamethod _ _gc. See the following example:

```
o = {x = "hi"}
setmetatable(o, {__gc = function (o) print(o.x) end})
o = nil
collectgarbage()    --> hi
```

In this example, we first create a table and set it with a metatable that has a _ _gc metamethod. Then we erase the only link to the table (global variable o) and force a complete garbage collection, calling collectgarbage. During the collection, Lua detects that the table is no more accessible, and therefore calls its finalizer (the _ _gc metamethod).

A subtleness of finalizers in Lua is the concept of marking an object for finalization. We mark an object for finalization when we set a metatable for it with a non-null _ _gc metamethod. If we do not mark the object, it will not be finalized. Most code we write works naturally, but some strange cases can occur, like here:

```
o = {x = "hi"}
mt = {}
setmetatable(o, mt)
mt.__gc = function (o) print(o.x) end
o = nil
collectgarbage()    --> (prints nothing)
```

In this example, the metatable we set for o does not have a _ _gc metamethod, so the object is not marked for finalization. Even if we later set a _ _gc field to the metatable, Lua does not detect that assignment as something special, so it will not mark the object. As we said, this is seldom a problem; it is not usual to change metamethods after using a metatable.

If you really need to set the metamethod later, you can provide any value for the _ _gc field, as a placeholder:

```
o = {x = "hi"}
mt = {__gc = true}
setmetatable(o, mt)
mt.__gc = function (o) print(o.x) end
o = nil
collectgarbage()    --> hi
```

Now, as the metatable has a _ _gc field, o is properly marked for finalization. There is no problem if you do not set a metamethod later; Lua only calls the finalizer if it is a proper function.

When the collector finalizes several objects in the same cycle, it calls their finalizers in the reverse order that the objects were marked for finalization. Consider the next example, which creates a linked list of objects with finalizers:

```
mt = {__gc = function (o) print(o[1]) end}
list = nil
for i = 1, 3 do
  list = setmetatable({i, link = list}, mt)
end
list = nil
collectgarbage()
  --> 3
  --> 2
  --> 1
```

The first object to be finalized is object 3, which was the last to be marked.

A common misconception is to think that links among objects being collected can affect the order that they are finalized. For instance, one can think that object 2 in the previous example must be finalized before object 1 because there is a link from 2 to 1. However, links can form cycles. Therefore, they do not impose any order to finalizers.

Another tricky point about finalizers is *resurrection*. When a finalizer is called, it gets the object being finalized as a parameter. So, the object becomes alive again, at least during the finalization. I call this a *transient resurrection*. While the finalizer runs, nothing stops it from storing the object in a global variable, for instance, so that it remains accessible after the finalizer returns. I call this a *permanent resurrection*.

Resurrection must be transitive. Consider the following piece of code:

```
A = {x = "this is A"}
B = {f = A}
setmetatable(B, {__gc = function (o) print(o.f.x) end})
A, B = nil
collectgarbage()    --> this is A
```

The finalizer for B accesses A, so A cannot be collected before the finalization of B. Lua must resurrect both B and A before running that finalizer.

Because of resurrection, objects with finalizers are collected in two phases. The first time the collector detects that an object with a finalizer is not reachable, the collector resurrects the object and queues it to be finalized. Once its finalizer runs, Lua marks the object as finalized. The next time the collector detects that the object is not reachable, it deletes the object. If you want to ensure that all garbage in your program has been actually released, you must call collectgarbage twice; the second call will delete the objects that were finalized during the first call.

The finalizer for each object runs exactly once, due to the mark that Lua puts on finalized objects. If an object is not collected until the end of a program, Lua will call its finalizer when the entire Lua state is closed. This last feature allows a form of atexit functions in Lua, that is, functions that will run immediately before the program terminates. All we have to do is to create a table with a finalizer and anchors it somewhere, for instance in a global variable:

```
_G.AA = {__gc = function ()
  -- your 'atexit' code comes here
  print("finishing Lua program")
end}
setmetatable(_G.AA, _G.AA)
```

Another interesting technique allows a program to call a given function every time Lua completes a collection cycle. As a finalizer runs only once, the trick here is to make the finalizer creates a new object to run the next finalizer:

```
do
  local mt = {__gc = function (o)
    -- whatever you want to do
    print("new cycle")
    -- creates new object for next cycle
    setmetatable({}, getmetatable(o))
  end}
  -- creates first object
  setmetatable({}, mt)
end

collectgarbage()    --> new cycle
collectgarbage()    --> new cycle
collectgarbage()    --> new cycle
```

The interaction of objects with finalizers and weak tables also has a subtlety. The collector clears the values in weak tables before the resurrection, while the keys are cleared after resurrection. The following fragment illustrates this behavior:

```
-- a table with weak keys
wk = setmetatable({}, {__mode = "k"})

-- a table with weak values
wv = setmetatable({}, {__mode = "v"})

o = {}    -- an object
wv[1] = o; wk[o] = 10    -- add it to both tables

setmetatable(o, {__gc = function (o)
  print(wk[o], wv[1])
end})

o = nil; collectgarbage()    --> 10    nil
```

When the object's finalizer runs, it finds the object in table wk, but not in table wv. The rationale for this behavior is that frequently we use tables with weak keys to keep properties of an object (as we discussed in Section 17.3), and finalizers may need to access those attributes. However, we use tables with weak values to reuse live objects; in this case, objects being finalized are not useful anymore.

Exercises

Exercise 17.1: Write an experiment to determine whether Lua actually implements ephemeron tables. (Remember to call `collectgarbage` to force a garbage collection cycle.) If possible, try your code both in Lua 5.1 and in Lua 5.2 to see the difference.

Exercise 17.2: Consider the first example of Section 17.6, which creates a table with a finalizer that only prints a message when activated. What happens if the program ends without a collection cycle? What happens if the program calls `os.exit`? What happens if the program ends with some error?

Exercise 17.3: Consider that you have to implement a memorizing table for a function from strings to strings. Doing the table weak will not allow the removal of entries, because weak tables do not consider strings as collectable objects. How can you implement memorization in that case?

Exercise 17.4: Explain the output of the following program:

```
local count = 0

local mt = {__gc = function () count = count - 1 end}
local a = {}

for i = 1, 10000 do
  count = count + 1
  a[i] = setmetatable({}, mt)
end

collectgarbage()
print(collectgarbage"count" * 1024, count)
a = nil
collectgarbage()
print(collectgarbage"count" * 1024, count)
collectgarbage()
print(collectgarbage"count" * 1024, count)
```

Part III

The Standard Libraries

18

The Mathematical Library

In this and the next chapters about the standard libraries, my purpose is not to give the complete specification of each function, but to show you what kind of functionality each library can provide. I may omit some subtle options or behaviors for clarity of exposition. The main idea is to spark your curiosity, which can then be satisfied by the Lua reference manual.

The math library comprises a standard set of mathematical functions, such as trigonometric functions (sin, cos, tan, asin, acos, etc.), exponentiation and logarithms (exp, log, log10), rounding functions (floor, ceil), max, min, functions for generating pseudo-random numbers (random, randomseed), plus variables pi and huge, which is the largest representable number. (huge may be the special value *inf* in some platforms.)

All trigonometric functions work in radians. You can use the functions deg and rad to convert between degrees and radians. If you want to work in degrees, you can redefine the trigonometric functions:

```
do
  local sin, asin, ... = math.sin, math.asin, ...
  local deg, rad = math.deg, math.rad
  math.sin = function (x) return sin(rad(x)) end
  math.asin = function (x) return deg(asin(x)) end
  ...
end
```

The math.random function generates pseudo-random numbers. We can call it in three ways. When we call it without arguments, it returns a pseudo-random real number with uniform distribution in the interval $[0, 1)$. When we call it with only one argument, an integer n, it returns a pseudo-random integer x

such that $1 \leq x \leq n$. For instance, you can simulate the result of tossing a die with random(6). Finally, we can call random with two integer arguments, l and u, to get a pseudo-random integer x such that $l \leq x \leq u$.

You can set a seed for the pseudo-random generator with the randomseed function; its numeric sole argument is the seed. Usually, when a program starts, it initializes the generator with a fixed seed. This means that, every time you run your program, it generates the same sequence of pseudo-random numbers. For debugging, this is a nice property; but in a game, you will have the same scenario over and over. A common trick to solve this problem is to use the current time as a seed, with the call math.randomseed(os.time()). The os.time function returns a number that represents the current time, usually as the number of seconds since some epoch.

The math.random function uses the rand function from the standard C library. In some implementations, this function produces numbers with not-so-good statistical properties. You can check for independent distributions of better pseudo-random generators for Lua. (The standard Lua distribution does not include any such generator to avoid copyright problems. It contains only code written by the Lua authors.)

Exercises

Exercise 18.1: Write a function to test whether a given number is a power of two.

Exercise 18.2: Write a function to compute the volume of a right circular cone, given its height and the angle between a generatrix and the axis.

Exercise 18.3: Implement a better random function in Lua. Search the Web for a good algorithm. (You may need the bitwise library; see Chapter 19.)

Exercise 18.4: Using math.random, write a function to produce a pseudo-random number with a standard normal (Gaussian) distribution.

Exercise 18.5: Write a function to shuffle a given list. Make sure that all permutations are equally probable.

19

The Bitwise Library

A source of constant complaints about Lua has been its lack of bitwise operations. That absence was not by accident. It is not easy to conciliate bitwise operations with floating-point numbers.

We can express some bitwise operations as arithmetic operations. For instance, left shifts correspond to multiplications by powers of two; right shifts correspond to divisions. However, bitwise-and and bitwise-or do not seem to have these translations. They are defined over the binary representation of integer numbers in base two. It seems impossible to extend them in any meaningful way to floating-point numbers in general. Even some simple operations seem out of place. What should be the complement of 0.0? Should it be -1? Or 0xFFFFFFFF (which is 4 294 967 295 in Lua, clearly different from -1)? Or maybe $2^{64} - 1$ (a number that cannot be exactly represented in a double)?

To amend this mismatch, Lua 5.2 offers bitwise operations through a library, not as predefined operations in the language. This interface makes it clear that such operations are not intrinsic to Lua numbers, but that they impose some specific interpretation to work over those numbers. Moreover, it allows alternative libraries to provide different interpretations for bitwise operations (e.g., by accepting more than 32 bits).

I will use hexadecimal notation for most examples in this chapter, to ease the interpretation of the results. I will use the word MAX to represent the number 0xFFFFFFFF (that is, $2^{32} - 1$). I will use also the following auxiliary function throughout the examples:

```
function printx (x)
  print(string.format("0x%X", x))
end
```

The bitwise library in Lua 5.2 is called `bit32`. This name makes it clear that it operates over 32-bit numbers. Because **and**, **or**, and **not** are reserved words in Lua, these operations are called respectively `band`, `bor`, and `bnot`. For consistency, the exclusive-or operation is called `bxor`:

```
printx(bit32.band(0xDF, 0xFD))        --> 0xDD
printx(bit32.bor(0xD0, 0x0D))         --> 0xDD
printx(bit32.bxor(0xD0, 0xFF))        --> 0x2F
printx(bit32.bnot(0))                 --> 0xFFFFFFFF
```

Functions `band`, `bor`, and `bxor` accept any number of arguments:

```
printx(bit32.bor(0xA, 0xA0, 0xA00))       --> 0xAAA
printx(bit32.band(0xFFA, 0xFAF, 0xAFF))   --> 0xAAA
printx(bit32.bxor(0, 0xAAA, 0))           --> 0xAAA
printx(bit32.bor())                       --> 0x0
printx(bit32.band())                      --> 0xFFFFFFFF
printx(bit32.bxor())                      --> 0x0
```

(They are all commutative and associative.)

The bitwise library operates with unsigned integers. Its operations convert any number given as an argument to an integer in the range 0–MAX. First, non-integer numbers are rounded in a non-specified way. Second, numbers out of the range 0–MAX are mapped into this range through a modulo operation: the integer n becomes $n \% 2^{32}$. This operation is equivalent to getting the two-complement representation of the number and then taking the least 32 bits. As expected, -1 becomes MAX. You can use the following operations to normalize a number (that is, to map it into the range 0–MAX):

```
printx(bit32.bor(2^32))        --> 0x0
printx(bit32.band(-1))         --> 0xFFFFFFFF
```

Of course, in standard Lua it is easier to do n%(2^32).

Unless noted otherwise, all operations in the library give results in the range 0–MAX, too. However, you should be cautious when using the results of bitwise operations as regular numbers. Sometimes, Lua is compiled with a different numerical type. In particular, restrained systems can use 32-bit integers as Lua numbers. In those systems, MAX is equal to -1. Moreover, some external bitwise libraries use different conventions for their results. So, whenever you need to handle the result of a bitwise operation as a number, take care. Avoid order comparisons: instead of x<0, write `bit32.btest(x,0x80000000)`. (We will see `btest` in a moment.) Use the bitwise library itself to normalize constants before equality comparisons, as in the next fragment:

```
if bit32.or(a, b) == bit32.or(-1) then
   <some code>
```

The bitwise library defines operations also to shift and rotate bits: `lshift` for shifts to the left; `rshift` and `arshift` (arithmetic shift) for shifts to the right; `lrotate` for rotations to the left; and `rrotate` for rotations to the right. Except for the arithmetic shift, all shifts fill vacant bits with zeros. The arithmetic shift fills its vacant bits on the left with copies of its last bit (the "signal bit"):

```
printx(bit32.rshift(0xDF, 4))              --> 0xD
printx(bit32.lshift(0xDF, 4))              --> 0xDF0
printx(bit32.rshift(-1, 28))               --> 0xF
printx(bit32.arshift(-1, 28))              --> 0xFFFFFFFF
printx(bit32.lrotate(0xABCDEF01, 4))       --> 0xBCDEF01A
printx(bit32.rrotate(0xABCDEF01, 4))       --> 0x1ABCDEF0
```

A shift (or rotate) with a negative displacement shifts (or rotates) to the opposite side. For instance, a shift of -1 bit to the right is equivalent to a shift of 1 bit to the left. The result of a shift by more than 31 bits is 0 or MAX, because all original bits are shifted out:

```
printx(bit32.lrotate(0xABCDEF01, -4))      --> 0x1ABCDEF0
printx(bit32.lrotate(0xABCDEF01, -36))     --> 0x1ABCDEF0
printx(bit32.lshift(0xABCDEF01, -36))      --> 0x0
printx(bit32.rshift(-1, 34))               --> 0x0
printx(bit32.arshift(-1, 34))              --> 0xFFFFFFFF
```

Besides those more or less standard bitwise operations, the bitwise library offers three convenience functions. Function btest performs the same operation as band, but returns a boolean indicating whether the result is different from zero:

```
print(bit32.btest(12, 1))       --> false
print(bit32.btest(13, 1))       --> true
```

Another common operation is to extract a bit field from a number. Usually this operation involves a shift followed by a mask; the bitwise library packs this extraction into a single function. The call bit32.extract(x,f,w) returns w bits from x, starting at bit f:

```
printx(bit32.extract(0xABCDEF01, 4, 8))      --> 0xF0
printx(bit32.extract(0xABCDEF01, 20, 12))    --> 0xABC
printx(bit32.extract(0xABCDEF01, 0, 12))     --> 0xF01
```

This operation counts bits from 0 to 31. If not provided, the field width defaults to one bit:

```
printx(bit32.extract(0x0000000F, 0))       --> 0x1
printx(bit32.extract(0xF0000000, 31))      --> 0x1
```

The reverse of extract is replace, which replaces a bit field into a number. The first parameter is the original number. The second parameter is the value to be inserted. The next two parameters, f and w, have the same meaning as in bit32.extract:

```
printx(bit32.replace(0xABCDEF01, 0x55, 4, 8))     --> 0xABCDE551
printx(bit32.replace(0xABCDEF01, 0x0, 4, 8))      --> 0xABCDE001
```

Note that, for any valid values for x, f and w, the following equality holds:

```
assert(bit32.replace(x, bit32.extract(x, f, w), f, w) == x)
```

Exercises

Exercise 19.1:   Write a function to test whether a given integer is a power of two.

Exercise 19.2:   Write a function to compute the Hamming weight of a given integer. (The *Hamming weight* of a number is the number of ones in its binary representation.)

Exercise 19.3:   Write a function to test whether the binary representation of a number is a palindrome.

Exercise 19.4:   Define the shift operations and the bitwise not using the arithmetic operators in Lua.

Exercise 19.5:   Write a function that receives a string coded in UTF-8 and returns its first code point as a number. The function should return nil if the string does not start with a valid UTF-8 sequence.

20

The Table Library

The `table` library comprises auxiliary functions to manipulate tables as arrays. It provides functions to insert and remove elements from lists, to sort the elements of an array, and to concatenate all strings in an array.

20.1 Insert and Remove

The `table.insert` function inserts an element in a given position of an array, moving up other elements to open space. For instance, if t is the array {10, 20, 30}, after the call `table.insert(t, 1, 15)` t will be {15, 10, 20, 30}. As a special (and frequent) case, if we call `insert` without a position, it inserts the element in the last position of the array (and, therefore, moves no elements). As an example, the following code reads the program input line by line, storing all lines in an array:

```
t = {}
for line in io.lines() do
  table.insert(t, line)
end
print(#t)          --> (number of lines read)
```

In Lua 5.0, this idiom was common. In more recent versions, I prefer the idiom `t[#t+1] = line` to append elements to a list.

The `table.remove` function removes (and returns) an element from a given position in an array, moving down other elements to close space. When called without a position, it removes the last element of the array.

With these two functions, it is straightforward to implement stacks, queues, and double queues. We can initialize such structures as `t = {}`. A push operation is equivalent to `table.insert(t, x)`; a pop operation is equivalent to `table.remove(t)`. The call `table.insert(t, 1, x)` inserts at the other end of the structure (its beginning, actually), and `table.remove(t, 1)` removes from this end. The last two operations are not particularly efficient, as they must move elements up and down. However, because the `table` library implements these functions in C, these loops are not too expensive, so that this implementation is good enough for small arrays (up to some hundred elements, say).

20.2   Sort

Another useful function on arrays is `table.sort`; we have seen it before. It takes the array to be sorted plus an optional order function. This order function takes two arguments and must return true when the first argument should come first in the sorted array. If this function is not provided, `sort` uses the default less-than operation (corresponding to the '<' operator).

A common confusion happens when programmers try to order the indices of a table. In a table, the indices form a set, and have no order whatsoever. If you want to order them, you have to copy them to an array and then sort the array. Let us see an example. Suppose that you read a source file and build a table that gives, for each function name, the line where this function is defined; something like this:

```
lines = {
  luaH_set = 10,
  luaH_get = 24,
  luaH_present = 48,
}
```

Now you want to print these function names in alphabetical order. If you traverse this table with `pairs`, the names appear in an arbitrary order. You cannot sort them directly, because these names are keys of the table. However, when you put them into an array, then you can sort them. First, you must create an array with these names, then sort it, and finally print the result:

```
a = {}
for n in pairs(lines) do a[#a + 1] = n end
table.sort(a)
for _, n in ipairs(a) do print(n) end
```

Some people get confused here. After all, for Lua, arrays also have no order (they are tables, after all). But we know how to count, so we impose an order when we access the array with ordered indices. That is why you should always traverse arrays with `ipairs`, rather than `pairs`. The first function imposes the key order 1, 2, ..., whereas the latter uses the natural arbitrary order of the table.

As a more advanced solution, we can write an iterator that traverses a table following the order of its keys. An optional parameter f allows the specification of an alternative order. It first sorts the keys into an array, and then iterates on the array. At each step, it returns the key and value from the original table:

```
function pairsByKeys (t, f)
  local a = {}
  for n in pairs(t) do a[#a + 1] = n end
  table.sort(a, f)
  local i = 0        -- iterator variable
  return function ()    -- iterator function
    i = i + 1
    return a[i], t[a[i]]
  end
end
```

With this function, it is easy to print those function names in alphabetical order:

```
for name, line in pairsByKeys(lines) do
  print(name, line)
end
```

20.3 Concatenation

We have already seen table.concat in Section 11.6. It takes a list of strings and returns the result of concatenating all these strings. An optional second argument specifies a string separator to be inserted between the strings of the list. The function also accepts two other optional arguments that specify the indices of the first and the last string to concatenate.

The next function is an interesting generalization of table.concat. It accepts nested lists of strings:

```
function rconcat (l)
  if type(l) ~= "table" then return l end
  local res = {}
  for i = 1, #l do
    res[i] = rconcat(l[i])
  end
  return table.concat(res)
end
```

For each list element, rconcat calls itself recursively to concatenate a possible nested list. Then it calls the original table.concat to concatenate all partial results.

```
print(rconcat{{"a", {" nice"}}, " and", {{" long"}, {" list"}}})
  --> a nice and long list
```

Exercises

Exercise 20.1: Rewrite function `rconcat` so that it can get a separator, just like `table.concat` does:

```
print(rconcat({{{"a", "b"}, {"c"}}, "d", {}, {"e"}}, ";")
  --> a;b;c;d;e
```

Exercise 20.2: A problem with `table.sort` is that the sort is not stable, that is, elements that the comparison function considers equal may not keep their original order in the array after the sort. How can you do a stable sort in Lua?

Exercise 20.3: Write a function to test whether a given table is a valid sequence.

21

The String Library

The power of a raw Lua interpreter to manipulate strings is quite limited. A program can create string literals, concatenate them, and get string lengths. But it cannot extract substrings or examine their contents. The full power to manipulate strings in Lua comes from its string library.

The string library exports its functions as a module called string. Since Lua 5.1, it also exports its functions as methods of the string type (using the metatable of that type). So, for instance, to translate a string to upper case we can write either string.upper(s) or s:upper(). Pick your choice.

21.1 Basic String Functions

Some functions in the string library are quite simple: the call string.len(s) returns the length of a string s. It is equivalent to #s. The call string.rep(s,n) (or s:rep(n)) returns the string s repeated n times. You can create a string with 1 MB (e.g., for tests) with string.rep("a",2^20). The call string.lower(s) returns a copy of s with the upper-case letters converted to lower case; all other characters in the string are unchanged. (Function string.upper converts to upper case.) As a typical use, if you want to sort an array of strings regardless of case, you may write something like this:

```
table.sort(a, function (a, b)
  return a:lower() < b:lower()
end)
```

The call string.sub(s,i,j) extracts a piece of the string s, from the i-th to the j-th character inclusive. In Lua, the first character of a string has index 1.

You can also use negative indices, which count from the end of the string: the index –1 refers to the last character in a string, –2 to the previous one, and so on. Therefore, the call `string.sub(s,1,j)` (or `s:sub(1,j)`) gets a prefix of the string s with length j; `string.sub(s,j,-1)` (or simply `s:sub(j)`, since the default for the last argument is –1) gets a suffix of the string, starting at the j-th character; and `string.sub(s,2,-2)` returns a copy of the string s with the first and last characters removed:

```
s = "[in brackets]"
print(s:sub(2, -2))    --> in brackets
```

Remember that strings in Lua are immutable. Function `string.sub`, like any other function in Lua, does not change the value of a string, but returns a new string. A common mistake is to write something like `s:sub(2,-2)` and to assume that it will modify the value of s. If you want to modify the value of a variable, you must assign the new value to it:

```
s = s:sub(2, -2)
```

The `string.char` and `string.byte` functions convert between characters and their internal numeric representations. Function `string.char` gets zero or more integers, converts each one to a character, and returns a string concatenating all these characters. Function `string.byte(s, i)` returns the internal numeric representation of the i-th character of the string s; the second argument is optional, so that the call `string.byte(s)` returns the internal numeric representation of the first (or single) character of s. In the following examples, we assume that characters are represented in ASCII:

```
print(string.char(97))                  --> a
i = 99; print(string.char(i, i+1, i+2))   --> cde
print(string.byte("abc"))               --> 97
print(string.byte("abc", 2))            --> 98
print(string.byte("abc", -1))           --> 99
```

In the last line, we used a negative index to access the last character of the string.

Since Lua 5.1, `string.byte` accepts an optional third argument. A call like `string.byte(s,i,j)` returns multiple values with the numeric representation of all characters between indices i and j (inclusive):

```
print(string.byte("abc", 1, 2))         --> 97 98
```

The default value for j is i, so a call without this argument returns only the i-th character. A nice idiom is `{s:byte(1,-1)}`, which creates a table with the codes of all characters in s. Given this table, we can recreate the original string by calling `string.char(table.unpack(t))`. This technique does not work for very long strings (say, longer than 1 MB), because Lua puts a limit on how many values a function can return.

Function `string.format` is a powerful tool for formatting strings, typically for output. It returns a formatted version of its variable number of arguments following the description given by its first argument, the so-called *format string*. The format string has rules similar to those of the `printf` function of standard C: it is composed of regular text and *directives*, which control where and how to place each argument in the formatted string. A directive is the character '%' plus a letter that tells how to format the argument: 'd' for a decimal number, 'x' for hexadecimal, 'o' for octal, 'f' for a floating-point number, 's' for strings, plus some other variants. Between the '%' and the letter, a directive can include other options that control the details of the formatting, such as the number of decimal digits of a floating-point number:

```
print(string.format("pi = %.4f", math.pi))        --> pi = 3.1416
d = 5; m = 11; y = 1990
print(string.format("%02d/%02d/%04d", d, m, y))    --> 05/11/1990
tag, title = "h1", "a title"
print(string.format("<%s>%s</%s>", tag, title, tag))
   --> <h1>a title</h1>
```

In the first example, the `%.4f` means a floating-point number with four digits after the decimal point. In the second example, the `%02d` means a decimal number with at least two digits and zero padding; the directive `%2d`, without the zero, would use blanks for padding. For a complete description of these directives, see the Lua reference manual. Or, better yet, see a C manual, as Lua calls the standard C library to do the hard work here.

21.2 Pattern-Matching Functions

The most powerful functions in the string library are `find`, `match`, `gsub` (*Global Substitution*), and `gmatch` (*Global Match*). They all are based on *patterns*.

Unlike several other scripting languages, Lua uses neither POSIX regex nor Perl regular expressions for pattern matching. The main reason for this decision is size: a typical implementation of POSIX regular expressions takes more than 4000 lines of code. This is about the size of all Lua standard libraries together. In comparison, the implementation of pattern matching in Lua has less than 600 lines. Of course, pattern matching in Lua cannot do all that a full POSIX implementation does. Nevertheless, pattern matching in Lua is a powerful tool, and includes some features that are difficult to match with standard POSIX implementations.

The `string.find` function

The `string.find` function searches for a pattern inside a given subject string. The simplest form of a pattern is a word, which matches only a copy of itself. For instance, the pattern 'hello' will search for the substring "hello" inside the subject string. When `find` finds its pattern, it returns two values: the index

where the match begins and the index where the match ends. If it does not find
a match, it returns nil:

```
s = "hello world"
i, j = string.find(s, "hello")
print(i, j)                        --> 1    5
print(string.sub(s, i, j))         --> hello
print(string.find(s, "world"))     --> 7    11
i, j = string.find(s, "l")
print(i, j)                        --> 3    3
print(string.find(s, "lll"))       --> nil
```

When a match succeeds, we can call `string.sub` with the values returned by
`string.find` to get the part of the subject string that matched the pattern. For
simple patterns, this is the pattern itself.

The `string.find` function has an optional third parameter: an index that
tells where in the subject string to start the search. This parameter is useful
when we want to process all the indices where a given pattern appears: we
search for a new match repeatedly, each time starting after the position where
we found the previous one. As an example, the following code makes a table
with the positions of all newlines in a string:

```
local t = {}                       -- table to store the indices
local i = 0
while true do
  i = string.find(s, "\n", i+1)    -- find next newline
  if i == nil then break end
  t[#t + 1] = i
end
```

We will see later a simpler way to write such loops, using the `string.gmatch`
iterator.

The `string.match` function

The `string.match` function is similar to `string.find`, in the sense that it also
searches for a pattern in a string. However, instead of returning the positions
where it found the pattern, it returns the part of the subject string that matched
the pattern:

```
print(string.match("hello world", "hello"))    --> hello
```

For fixed patterns like 'hello', this function is pointless. It shows its power when
used with variable patterns, as in the next example:

```
date = "Today is 17/7/1990"
d = string.match(date, "%d+/%d+/%d+")
print(d)   --> 17/7/1990
```

Shortly we will discuss the meaning of the pattern '%d+/%d+/%d+' and more advanced uses for string.match.

The string.gsub **function**

The string.gsub function has three mandatory parameters: a subject string, a pattern, and a replacement string. Its basic use is to substitute the replacement string for all occurrences of the pattern inside the subject string:

```
s = string.gsub("Lua is cute", "cute", "great")
print(s)             --> Lua is great
s = string.gsub("all lii", "l", "x")
print(s)             --> axx xii
s = string.gsub("Lua is great", "Sol", "Sun")
print(s)             --> Lua is great
```

An optional fourth parameter limits the number of substitutions to be made:

```
s = string.gsub("all lii", "l", "x", 1)
print(s)             --> axl lii
s = string.gsub("all lii", "l", "x", 2)
print(s)             --> axx lii
```

The string.gsub function also returns as a second result the number of times it made the substitution. For instance, an easy way to count the number of spaces in a string is

```
count = select(2, string.gsub(str, " ", " "))
```

The string.gmatch **function**

The string.gmatch function returns a function that iterates over all occurrences of a pattern in a string. For instance, the following example collects all words in a given string s:

```
words = {}
for w in string.gmatch(s, "%a+") do
  words[#words + 1] = w
end
```

As we will discuss shortly, the pattern '%a+' matches sequences of one or more alphabetic characters (that is, words). So, the **for** loop will iterate over all words of the subject string, storing them in the list words.

The next example implements a function similar to package.searchpath, using gmatch and gsub:

```
function search (modname, path)
  modname = string.gsub(modname, "%.", "/")
  for c in string.gmatch(path, "[^;]+") do
    local fname = string.gsub(c, "?", modname)
    local f = io.open(fname)
    if f then
      f:close()
      return fname
    end
  end
  return nil     -- not found
end
```

The first step is to substitute the directory separator, assumed to be '/' in this example, for any dots. (As we will see later, a dot has a special meaning in a pattern. To match a literal dot we must write '%.'.) Then the function loops over all components of the path, wherein each component is a maximum expansion of non-semicolon characters. For each component, the function substitutes the module name for the question marks to get the final file name, and then it checks whether there is such a file. If so, the function closes the file and returns its name.

21.3   Patterns

You can make patterns more useful with *character classes*. A character class is an item in a pattern that can match any character in a specific set. For instance, the class %d matches any digit. Therefore, you can search for a date in the format dd/mm/yyyy with the pattern '%d%d/%d%d/%d%d%d%d':

```
s = "Deadline is 30/05/1999, firm"
date = "%d%d/%d%d/%d%d%d%d"
print(string.sub(s, string.find(s, date)))   --> 30/05/1999
```

The following table lists all character classes:

.	all characters
%a	letters
%c	control characters
%d	digits
%g	printable characters except spaces
%l	lower-case letters
%p	punctuation characters
%s	space characters
%u	upper-case letters
%w	alphanumeric characters
%x	hexadecimal digits

An upper-case version of any of these classes represents the complement of the
class. For instance, '%A' represents all non-letter characters:

```
print(string.gsub("hello, up-down!", "%A", "."))
  --> hello..up.down.    4
```

(The 4 is not part of the result string. It is the second result of gsub, the total
number of substitutions. I will omit this count in other examples that print the
result of gsub.)

Some characters, called *magic characters*, have special meanings when used
in a pattern. The magic characters are

```
( )  . % + - * ? [ ] ^ $
```

The character '%' works as an escape for these magic characters. So, '%.' matches
a dot; '%%' matches the character '%' itself. You can use the escape '%' not only
for the magic characters, but also for any non-alphanumeric character. When in
doubt, play safe and use an escape.

For the Lua parser, patterns are regular strings. They have no special
treatment, following the same rules as other strings. Only the pattern functions
interpret them as patterns, and only these functions treat the '%' as an escape.
To put a quote inside a pattern, you use the same techniques that you use to put
a quote inside other strings; for instance, you can escape the quote with a '\',
which is the escape character for Lua.

A *char-set* allows you to create your own character classes, grouping different
classes and single characters inside square brackets. For instance, the char-
set '[%w_]' matches both alphanumeric characters and underscores; the char-set
'[01]' matches binary digits; and the char-set '[%[%]]' matches square brackets.
To count the number of vowels in a text, you can write

```
nvow = select(2, string.gsub(text, "[AEIOUaeiou]", ""))
```

You can also include character ranges in a char-set, by writing the first and the
last characters of the range separated by a hyphen. I seldom use this facility,
because most useful ranges are already predefined; for instance, '[0-9]' is the
same as '%d', and '[0-9a-fA-F]' is the same as '%x'. However, if you need to find
an octal digit, then you may prefer '[0-7]' instead of an explicit enumeration
like '[01234567]'. You can get the complement of any char-set by starting it
with '^': the pattern '[^0-7]' finds any character that is not an octal digit and
'[^\n]' matches any character different from newline. But remember that you
can negate simple classes with its upper-case version: '%S' is simpler than '[^%s]'.

You can make patterns still more useful with modifiers for repetitions and
optional parts. Patterns in Lua offer four modifiers:

+	1 or more repetitions
*	0 or more repetitions
-	0 or more lazy repetitions
?	optional (0 or 1 occurrence)

The '+' modifier matches one or more characters of the original class. It will always get the longest sequence that matches the pattern. For instance, the pattern '%a+' means one or more letters, or a word:

```
print(string.gsub("one, and two; and three", "%a+", "word"))
  --> word, word word; word word
```

The pattern '%d+' matches one or more digits (an integer numeral):

```
print(string.match("the number 1298 is even", "%d+"))    --> 1298
```

The modifier '*' is similar to '+', but it also accepts zero occurrences of characters of the class. A typical use is to match optional spaces between parts of a pattern. For instance, to match an empty parenthesis pair, such as () or ( ), you can use the pattern '%(%s*%)': the pattern '%s*' matches zero or more spaces. (Parentheses also have a special meaning in a pattern, so we must escape them.) As another example, the pattern '[_%a] [_%w]*' matches identifiers in a Lua program: a sequence starting with a letter or an underscore, followed by zero or more underscores or alphanumeric characters.

Like '*', the modifier '-' also matches zero or more occurrences of characters of the original class. However, instead of matching the longest sequence, it matches the shortest one. Sometimes, there is no difference between '*' and '-', but usually they present rather different results. For instance, if you try to find an identifier with the pattern '[_%a] [_%w]-', you will find only the first letter, because the '[_%w]-' will always match the empty sequence. On the other hand, suppose you want to find comments in a C program. Many people would first try '/%*.*%*/' (that is, a "/*" followed by a sequence of any characters followed by "*/", written with the appropriate escapes). However, because the '.*' expands as far as it can, the first "/*" in the program would close only with the last "*/":

```
test = "int x; /* x */  int y; /* y */"
print(string.match(test, "/%*.*%*/"))
  --> /* x */  int y; /* y */
```

The pattern '.-', instead, will expand the least amount necessary to find the first "*/", so that you get the desired result:

```
test = "int x; /* x */  int y; /* y */"
print(string.gsub(test, "/%*.-%*/", ""))
  --> int x;    int y;
```

The last modifier, '?', matches an optional character. As an example, suppose we want to find an integer in a text, where the number can contain an optional sign. The pattern '[+-]?%d+' does the job, matching numerals like "-12", "23", and "+1009". The character class '[+-]' matches either a '+' or a '-' sign; the following '?' makes this sign optional.

Unlike some other systems, in Lua a modifier can be applied only to a character class; there is no way to group patterns under a modifier. For instance, there is no pattern that matches an optional word (unless the word has only one letter). Usually you can circumvent this limitation using some of the advanced techniques that we will see in the end of this chapter.

If a pattern begins with a '^', it will match only at the beginning of the subject string. Similarly, if it ends with a '$', it will match only at the end of the subject string. You can use these marks both to restrict the patterns that you find and to anchor patterns. For instance, the next test checks whether the string s starts with a digit:

```
if string.find(s, "^%d") then ...
```

This one checks whether that string represents an integer number, without any other leading or trailing characters:

```
if string.find(s, "^[+-]?%d+$") then ...
```

The characters '^' and '$' are magic only when used in the beginning or end of the pattern. Otherwise, they act as regular characters matching themselves.

Another item in a pattern is '%b', which matches balanced strings. We write this item as '%bxy', where x and y are any two distinct characters; the x acts as an opening character and the y as the closing one. For instance, the pattern '%b()' matches parts of the string that start with a '(' and finish at the respective ')':

```
s = "a (enclosed (in) parentheses) line"
print(string.gsub(s, "%b()", ""))      --> a  line
```

Typically, we use this pattern as '%b()', '%b[]', '%b{}', or '%b<>', but you can use any two distinct characters as delimiters.

Finally, the item '%f[*char-set*]' represents a *frontier pattern*. It matches an empty string only if the next character is in *char-set* but the previous one is not:

```
s = "the anthem is the theme"
print(s:gsub("%f[%w]the%f[%W]", "one"))
   --> one anthem is one theme
```

The pattern '%f[%w]' matches a frontier between a non-alphanumeric and an alphanumeric character, and the pattern '%f[%W]' matches a frontier between an alphanumeric and a non-alphanumeric character. Therefore, the given pattern matches the string "the" only as an entire word. Note that we must write the char-set inside brackets, even when it is a single class.

The positions before the first and after the last characters in the subject string are treated as if they had the null character (ASCII code zero). In the previous example, the first "the" starts with a frontier between a null character (not in the set '[%w]') and a 't' (in the set '[%w]').

The frontier pattern was already implemented in Lua 5.1, but was undocumented. It became official only in Lua 5.2.

21.4 Captures

The *capture* mechanism allows a pattern to yank parts of the subject string that match parts of the pattern for further use. You specify a capture by writing the parts of the pattern that you want to capture between parentheses.

When a pattern has captures, the function `string.match` returns each captured value as a separate result; in other words, it breaks a string into its captured parts.

```
pair = "name = Anna"
key, value = string.match(pair, "(%a+)%s*=%s*(%a+)")
print(key, value)   --> name  Anna
```

The pattern '%a+' specifies a non-empty sequence of letters; the pattern '%s*' specifies a possibly empty sequence of spaces. So, in the example above, the whole pattern specifies a sequence of letters, followed by a sequence of spaces, followed by '=', again followed by spaces, plus another sequence of letters. Both sequences of letters have their patterns enclosed in parentheses, so that they will be captured if a match occurs. Below is a similar example:

```
date = "Today is 17/7/1990"
d, m, y = string.match(date, "(%d+)/(%d+)/(%d+)")
print(d, m, y)   --> 17  7  1990
```

In a pattern, an item like '%d', where *d* is a single digit, matches only a copy of the *d*-th capture. As a typical use, suppose you want to find, inside a string, a substring enclosed between single or double quotes. You could try a pattern such as '["'].-["']', that is, a quote followed by anything followed by another quote; but you would have problems with strings like "it's all right". To solve this problem, you can capture the first quote and use it to specify the second one:

```
s = [[then he said: "it's all right"!]]
q, quotedPart = string.match(s, "([\"']) (.-)%1")
print(quotedPart)    --> it's all right
print(q)             --> "
```

The first capture is the quote character itself and the second capture is the contents of the quote (the substring matching the '.-').

A similar example is the pattern that matches long strings in Lua:

```
%[(=*)%[(.-)%]%1%]
```

It will match an opening square bracket followed by zero or more equal signs, followed by another opening square bracket, followed by anything (the string content), followed by a closing square bracket, followed by the same number of equal signs, followed by another closing square bracket:

```
p = "%[(=*)%[(.-)%]%1%]"
s = "a = [=[[[ something ]] ]==] ]=]; print(a)"
print(string.match(s, p))    --> =        [[ something ]] ]==]
```

The first capture is the sequence of equal signs (only one sign in this example); the second is the string content.

The third use of captured values is in the replacement string of gsub. Like the pattern, also the replacement string can contain items like "%d", which are changed to the respective captures when the substitution is made. In particular, the item "%0" is changed to the whole match. (By the way, a '%' in the replacement string must be escaped as "%%".) As an example, the following command duplicates every letter in a string, with a hyphen between the copies:

```
print(string.gsub("hello Lua!", "%a", "%0-%0"))
--> h-he-el-ll-lo-o L-Lu-ua-a!
```

This one interchanges adjacent characters:

```
print(string.gsub("hello Lua", "(.)(.)", "%2%1"))  --> ehll ouLa
```

As a more useful example, let us write a primitive format converter, which gets a string with commands written in a LaTeX style and changes them to a format in XML style:

```
\command{some text}    -->    <command>some text</command>
```

If we disallow nested commands, the following call to string.gsub does the job:

```
s = [[the \quote{task} is to \em{change} that.]]
s = string.gsub(s, "\\(%a+){(.-)}", "<%1>%2</%1>")
print(s)
--> the <quote>task</quote> is to <em>change</em> that.
```

(In the next section, we will see how to handle nested commands.)

Another useful example is how to trim a string:

```
function trim (s)
   return (string.gsub(s, "^%s*(.-)%s*$", "%1"))
end
```

Note the judicious use of pattern formats. The two anchors ('^' and '$') ensure that we get the whole string. Because the '.-' tries to expand as little as possible, the two patterns '%s*' match all spaces at both extremities. Note also that, because gsub returns two values, we parenthesize the call to discard the extra result (the count).

21.5 Replacements

Instead of a string, we can use either a function or a table as the third argument to string.gsub. When invoked with a function, string.gsub calls the function every time it finds a match; the arguments to each call are the captures, and the value that the function returns is used as the replacement string. When invoked with a table, string.gsub looks up the table using the first capture as the key,

and the associated value is used as the replacement string. If the result from
the call or from the table lookup is nil, gsub does not change this match.

As a first example, the following function does variable expansion: it substitutes the value of the global variable varname for every occurrence of $varname
in a string:

```
function expand (s)
  return (string.gsub(s, "$(%w+)", _G))
end

name = "Lua"; status = "great"
print(expand("$name is $status, isn't it?"))
  --> Lua is great, isn't it?
```

For each match with '$(%w+)' (a dollar sign followed by a name), gsub looks up
the captured name in the global table _G; the result replaces the match. When
the table does not have the key, there is no replacement:

```
print(expand("$othername is $status, isn't it?"))
  --> $othername is great, isn't it?
```

If you are not sure whether the given variables have string values, you may
want to apply tostring to their values. In this case, you can use a function as
the replacement value:

```
function expand (s)
  return (string.gsub(s, "$(%w+)", function (n)
            return tostring(_G[n])
          end))
end

print(expand("print = $print; a = $a"))
  --> print = function: 0x8050ce0; a = nil
```

Now, for each match with '$(%w+)', gsub calls the given function with the cap-
tured name as argument; the return replaces the match.

The last example goes back to our format converter, from the previous section. Again, we want to convert commands in LaTeX style (\example{text})
to XML style (<example>text</example>), but allowing nested commands this
time. The following function uses recursion to do the job:

```
function toxml (s)
  s = string.gsub(s, "\\(%a+)(%b{})", function (tag, body)
        body = string.sub(body, 2, -2)  -- remove brackets
        body = toxml(body)              -- handle nested commands
        return string.format("<%s>%s</%s>", tag, body, tag)
      end)
  return s
end

print(toxml("\\title{The \\bold{big} example}"))
  --> <title>The <bold>big</bold> example</title>
```

URL encoding

For our next example, we use *URL encoding*, which is the encoding used by HTTP to send parameters in a URL. This encoding encodes special characters (such as '=', '&', and '+') as "%*xx*", where *xx* is the character code in hexadecimal. After that, it changes spaces to '+'. For instance, it encodes the string "a+b = c" as "a%2Bb+%3D+c". Finally, it writes each parameter name and parameter value with an equal in between and appends all resulting pairs name=value with an ampersand in between. For instance, the values

```
name = "al";  query = "a+b = c"; q="yes or no"
```

are encoded as "name=al&query=a%2Bb+%3D+c&q=yes+or+no".

Now, suppose we want to decode this URL and store each value in a table, indexed by its corresponding name. The following function does the basic decoding:

```
function unescape (s)
  s = string.gsub(s, "+", " ")
  s = string.gsub(s, "%%(%x%x)", function (h)
        return string.char(tonumber(h, 16))
      end)
  return s
end
```

The first statement changes each '+' in the string to a space. The second gsub matches all two-digit hexadecimal numerals preceded by '%' and calls an anonymous function for each match. This function converts the hexadecimal numeral into a number (tonumber, with base 16) and returns the corresponding character (string.char). For instance,

```
print(unescape("a%2Bb+%3D+c"))   --> a+b = c
```

To decode the pairs name=value we use gmatch. Because both names and values cannot contain either '&' or '=', we can match them with the pattern '[^&=]+':

```
cgi = {}
function decode (s)
  for name, value in string.gmatch(s, "([^&=]+)=([^&=]+)") do
    name = unescape(name)
    value = unescape(value)
    cgi[name] = value
  end
end
```

The call to gmatch matches all pairs in the form name=value. For each pair, the iterator returns the corresponding captures (as marked by the parentheses in the matching string) as the values for name and value. The loop body simply calls unescape on both strings and stores the pair in the cgi table.

The corresponding encoding is also easy to write. First, we write the escape function; this function encodes all special characters as a '%' followed by the character code in hexadecimal (the format option "%02X" makes a hexadecimal number with two digits, using 0 for padding), and then changes spaces to '+':

```
function escape (s)
  s = string.gsub(s, "[&=+%%%c]", function (c)
        return string.format("%%02X", string.byte(c))
      end)
  s = string.gsub(s, " ", "+")
  return s
end
```

The encode function traverses the table to be encoded, building the resulting string:

```
function encode (t)
  local b = {}
  for k,v in pairs(t) do
    b[#b + 1] = (escape(k) .. "=" .. escape(v))
  end
  return table.concat(b, "&")
end

t = {name = "al",  query = "a+b = c", q = "yes or no"}
print(encode(t)) --> q=yes+or+no&query=a%2Bb+%3D+c&name=al
```

Tab expansion

An empty capture like '()' has a special meaning in Lua. Instead of capturing nothing (a quite useless task), this pattern captures its position in the subject string, as a number:

```
print(string.match("hello", "()ll()"))   --> 3  5
```

(Note that the result of this example is not the same as what you get from string.find, because the position of the second empty capture is *after* the match.)

A nice example of the use of position captures is for expanding tabs in a string:

```
function expandTabs (s, tab)
  tab = tab or 8       -- tab "size" (default is 8)
  local corr = 0
  s = string.gsub(s, "()\t", function (p)
        local sp = tab - (p - 1 + corr)%tab
        corr = corr - 1 + sp
        return string.rep(" ", sp)
      end)
  return s
end
```

The gsub pattern matches all tabs in the string, capturing their positions. For each tab, the inner function uses this position to compute the number of spaces needed to arrive at a column that is a multiple of tab: it subtracts one from the position to make it relative to zero and adds corr to compensate for previous tabs. (The expansion of each tab affects the position of the next ones.) It then updates the correction for the next tab: minus one for the tab being removed, plus sp for the spaces being added. Finally, it returns a string with the appropriate number of spaces.

Just for completeness, let us see how to reverse this operation, converting spaces to tabs. A first approach could also involve the use of empty captures to manipulate positions, but there is a simpler solution: at every eighth character, we insert a mark in the string. Then, wherever the mark is preceded by spaces, we replace the sequence spaces–mark by a tab:

```
function unexpandTabs (s, tab)
  tab = tab or 8
  s = expandTabs(s)
  local pat = string.rep(".", tab)
  s = string.gsub(s, pat, "%0\1")
  s = string.gsub(s, " +\1", "\t")
  s = string.gsub(s, "\1", "")
  return s
end
```

The function starts by expanding the string to remove any previous tabs. Then it computes an auxiliary pattern for matching all sequences of tab characters, and uses this pattern to add a mark (the control character \1) after every tab characters. It then substitutes a tab for all sequences of spaces followed by a mark. Finally, it removes the marks left (those not preceded by spaces).

21.6 Tricks of the Trade

Pattern matching is a powerful tool for manipulating strings. You can perform many complex operations with only a few calls to string.gsub. However, as with any power, you must use it carefully.

Pattern matching is not a replacement for a proper parser. For quick-and-dirty programs, you can do useful manipulations on source code, but it is hard to build a product with quality. As a good example, consider the pattern we used to match comments in a C program: '/%*.-%*/'. If your program has a literal string containing "/*", you may get a wrong result:

```
test = [[char s[] = "a /* here";  /* a tricky string */]]
print(string.gsub(test, "/%*.-%*/", "<COMMENT>"))
  --> char s[] = "a <COMMENT>
```

Strings with such contents are rare and, for your own use, that pattern will probably do its job. But you should not distribute a program with such a flaw.

Usually, pattern matching is efficient enough for Lua programs: my old
Pentium machine takes less than 0.3 second to match all words in a text with
4.4 MB (850K words). But you can take precautions. You should always make
the pattern as specific as possible; loose patterns are slower than specific ones.
An extreme example is '(.-)%$', to get all text in a string up to the first dollar
sign. If the subject string has a dollar sign, everything goes fine; but suppose
that the string does not contain any dollar signs. The algorithm will first try to
match the pattern starting at the first position of the string. It will go through
all the string, looking for a dollar. When the string ends, the pattern fails *for the
first position* of the string. Then, the algorithm will do the whole search again,
starting at the second position of the string, only to discover that the pattern
does not match there, too; and so on. This will take a quadratic time, resulting
in more than four minutes in my old Pentium machine for a string with 100K
characters. You can correct this problem simply by anchoring the pattern at the
first position of the string, with '^(.-)%$'. The anchor tells the algorithm to stop
the search if it cannot find a match at the first position. With the anchor, the
pattern runs in a hundredth of a second.

Beware also of *empty* patterns, that is, patterns that match the empty string.
For instance, if you try to match names with a pattern like '%a*', you will find
names everywhere:

```
i, j = string.find(";$%  **#$hello13", "%a*")
print(i,j)   --> 1  0
```

In this example, the call to string.find has correctly found an empty sequence
of letters at the beginning of the string.

It never makes sense to write a pattern that begins or ends with the modifier
'-', because it will match only the empty string. This modifier always needs
something around it to anchor its expansion. Similarly, patterns that include '.*'
are tricky, because this construction can expand much more than you intended.

Sometimes, it is useful to use Lua itself to build a pattern. We already
used this trick in our function to convert spaces to tabs. As another example,
let us see how we can find long lines in a text, say lines with more than 70
characters. Well, a long line is a sequence of 70 or more characters different
from newline. We can match a single character different from newline with
the character class '[^\n]'. Therefore, we can match a long line with a pattern
that repeats 70 times the pattern for one character, followed by zero or more of
these characters. Instead of writing this pattern by hand, we can create it with
string.rep:

```
pattern = string.rep("[^\n]", 70) .. "[^\n]*"
```

As another example, suppose you want to make a case-insensitive search. A
way of doing this is to change any letter *x* in the pattern for the class '[*xX*]', that
is, a class including both the lower and the upper-case versions of the original
letter. We can automate this conversion with a function:

```
function nocase (s)
  s = string.gsub(s, "%a", function (c)
        return "[" .. string.lower(c) .. string.upper(c) .. "]"
      end)
  return s
end

print(nocase("Hi there!"))   --> [hH][iI] [tT][hH][eE][rR][eE]!
```

Sometimes, you want to change every plain occurrence of s1 to s2, without regarding any character as magic. If the strings s1 and s2 are literals, you can add proper escapes to magic characters while you write the strings. But if these strings are variable values, you can use another gsub to put the escapes for you:

```
s1 = string.gsub(s1, "(%W)", "%%1")
s2 = string.gsub(s2, "%%", "%%%%")
```

In the search string, we escape all non-alphanumeric characters (thus the upper-case 'W'). In the replacement string, we escape only the '%'.

Another useful technique for pattern matching is to preprocess the subject string before the real work. Suppose we want to change to upper case all quoted strings in a text, where a quoted string starts and ends with a double quote (""'), but may contain escaped quotes ("\""):

```
follows a typical string: "This is \"great\"!".
```

One approach for handling such cases is to preprocess the text so as to encode the problematic sequence to something else. For instance, we could code "\"" as "\1". However, if the original text already contains a "\1", we are in trouble. An easy way to do the encoding and avoid this problem is to code all sequences "\x" as "\ddd", where ddd is the decimal representation of the character x:

```
function code (s)
  return (string.gsub(s, "\\(.)", function (x)
          return string.format("\\%03d", string.byte(x))
        end))
end
```

Now any sequence "\ddd" in the encoded string must have come from the coding, because any "\ddd" in the original string has been coded, too. So, the decoding is an easy task:

```
function decode (s)
  return (string.gsub(s, "\\(%d%d%d)", function (d)
          return "\\" .. string.char(tonumber(d))
        end))
end
```

Now we can complete our task. As the encoded string does not contain any escaped quote ("\""), we can search for quoted strings simply with "".-"":

```
s = [[follows a typical string: "This is \"great\"!".]]
s = code(s)
s = string.gsub(s, '".-"', string.upper)
s = decode(s)
print(s)     --> follows a typical string: "THIS IS \"GREAT\"!".
```

Or, in a more compact notation,

```
print(decode(string.gsub(code(s), '".-"', string.upper)))
```

21.7 Unicode

Currently, the string library does not offer any explicit support for Unicode.
Nevertheless, it is not difficult to code several useful simple tasks over Unicode
strings encoded in UTF-8 without extra libraries.

UTF-8 is the dominant encoding for Unicode on the Web. Because of its
compatibility with ASCII, UTF-8 is also the ideal encoding for Lua. That compatibility is enough to ensure that several string-manipulation techniques that
work on ASCII strings also work on UTF-8 with no modifications.

UTF-8 represents each Unicode character using a variable number of bytes.
For instance, it represents 'A' by one byte, 65; it represents the Hebrew character
Aleph, which has code 1488 in Unicode, by the two-byte sequence 215–144. UTF-
8 represents all characters in the ASCII range as in ASCII, that is, a single
byte smaller than 128. It represents all other characters using sequences of
bytes where the first byte is in the range $[194, 244]$ and continuation bytes are
in the range $[128, 191]$. Specifically, the range of the starting bytes for two-byte
sequences is $[194, 223]$; for three-byte sequences, the range is $[224, 239]$; and for
four-byte sequences, it is $[240, 244]$. This construction ensures that the code
sequence of any character never appears inside the code sequence of any other
character. For instance, a byte smaller than 128 never appears in a multibyte
sequence; it always represents its corresponding ASCII character.

Because Lua is 8-bit clean, it can read, write, and store UTF-8 strings just
like regular strings. Literal strings can contain UTF-8 data. (Of course, you
probably will want to edit your source code as a UTF-8 file.) The concatenation
operation works correctly for UTF-8 strings. String order operators (less than,
less equal, etc.) compare UTF-8 strings following the order of the character
codes in Unicode.

The operating-system library and the I/O library are mainly interfaces to
the underlying system, so their support for UTF-8 strings depends on that
underlying system. On Linux, for instance, we can use UTF-8 for file names,
but Windows uses UTF-16. So, to manipulate Unicode file names in Windows,
we need either extra libraries or some changes in the standard Lua libraries.

Let us now see how functions from the string library handle UTF-8 strings.

Functions `string.reverse`, `string.byte`, `string.char`, `string.upper`, and `string.lower`, do not work for UTF-8 strings, as all of them assume that one character is equivalent to one byte.

Functions `string.format` and `string.rep` work without problems with UTF-8 strings except for the format option '%c', which assumes that one character is one byte. Functions `string.len` and `string.sub` work correctly with UTF-8 strings, with indices referring to byte counts (not character counts). Frequently, this is what you need. But we can count the number of characters, too, as we will see in a moment.

For the pattern-matching functions, their applicability to UTF-8 strings depends on the pattern. Literal patterns work without problems, due to the key property of UTF-8 that the encoding of any character never appears inside the encoding of any other character. Character classes and character sets work only for ASCII characters. For instance, the pattern '%s' works on UTF-8 strings, but it will match only the ASCII white spaces; it will not match extra Unicode white spaces such as a non-break space (U+00A0), a paragraph separator (U+2029), or a Mongolian vowel separator (U+180E).

Some patterns can put the particularities of UTF-8 for good use. For instance, if you want to count the number of characters in a string, you can use the following expression:

```
#(string.gsub(s, "[\128-\191]", ""))
```

The gsub removes the continuation bytes from the string, so that what are left are the one-byte sequences and the starting bytes of multi-line sequences: one byte for each character.

Using similar ideas, the following example shows how we can iterate over each character in a UTF-8 string:

```
for c in string.gmatch(s, ".[\128-\191]*") do
  print(c)
end
```

Listing 21.1 illustrates some techniques to manipulate UTF-8 strings in Lua. Of course, to run those examples you need a platform where `print` understands UTF-8.

Unfortunately, there is not much more that Lua can offer. Adequate support for Unicode demands huge tables, which are incompatible with the small size of Lua. Unicode has too many peculiarities. It is virtually impossible to abstract almost any concept from specific languages. Even the concept of what is a character is vague, because there is no one-to-one correspondence between Unicode coded characters and graphemes (e.g., characters with diacritical marks and "completely ignorable" characters). Other apparently basic concepts, such as what is a letter, also change across different languages.

What is missing most in Lua, in my opinion, are functions to convert between UTF-8 sequences and Unicode code points and to check the validity of UTF-8 strings. Probably the next version of Lua will include them. For anything fancier, the best approach seems to be an external library, such as the slnunicode library.

Listing 21.1. Examples of basic UTF-8 manipulation in Lua.:

```
local a = {}
a[#a + 1] = "Nähdään"
a[#a + 1] = "ação"
a[#a + 1] = "ÃøÆËĐ"

local l = table.concat(a, ";")

print(l, #(string.gsub(l, "[\128-\191]", "")))
  --> Nähdään;ação;ÃøÆËĐ         18

for w in string.gmatch(l, "[^;]+") do
  print(w)
end
  --> Nähdään
  --> ação
  --> ÃøÆËĐ

for c in string.gmatch(a[3], ".[\128-\191]*") do
  print(c)
end
  --> Ã
  --> ø
  --> Æ
  --> Ë
  --> Đ
```

Exercises

Exercise 21.1: Write a split function that receives a string and a delimiter pattern and returns a sequence with the chunks in the original string separated by the delimiter:

```
t = split("a whole new world", " ")
-- t = {"a", "whole", "new", "world"}
```

How does your function handle empty strings? (In particular, is an empty string an empty sequence or a sequence with one empty string?)

Exercise 21.2: The patterns '%D' and '[^%d]' are equivalent. What about the patterns '[^%d%u]' and '[%D%U]'?

Exercise 21.3: Write a transliterate function. This function receives a string and replaces each character in that string by another character, according to a table given as a second argument. If the table maps 'a' to 'b', the function should replace any occurrence of 'a' by 'b'. If the table maps 'a' to **false**, the function should remove occurrences of 'a' from the resulting string.

Exercise 21.4: Write a function to reverse a UTF-8 string.

Exercise 21.5: Rewrite the transliterate function for UTF-8 characters.

22

The I/O Library

The I/O library offers two different models for file manipulation. The simple model assumes a *current input file* and a *current output file*, and its I/O operations operate on these files. The complete model uses explicit file handles; it adopts an object-oriented style that defines all operations as methods on file handles.

The simple model is convenient for simple things; we have been using it throughout the book until now. But it is not enough for more advanced file manipulation, such as reading from or writing to several files simultaneously. For these manipulations, we need the complete model.

22.1 The Simple I/O Model

The simple model does all its operations on two current files. The library initializes the current input file as the process standard input (stdin) and the current output file as the process standard output (stdout). Therefore, when we execute something like io.read(), we read a line from the standard input.

We can change these current files with the io.input and io.output functions. A call like io.input(filename) opens the given file in read mode and sets it as the current input file. From this point on, all input will come from this file, until another call to io.input; io.output does a similar job for output. In case of an error, both functions raise the error. If you want to handle errors directly, you must use the complete model.

As write is simpler than read, we will look at it first. The io.write function simply gets an arbitrary number of string arguments and writes them to the current output file. It converts numbers to strings following the usual conversion rules; for full control over this conversion, you should use the string.format function:

```
> io.write("sin (3) = ", math.sin(3), "\n")
--> sin (3) = 0.14112000805987
> io.write(string.format("sin (3) = %.4f\n", math.sin(3)))
--> sin (3) = 0.1411
```

Avoid code like io.write(a..b..c); the call io.write(a,b,c) accomplishes the same effect with fewer resources, as it avoids the concatenations.

As a rule, you should use print for quick-and-dirty programs or debugging, and write when you need full control over your output:

```
> print("hello", "Lua"); print("Hi")
--> hello    Lua
--> Hi

> io.write("hello", "Lua"); io.write("Hi", "\n")
--> helloLuaHi
```

Unlike print, write adds no extra characters to the output, such as tabs or newlines. Moreover, write allows you to redirect your output, whereas print always uses the standard output. Finally, print automatically applies tostring to its arguments; this is handy for debugging, but it can hide bugs if you are not paying attention to your output.

The io.read function reads strings from the current input file. Its arguments control what to read:

"*a"	reads the whole file
"*l"	reads the next line (without newline)
"*L"	reads the next line (with newline)
"*n"	reads a number
num	reads a string with up to *num* characters

The call io.read("*a") reads the whole current input file, starting at its current position. If we are at the end of the file, or if the file is empty, the call returns an empty string.

Because Lua handles long strings efficiently, a simple technique for writing filters in Lua is to read the whole file into a string, do the processing to the string (typically with gsub), and then write the string to the output:

```
t = io.read("*a")          -- read the whole file
t = string.gsub(t, ...)    -- do the job
io.write(t)                -- write the file
```

As an example, the following chunk is a complete program to code a file's content using the MIME *quoted-printable* encoding. This encoding codes each non-ASCII byte as =*xx*, where *xx* is the value of the byte in hexadecimal. To keep the consistency of the encoding, the '=' character must be encoded as well:

```
t = io.read("*a")
t = string.gsub(t, "([\128-\255=])", function (c)
      return string.format("=%02X", string.byte(c))
    end)
io.write(t)
```

The pattern used in the gsub captures all bytes from 128 to 255, plus the equal sign.

The call io.read("*l") returns the next line from the current input file, without the newline character; the call io.read("*L") is similar, but it keeps the newline character (if present in the file). When we reach the end of file, the call returns nil (as there is no next line to return). The pattern "*l" is the default for read. Usually, I use this pattern only when the algorithm naturally handles the file line by line; otherwise, I favor reading the whole file at once, with *a, or in blocks, as we will see later.

As a simple example of the use of this pattern, the following program copies its current input to the current output, numbering each line:

```
for count = 1, math.huge do
  local line = io.read()
  if line == nil then break end
  io.write(string.format("%6d  ", count), line, "\n")
end
```

However, to iterate on a whole file line by line, we do better to use the io.lines iterator. For instance, we can write a complete program to sort the lines of a file as follows:

```
local lines = {}
-- read the lines in table 'lines'
for line in io.lines() do lines[#lines + 1] = line end
-- sort
table.sort(lines)
-- write all the lines
for _, l in ipairs(lines) do io.write(l, "\n") end
```

The call io.read("*n") reads a number from the current input file. This is the only case where read returns a number, instead of a string. When a program needs to read many numbers from a file, the absence of the intermediate strings improves its performance. The *n option skips any spaces before the number and accepts number formats like -3, +5.2, 1000, and -3.4e-23. If it cannot find a number at the current file position (because of bad format or end of file), it returns nil.

You can call read with multiple options; for each argument, the function will return the respective result. Suppose you have a file with three numbers per line:

```
6.0       -3.23     15e12
4.3       234       1000001
...
```

Now you want to print the maximum value of each line. You can read all three numbers with a single call to read:

```
while true do
  local n1, n2, n3 = io.read("*n", "*n", "*n")
  if not n1 then break end
  print(math.max(n1, n2, n3))
end
```

Besides the basic read patterns, you can call read with a number n as an argument: in this case, read tries to read n characters from the input file. If it cannot read any character (end of file), read returns nil; otherwise, it returns a string with at most n characters. As an example of this read pattern, the following program is an efficient way (in Lua, of course) to copy a file from stdin to stdout:

```
while true do
  local block = io.read(2^13)               -- buffer size is 8K
  if not block then break end
  io.write(block)
end
```

As a special case, io.read(0) works as a test for end of file: it returns an empty string if there is more to be read or nil otherwise.

22.2   The Complete I/O Model

For more control over I/O, you can use the complete model. A central concept in this model is the *file handle*, which is equivalent to streams (FILE*) in C: it represents an open file with a current position.

To open a file, you use the io.open function, which mimics the fopen function in C. It takes as arguments the name of the file to open plus a *mode* string. This mode string can contain an 'r' for reading, a 'w' for writing (which also erases any previous content of the file), or an 'a' for appending, plus an optional 'b' to open binary files. The open function returns a new handle for the file. In case of an error, open returns nil, plus an error message and an error number:

```
print(io.open("non-existent-file", "r"))
  --> nil     non-existent-file: No such file or directory     2

print(io.open("/etc/passwd", "w"))
  --> nil     /etc/passwd: Permission denied   13
```

The interpretation of the error numbers is system dependent.

A typical idiom to check for errors is

```
local f = assert(io.open(filename, mode))
```

If the open fails, the error message goes as the second argument to assert, which then shows the message.

After you open a file, you can read from it or write to it with the methods read/write. They are similar to the read/write functions, but you call them as methods on the file handle, using the colon syntax. For instance, to open a file and read it all, you can use a chunk like this:

```
local f = assert(io.open(filename, "r"))
local t = f:read("*a")
f:close()
```

The I/O library offers handles for the three predefined C streams: io.stdin, io.stdout, and io.stderr. So, you can send a message directly to the error stream with a code like this:

```
io.stderr:write(message)
```

We can mix the complete model with the simple model. We get the current input file handle by calling io.input(), without arguments. We set this handle with the call io.input(handle). (Similar calls are also valid for io.output.) For instance, if you want to change the current input file temporarily, you can write something like this:

```
local temp = io.input()     -- save current file
io.input("newinput")        -- open a new current file
<do something with new input>
io.input():close()          -- close current file
io.input(temp)              -- restore previous current file
```

Instead of io.read, we can also use io.lines to read from a file. As we have seen in previous examples, io.lines gives an iterator that repeatedly reads from a file.

The first argument to io.lines can be a file name or a file handle. Given a file name, io.lines will open the file in read mode and will close the file after reaching end of file. Given a file handle, io.lines will use that file for reading; in this case, io.lines will not close the file after reading it. When called with no arguments, io.lines will read from the current input file.

Starting in Lua 5.2, io.lines also accepts the same options that io.read accepts, after the file argument. As an example, the next fragment copies a file to the current output: using io.lines:

```
for block in io.lines(filename, 2^13) do
  io.write(block)
end
```

A small performance trick

Usually, in Lua, it is faster to read a file as a whole than to read it line by line. However, sometimes we must face a big file (say, tens or hundreds megabytes)

Listing 22.1. The wc program:

```
local BUFSIZE = 2^13          -- 8K
local f = io.input(arg[1])    -- open input file
local cc, lc, wc = 0, 0, 0    -- char, line, and word counts
for lines, rest in io.lines(arg[1], BUFSIZE, "*L") do
  if rest then lines = lines .. rest end
  cc = cc + #lines
  -- count words in the chunk
  local _, t = string.gsub(lines, "%S+", "")
  wc = wc + t
  -- count newlines in the chunk
  _,t = string.gsub(lines, "\n", "\n")
  lc = lc + t
end
print(lc, wc, cc)
```

for which it is not reasonable to read it all at once. If you want to handle such big files with maximum performance, the fastest way is to read them in reasonably large chunks (e.g., 8 kB each). To avoid the problem of breaking lines in the middle, you simply ask to read a chunk plus a line:

```
local lines, rest = f:read(BUFSIZE, "*l")
```

The variable rest will get the rest of any line broken by the chunk. We then concatenate the chunk and this rest of line. This way, the resulting chunk will always break at line boundaries.

The example in Listing 22.1 uses this technique to implement wc, a program that counts the number of characters, words, and lines in a file. Note the use of io.lines to do the iteration and of the option "*L" to read a line with the newline; both features are new in Lua 5.2.

Binary files

The simple-model functions io.input and io.output always open a file in text mode (the default). In UNIX, there is no difference between binary files and text files. But in some systems, notably Windows, binary files must be opened with a special flag. To handle such binary files, you must use io.open, with the letter 'b' in the mode string.

Lua handles binary data similarly to text. A string in Lua can contain any bytes, and almost all functions in the libraries can handle arbitrary bytes. You can even do pattern matching over binary data, as long as the pattern does not contain a zero byte. If you want to match this byte in the subject, you can use the class %z instead.

Typically, you read binary data either with the *a pattern, that reads the whole file, or with the pattern *n*, that reads *n* bytes. As a simple example, the following program converts a text file from Windows format to UNIX format (that is, it translates sequences of carriage return–newlines to newlines). It does not use the standard I/O files (stdin–stdout), because these files are open in text mode. Instead, it assumes that the names of the input file and the output file are given as arguments to the program:

```
local inp = assert(io.open(arg[1], "rb"))
local out = assert(io.open(arg[2], "wb"))

local data = inp:read("*a")
data = string.gsub(data, "\r\n", "\n")
out:write(data)

assert(out:close())
```

You can call this program with the following command line:

```
> lua prog.lua file.dos file.unix
```

As another example, the following program prints all strings found in a binary file:

```
local f = assert(io.open(arg[1], "rb"))
local data = f:read("*a")
local validchars = "[%g%s]"
local pattern = "(" .. string.rep(validchars, 6) .. "+)\0"
for w in string.gmatch(data, pattern) do
  print(w)
end
```

The program assumes that a string is any zero-terminated sequence of six or more valid characters, where a valid character is any character accepted by the pattern validchars. In our example, this pattern comprises the printable characters. We use string.rep and concatenation to create a pattern that matches all sequences of six or more validchars followed by a zero. The parentheses in the pattern capture the string (but not the zero).

As a last example, the following program makes a dump of a binary file:

```
local f = assert(io.open(arg[1], "rb"))
local block = 16
for bytes in f:lines(block) do
  for c in string.gmatch(bytes, ".") do
    io.write(string.format("%02X ", string.byte(c)))
  end
  io.write(string.rep("   ", block - string.len(bytes)))
  io.write(" ", string.gsub(bytes, "%c", "."), "\n")
end
```

Listing 22.2. Dumping the `dump` program:

```
6C 6F 63 61 6C 20 66 20 3D 20 61 73 73 65 72 74    local f = assert
28 69 6F 2E 6F 70 65 6E 28 61 72 67 5B 31 5D 2C    (io.open(arg[1],
20 22 72 62 22 29 29 0A 6C 6F 63 61 6C 20 62 6C     "rb")).local bl
6F 63 6B 20 3D 20 31 36 0A 66 6F 72 20 62 79 74    ock = 16.for byt
65 73 20 69 6E 20 66 3A 6C 69 6E 65 73 28 62 6C    es in f:lines(bl

  . . .

20 22 2C 20 73 74 72 69 6E 67 2E 67 73 75 62 28     ", string.gsub(
62 79 74 65 73 2C 20 22 25 63 22 2C 20 22 2E 22    bytes, "%c", "."
29 2C 20 22 5C 6E 22 29 0A 65 6E 64 0A 0A          ), "\n").end..
```

Again, the first program argument is the input file name; the output goes to the standard output. The program reads the file in chunks of 16 bytes. For each chunk, it writes the hexadecimal representation of each byte, and then it writes the chunk as text, changing control characters to dots.

Listing 22.2 shows the result of applying this program over itself (in a UNIX machine).

22.3   Other Operations on Files

The `tmpfile` function returns a handle for a temporary file, open in read/write mode. This file is automatically removed (deleted) when your program ends.

The `flush` function executes all pending writes to a file. Like the `write` function, you can call it as a function, `io.flush()`, to flush the current output file; or as a method, `f:flush()`, to flush a particular file `f`.

The `setvbuf` method sets the buffering mode of a stream. Its first argument is a string: "no" means no buffering; "full" means that the stream is only written out when the buffer is full or when you explicitly flush the file; "line" means that the output is buffered until a newline is output or there is any input from some special files (such as a terminal device). For the last two options, `setvbuf` accepts an optional second argument with the buffer size.

In most systems, the standard error stream (`io.stderr`) is not buffered, while the standard output stream (`io.stdout`) is buffered in line mode. So, if you write incomplete lines to the standard output (e.g., a progress indicator), you may need to flush the stream to see that output.

The `seek` method can both get and set the current position of a file. Its general form is `f:seek(whence, offset)`, where the `whence` parameter is a string that specifies how to interpret the offset. Its valid values are "set", when offsets are interpreted from the beginning of the file; "cur", when offsets are interpreted from the current position of the file; and "end", when offsets are interpreted from the end of the file. Independently of the value of `whence`, the call returns the new current position of the file, measured in bytes from the beginning of the file.

The default value for whence is "cur" and for offset is zero. Therefore, the call file:seek() returns the current file position, without changing it; the call file:seek("set") resets the position to the beginning of the file (and returns zero); and the call file:seek("end") sets the position to the end of the file and returns its size. The following function gets the file size without changing its current position:

```
function fsize (file)
  local current = file:seek()      -- get current position
  local size = file:seek("end")    -- get file size
  file:seek("set", current)        -- restore position
  return size
end
```

All these functions return nil plus an error message in case of error.

Exercises

Exercise 22.1: Write a program that reads a text file and rewrites it with their lines sorted in alphabetical order. When called with no arguments, it should read from the standard input file and write to the standard output file. When called with one file-name argument, it should read from that file and write to the standard output file. When called with two file-name arguments, it should read from the first file and write to the second one.

Exercise 22.2: Change the previous program so that it asks for a confirmation if the user gives the name of an existing file for its output.

Exercise 22.3: Compare the performance of Lua programs that copy the standard input file to the standard output file in the following ways:

- byte by byte;

- line by line;

- in chunks of 8 kB;

- the whole file at once.

For the last option, how large can be the input file?

Exercise 22.4: Write a program that prints the last line of a text file. Try to avoid reading the entire file when the file is large and seekable.

Exercise 22.5: Generalize the previous program so that it prints the last n lines of a text file. Again, try to avoid reading the entire file when the file is large and seekable.

23

The Operating System Library

The Operating System library includes functions for file (not stream) manipulation, for getting the current date and time, and other facilities related to the operating system. It is defined in table `os`. This library pays a price for Lua portability: because Lua is written in ANSI C, it uses only the functionality that the ANSI standard offers. Many OS facilities, such as directory manipulation and sockets, are not part of this standard; therefore, the system library does not provide them. There are other Lua libraries, not included in the main distribution, that provide extended OS access. Examples are the `posix` library, which offers all functionality of the POSIX.1 standard to Lua; `luasocket`, for network support; and `LuaFileSystem`, for basic manipulation of directories and file attributes.

For file manipulation, all that this OS library provides is an `os.rename` function, which changes the name of a file; and `os.remove`, which removes (deletes) a file.

23.1 Date and Time

Two functions, `time` and `date`, provide all date and time functionality in Lua.

The `time` function, when called without arguments, returns the current date and time, coded as a number. (In most systems, this number is the number of seconds since some epoch.) When called with a table, it returns the number representing the date and time described by the table. Such *date tables* have the following significant fields:

year	a full year
month	01–12
day	01–31
hour	00–23
min	00–59
sec	00–59
isdst	a boolean, true if daylight saving is on

The first three fields are mandatory; the others default to noon (12:00:00) when not provided. In a UNIX system (where the epoch is 00:00:00 UTC, January 1, 1970) running in Rio de Janeiro (which is three hours west of Greenwich), we have the following examples:

```
print(os.time{year=1970, month=1, day=1, hour=0})     --> 10800
print(os.time{year=1970, month=1, day=1, hour=0, sec=1})
   --> 10801
print(os.time{year=1970, month=1, day=1})             --> 54000
```

(Note that 10 800 are 3 hours in seconds, and 54 000 are 10 800 plus 12 hours in seconds.)

The date function, despite its name, is a kind of a reverse of the time function: it converts a number representing the date and time back to some higher-level representation. Its first parameter is a *format string*, describing the representation we want. The second is the numeric date–time; it defaults to the current date and time.

To produce a date table, we use the format string "*t". For instance, the call os.date("*t",906000490) returns the following table:

```
{year = 1998, month = 9, day = 16, yday = 259, wday = 4,
 hour = 23, min = 48, sec = 10, isdst = false}
```

Notice that, besides the fields used by os.time, the table created by os.date also gives the day of week (wday, 1 is Sunday) and the day of year (yday, 1 is January 1st).

For other format strings, os.date formats the date as a string that is a copy of the format string where specific tags were replaced by information about time and date. A tag consists of a '%' followed by a letter, as in the next examples:

```
print(os.date("a %A in %B"))          --> a Tuesday in May
print(os.date("%x", 906000490))       --> 09/16/1998
```

All representations follow the current locale. For instance, in a locale for Brazil–Portuguese, %B would result in "setembro" and %x in "16/09/98".

The following table shows each tag, its meaning, and its value for September 16, 1998 (a Wednesday), at 23:48:10. For numeric values, the table shows also their range of possible values:

%a	abbreviated weekday name (e.g., Wed)
%A	full weekday name (e.g., Wednesday)
%b	abbreviated month name (e.g., Sep)
%B	full month name (e.g., September)
%c	date and time (e.g., 09/16/98 23:48:10)
%d	day of the month (16) [01–31]
%H	hour, using a 24-hour clock (23) [00–23]
%I	hour, using a 12-hour clock (11) [01–12]
%j	day of the year (259) [001–366]
%M	minute (48) [00–59]
%m	month (09) [01–12]
%p	either "am" or "pm" (pm)
%S	second (10) [00–60]
%w	weekday (3) [0–6 = Sunday–Saturday]
%x	date (e.g., 09/16/98)
%X	time (e.g., 23:48:10)
%y	two-digit year (98) [00–99]
%Y	full year (1998)
%%	the character '%'

If you call date without any arguments, it uses the %c format, that is, complete date and time information in a reasonable format. Note that the representations for %x, %X, and %c change according to the locale and the system. If you want a fixed representation, such as mm/dd/yyyy, use an explicit format string, such as "%m/%d/%Y".

The os.clock function returns the number of seconds of CPU time for the program. Its typical use is to benchmark a piece of code:

```
local x = os.clock()
local s = 0
for i = 1, 100000 do s = s + i end
print(string.format("elapsed time: %.2f\n", os.clock() - x))
```

23.2 Other System Calls

The os.exit function terminates the execution of a program. Its optional first argument is the return status of the program. It can be a number (zero means a successful execution) or a boolean (**true** means a successful execution). An optional second argument, if true, closes the Lua state, calling all finalizers and releasing all memory used by that state. (Usually this finalization is not necessary, because most operating systems release all resources used by a process when it exits.)

The os.getenv function gets the value of an environment variable. It takes the name of the variable and returns a string with its value:

```
print(os.getenv("HOME"))    --> /home/lua
```

The call returns nil for undefined variables.

Function os.execute runs a system command; it is equivalent to the system function in C. It takes a string with the command and returns information regarding how the command terminated. The first return is a boolean: **true** means the program exited with no errors. The second return is a string: "exit" if the program terminated normally or "signal" if it was interrupted by a signal. A third return is the return status (if the program terminated normally) or the number of the signal that terminated the program. As an example of use, both in UNIX and in Windows you can use the following function to create new directories:

```
function createDir (dirname)
    os.execute("mkdir " .. dirname)
end
```

The os.execute function is powerful, but it is also highly system dependent.

The os.setlocale function sets the current locale used by a Lua program. Locales define behavior that is sensitive to cultural or linguistic differences. The setlocale function has two string parameters: the locale name and a category that specifies what features the locale will affect. There are six categories of locales:

"collate" controls the alphabetic order of strings;

"ctype" controls the types of individual characters (e.g., what is a letter) and the conversion between lower and upper cases;

"monetary" has no influence in Lua programs;

"numeric" controls how numbers are formatted;

"time" controls how date and time are formatted (i.e., function os.date);

"all" controls all the above functions.

The default category is "all", so that if you call setlocale with only the locale name it will set all categories. The setlocale function returns the locale name or nil if it fails (usually because the system does not support the given locale).

```
print(os.setlocale("ISO-8859-1", "collate"))   --> ISO-8859-1
```

The category "numeric" is a little tricky. As Portuguese and other Latin languages use a comma instead of a point to represent decimal numbers, the locale changes the way Lua prints and reads these numbers. But the locale does not change the way that Lua parses numbers in programs (among other reasons because expressions like print(3,4) already have a meaning in Lua). If you are using Lua to create pieces of Lua code, you may have problems here:

```
print(os.setlocale("pt_BR"))      --> pt_BR
s = "return (" .. 3.4 .. ")"
print(s)                          --> return (3,4)
print(loadstring(s))
   --> nil    [string "return (3,4)"]:1: ')' expected near ','
```

To avoid those problems, make sure that your program is using the standard "C" locale when creating pieces of code.

Exercises

Exercise 23.1: Write a function that returns the date/time exactly one month after a given date/time. (Assume the usual coding of date/time as a number.)

Exercise 23.2: Write a function that receives a date/time (coded as a number) and returns the number of seconds passed since the beginning of its respective day.

Exercise 23.3: Can you use the `os.execute` function to change the current directory of your Lua program? Why?

24

The Debug Library

The debug library does not give you a debugger for Lua, but it offers all the primitives that you need for writing your own debugger. For performance reasons, the official interface to these primitives is through the C API. The debug library in Lua is a way to access them directly within Lua code.

Unlike the other libraries, you should use the debug library with parsimony. First, some of its functionality is not exactly famous for performance. Second, it breaks some sacred truths of the language, such as that you cannot access a local variable from outside its lexical scope. Frequently, you may not want to open this library in your final version of a product, or else you may want to erase it.

The debug library comprises two kinds of functions: *introspective functions* and *hooks*. Introspective functions allow us to inspect several aspects of the running program, such as its stack of active functions, current line of execution, and values and names of local variables. Hooks allow us to trace the execution of a program.

An important concept in the debug library is the *stack level*. A stack level is a number that refers to a particular function that is active at that moment: the function calling the debug library has level 1, the function that called it has level 2, and so on.

24.1 Introspective Facilities

The main introspective function in the debug library is the `debug.getinfo` function. Its first parameter can be a function or a stack level. When you call `debug.getinfo(foo)` for some function `foo`, you get a table with some data about this function. The table can have the following fields:

source: where the function was defined. If the function was defined in a string (through loadstring), source is this string. If the function was defined in a file, source is the file name prefixed with a '@'.

short_src: a short version of source (up to 60 characters), useful for error messages.

linedefined: number of the first line of the source where the function was defined.

lastlinedefined: number of the last line of the source where the function was defined.

what: what this function is. Options are "Lua" if foo is a regular Lua function, "C" if it is a C function, or "main" if it is the main part of a Lua chunk.

name: a reasonable name for the function.

namewhat: what the previous field means. This field can be "global", "local", "method", "field", or "" (the empty string). The empty string means that Lua did not find a name for the function.

nups: number of upvalues of that function.

activelines: a table representing the set of active lines of the function. An *active line* is a line with some code, as opposed to empty lines or lines containing only comments. (A typical use of this information is for setting breakpoints. Most debuggers do not allow you to set a breakpoint outside an active line, as it would be unreachable.)

func: the function itself; see later.

When foo is a C function, Lua does not have much data about it. For such functions, only the fields what, name, and namewhat are relevant.

When you call debug.getinfo(n) for some number n, you get data about the function active at that stack level. For instance, if n is 1, you get data about the function doing the call. (When n is 0, you get data about getinfo itself, a C function.) If n is larger than the number of active functions in the stack, debug.getinfo returns nil. When you query an active function, calling debug.getinfo with a number, the result table has an extra field, currentline, with the line where the function is at that moment. Moreover, func has the function that is active at that level.

The field name is tricky. Remember that, because functions are first-class values in Lua, a function may not have a name, or may have several names. Lua tries to find a name for a function by looking into the code that called the function, to see how it was called. This method works only when we call getinfo with a number, that is, when we ask information about a particular invocation.

The getinfo function is not efficient. Lua keeps debug information in a form that does not impair program execution; efficient retrieval is a secondary goal here. To achieve better performance, getinfo has an optional second parameter that selects what information to get. In this way, the function does not waste time collecting data that the user does not need. The format of this parameter is a string, where each letter selects a group of fields, according to the following table:

'n'	selects name and namewhat
'f'	selects func
'S'	selects source, short_src, what, linedefined, and lastlinedefined
'l'	selects currentline
'L'	selects activelines
'u'	selects nup

The following function illustrates the use of debug.getinfo. It prints a primitive traceback of the active stack:

```
function traceback ()
  for level = 1, math.huge do
    local info = debug.getinfo(level, "Sl")
    if not info then break end
    if info.what == "C" then    -- is a C function?
      print(level, "C function")
    else    -- a Lua function
      print(string.format("[%s]:%d", info.short_src,
                                       info.currentline))
    end
  end
end
```

It is not difficult to improve this function, by including more data from getinfo. Actually, the debug library offers such an improved version, the traceback function. Unlike our version, debug.traceback does not print its result; instead, it returns a (usually long) string with the traceback.

Accessing local variables

We can inspect the local variables of any active function with debug.getlocal. This function has two parameters: the stack level of the function you are querying and a variable index. It returns two values: the name and the current value of this variable. If the variable index is larger than the number of active variables, getlocal returns nil. If the stack level is invalid, it raises an error. (We can use debug.getinfo to check the validity of the stack level.)

Lua numbers local variables in the order that they appear in a function, counting only the variables that are active in the current scope of the function. For instance, consider the following function:

```
function foo (a, b)
  local x
  do local c = a - b end
  local a = 1
  while true do
    local name, value = debug.getlocal(1, a)
    if not name then break end
    print(name, value)
    a = a + 1
  end
end
```

The call foo(10, 20) will print this:

```
a         10
b         20
x         nil
a         4
```

The variable with index 1 is a (the first parameter), 2 is b, 3 is x, and 4 is the other a. At the point where getlocal is called, c is already out of scope, while name and value are not yet in scope. (Remember that local variables are only visible *after* their initialization code.)

Starting with Lua 5.2, negative indices get information about the extra arguments of the function: index -1 refers to the first extra argument. The name in this case is always "(*vararg)".

You can also change the values of local variables, with debug.setlocal. Its first two parameters are a stack level and a variable index, like in getlocal. Its third parameter is the new value for this variable. It returns the variable name or nil if the variable index is out of scope.

Accessing non-local variables

The debug library also allows us to access the non-local variables used by a Lua function, with getupvalue. Unlike local variables, the non-local variables referred by a function exist even when the function is not active (this is what closures are about, after all). Therefore, the first argument for getupvalue is not a stack level, but a function (a closure, more precisely). The second argument is the variable index. Lua numbers non-local variables in the order they are first referred in a function, but this order is not relevant, because a function cannot access two non-local variables with the same name.

You can also update non-local variables, with debug.setupvalue. As you might expect, it has three parameters: a closure, a variable index, and the new value. Like setlocal, it returns the name of the variable, or nil if the variable index is out of range.

Listing 24.1 shows how we can access the value of any given variable of a calling function, given the variable name. The parameter level tells where in the stack the function should look; the plus one corrects the level to include the

Listing 24.1. Getting the value of a variable:

```
function getvarvalue (name, level)
  local value
  local found = false

  level = (level or 1) + 1

  -- try local variables
  for i = 1, math.huge do
    local n, v = debug.getlocal(level, i)
    if not n then break end
    if n == name then
      value = v
      found = true
    end
  end
  if found then return value end

  -- try non-local variables
  local func = debug.getinfo(level, "f").func
  for i = 1, math.huge do
    local n, v = debug.getupvalue(func, i)
    if not n then break end
    if n == name then return v end
  end

  -- not found; get value from the environment
  local env = getvarvalue("_ENV", level)
  return env[name]
end
```

call to function getvarvalue itself. Function getvarvalue starts trying a local variable. If there is more than one variable with the given name, it must get the one with the highest index; so, it must always go through the whole loop. If it cannot find any local variable with that name, then it tries the non-local variables. For that, it gets the calling closure, with debug.getinfo, and then it traverses its non-local variables. Finally, if it cannot find a non-local variable with that name, then it goes for a global variable: it calls itself recursively to access the proper _ENV variable and then looks up the name in that environment.

Accessing other coroutines

All introspective functions from the debug library accept an optional coroutine as their first argument, so that we can inspect the coroutine from outside. For instance, consider the next example:

```
co = coroutine.create(function ()
  local x = 10
  coroutine.yield()
  error("some error")
end)

coroutine.resume(co)
print(debug.traceback(co))
```

The call to traceback will work on coroutine co, resulting in something like this:

```
stack traceback:
        [C]: in function 'yield'
        temp:3: in function <temp:1>
```

The trace does not go through the call to resume, because the coroutine and the main program run in different stacks.

When a coroutine raises an error, it does not unwind its stack. This means that we can inspect it after the error. Continuing our example, if we resume the coroutine again it hits the error:

```
print(coroutine.resume(co))      --> false    temp:4: some error
```

Now if we print its traceback we get something like this:

```
stack traceback:
        [C]: in function 'error'
        temp:4: in function <temp:1>
```

We can also inspect local variables from a coroutine, even after an error:

```
print(debug.getlocal(co, 1, 1))     --> x       10
```

24.2 Hooks

The hook mechanism of the debug library allows us to register a function to be called at specific events as a program runs. There are four kinds of events that can trigger a hook:

- *call* events happen every time Lua calls a function;

- *return* events happen every time a function returns;

- *line* events happen when Lua starts executing a new line of code;

- *count* events happen after a given number of instructions.

Lua calls hooks with a single argument, a string describing the event that generated the call: "call" (or "tail call"), "return", "line", or "count". For line events, it also passes a second argument, the new line number. To get more information inside a hook we must call debug.getinfo.

To register a hook, we call debug.sethook with two or three arguments: the first argument is the hook function; the second argument is a mask string, which describes the events we want to monitor; and the optional third argument is a number that describes at what frequency we want to get count events. To monitor the call, return, and line events, we add their first letters ('c', 'r', or 'l') in the mask string. To monitor the count event, we simply supply a counter as the third argument. To turn off hooks, we call sethook with no arguments.

As a simple example, the following code installs a primitive tracer, which prints each line the interpreter executes:

```
debug.sethook(print, "l")
```

This call simply installs print as the hook function and instructs Lua to call it only at line events. A more elaborated tracer can use getinfo to add the current file name to the trace:

```
function trace (event, line)
  local s = debug.getinfo(2).short_src
  print(s .. ":" .. line)
end

debug.sethook(trace, "l")
```

A useful function to use with hooks is debug.debug. This simple function prints a prompt that executes arbitrary Lua commands. It is roughly equivalent to the following code:

```
function debug1 ()
  while true do
    io.write("debug> ")
    local line = io.read()
    if line == "cont" then break end
    assert(load(line))()
  end
end
```

When the user enters the "command" cont, the function returns. The standard implementation is very simple and runs the commands in the global environment, outside the scope of the code being debugged. Exercise 24.5 discusses a better implementation.

24.3 Profiles

Despite its name, the debug library is useful also for tasks other than debugging. A common such task is profiling. For a profile with timing, it is better to use the C interface: the overhead of a Lua call for each hook is too high and may invalidate any measure. However, for counting profiles, Lua code does a decent job. In this section, we will develop a rudimentary profiler that lists the number of times each function in a program is called in a run.

The main data structures of our program are two tables: one associates functions to their call counters, and the other associates functions to their names. The indices to both tables are the functions themselves.

```
local Counters = {}
local Names = {}
```

We could retrieve the function names after the profiling, but remember that we get better results if we get the name of a function while it is active, because then Lua can look at the code that is calling the function to find its name.

Now we define the hook function. Its job is to get the function being called and increment the corresponding counter; it also collects the function name:

```
local function hook ()
  local f = debug.getinfo(2, "f").func
  local count = Counters[f]
  if count == nil then     -- first time 'f' is called?
    Counters[f] = 1
    Names[f] = debug.getinfo(2, "Sn")
  else     -- only increment the counter
    Counters[f] = count + 1
  end
end
```

The next step is to run the program with this hook. We will assume that the main chunk of the program is in a file and that the user gives this file name as an argument to the profiler, like this:

```
% lua profiler main-prog
```

With this scheme, the profiler can get the file name in arg[1], turn on the hook, and run the file:

```
local f = assert(loadfile(arg[1]))
debug.sethook(hook, "c")   -- turn on the hook for calls
f()                        -- run the main program
debug.sethook()            -- turn off the hook
```

The last step is to show the results. Function getname in Listing 24.2 produces a name for a function. Because function names in Lua are so uncertain, we add to each function its location, given as a pair *file:line*. If a function has no name, then we use only its location. If a function is a C function, we use only its name (as it has no location). After that definition, we print each function with its counter:

```
for func, count in pairs(Counters) do
  print(getname(func), count)
end
```

Listing 24.2. Getting the name of a function:

```
function getname (func)
  local n = Names[func]
  if n.what == "C" then
    return n.name
  end
  local lc = string.format("[%s]:%d", n.short_src, n.linedefined)
  if n.what ~= "main" and n.namewhat ~= "" then
    return string.format("%s (%s)", lc, n.name)
  else
    return lc
  end
end
```

If we apply our profiler to the Markov example that we developed in Section 10.3, we get a result like this:

```
[markov.lua]:4 884723
write    10000
[markov.lua]:0 1
read     31103
sub      884722
[markov.lua]:1 (allwords)        1
[markov.lua]:20 (prefix)         894723
find     915824
[markov.lua]:26 (insert)         884723
random   10000
sethook 1
insert   884723
```

This result means that the anonymous function at line 4 (which is the iterator function defined inside `allwords`) was called 884 723 times, `write` (`io.write`) was called 10 000 times, and so on.

There are several improvements that you can make to this profiler, such as to sort the output, to print better function names, and to embellish the output format. Nevertheless, this basic profiler is already useful as it is, and can be used as a base for more advanced tools.

Exercises

Exercise 24.1: Why the recursion in function `getvarvalue` (Listing 24.1) is guaranteed to stop?

Exercise 24.2: Adapt function `getvarvalue` (Listing 24.1) to work with different coroutines (like other functions from the `debug` library).

Exercise 24.3:   Write a function `setvarvalue` similar to `getvarvalue` (Listing 24.1).

Exercise 24.4:   Write a modification of `getvarvalue` (Listing 24.1), called `getallvars`, that returns a table with all variables that are visible at the calling function. (The returned table should not include environmental variables; instead, it should inherit them from the original environment.)

Exercise 24.5: Write an improved version of `debug.debug` that runs the given commands as if they were in the lexical scope of the calling function. (Hint: run the commands in an empty environment and use the `__index` metamethod attached to function `getvarvalue` to do all accesses to variables.)

Exercise 24.6: Improve the previous exercise to handle updates, too.

Exercise 24.7:   Implement some of the suggested improvements for the basic profiler in Section 24.3.

Exercise 24.8:   Write a library for breakpoints. It should offer at least two functions:

```
setbreakpoint(function, line)    --> returns handle
removebreakpoint(handle)
```

A breakpoint is specified by a function and a line inside that function. When the program hits a breakpoint, the library should call `debug.debug`. (Hint: for a basic implementation, use a line hook that checks whether it is in a breakpoint; to improve performance, use a call hook to trace the program execution and only turn the line hook when the program is running the target function.)

Part IV

The C API

25

An Overview of the C API

Lua is an *embedded language*. This means that Lua is not a stand-alone package, but a library that we can link with other applications to incorporate Lua facilities into them.

You may be wondering: if Lua is not a stand-alone program, how come we have been using Lua stand-alone through the whole book until now? The solution to this puzzle is the Lua interpreter (the executable lua). This interpreter is a tiny application (with less than five hundred lines of code) that uses the Lua library to implement the stand-alone interpreter. This program handles the interface with the user, taking her files and strings to feed them to the Lua library, which does the bulk of the work (such as actually running Lua code).

This ability to be used as a library to extend an application is what makes Lua an *extension language*. At the same time, a program that uses Lua can register new functions in the Lua environment; such functions are implemented in C (or another language), so that they can add facilities that cannot be written directly in Lua. This is what makes Lua an *extensible language*.

These two views of Lua (as an extension language and as an extensible language) correspond to two kinds of interaction between C and Lua. In the first kind, C has the control and Lua is the library. The C code in this kind of interaction is what we call *application code*. In the second kind, Lua has the control and C is the library. Here, the C code is called *library code*. Both application code and library code use the same API to communicate with Lua, the so-called C API.

The C API is the set of functions that allow C code to interact with Lua.[1] It comprises functions to read and write Lua global variables, to call Lua functions,

---

[1]Throughout this text, the term "function" actually means "function or macro". The API implements several facilities as macros.

to run pieces of Lua code, to register C functions so that they can later be called by Lua code, and so on. Virtually anything that Lua code can do can also be done by C code through the C API.

The C API follows the *modus operandi* of C, which is quite different from the *modus operandi* of Lua. When programming in C, we must care about type checking, error recovery, memory-allocation errors, and several other sources of complexity. Most functions in the API do not check the correctness of their arguments; it is your responsibility to make sure that the arguments are valid before calling a function.[2] If you make mistakes, you can get a "segmentation fault" error or something similar, instead of a well-behaved error message. Moreover, the API emphasizes flexibility and simplicity, sometimes at the cost of ease of use. Common tasks may involve several API calls. This may be boring, but it gives you full control over all details.

As its title says, the goal of this chapter is to give an overview of what is involved when you use Lua from C. Do not bother understanding all the details of what is going on now. Later we will fill in the details. Nevertheless, do not forget that you always can find more details about specific functions in the Lua reference manual. Moreover, you can find several examples of the use of the API in the Lua distribution itself. The Lua stand-alone interpreter (lua.c) provides examples of application code, while the standard libraries (lmathlib.c, lstrlib.c, etc.) provide examples of library code.

From now on, we are wearing a C programmers' hat. When I talk about "you", I mean you when programming in C, or you impersonated by the C code you write.

A major component in the communication between Lua and C is an omnipresent virtual *stack*. Almost all API calls operate on values on this stack. All data exchange from Lua to C and from C to Lua occurs through this stack. Moreover, you can use the stack to keep intermediate results too. The stack helps to solve two impedance mismatches between Lua and C: the first is caused by Lua being garbage collected, whereas C requires explicit deallocation; the second results from the shock between dynamic typing in Lua versus the static typing of C. We will discuss the stack in more detail in Section 25.2.

25.1   A First Example

We will start this overview with a simple example of an application program: a stand-alone Lua interpreter. We can write a primitive stand-alone interpreter as in Listing 25.1. The header file lua.h defines the basic functions provided by Lua. It includes functions to create a new Lua environment, to invoke Lua functions (such as lua_pcall), to read and write global variables in the Lua environment, to register new functions to be called by Lua, and so on. Everything defined in lua.h has a lua_ prefix.

---

[2]You can compile with the macro LUA_USE_APICHECK defined to enable some checks; this option is particularly useful when debugging your C code. Nevertheless, several errors simply cannot be detected in C, such as invalid pointers.

Listing 25.1. A simple stand-alone Lua interpreter:

```
#include <stdio.h>
#include <string.h>
#include "lua.h"
#include "lauxlib.h"
#include "lualib.h"

int main (void) {
  char buff[256];
  int error;
  lua_State *L = luaL_newstate();          /* opens Lua */
  luaL_openlibs(L);          /* opens the standard libraries */

  while (fgets(buff, sizeof(buff), stdin) != NULL) {
    error = luaL_loadstring(L, buff) || lua_pcall(L, 0, 0, 0);
    if (error) {
      fprintf(stderr, "%s\n", lua_tostring(L, -1));
      lua_pop(L, 1);  /* pop error message from the stack */
    }
  }

  lua_close(L);
  return 0;
}
```

The header file `lauxlib.h` defines the functions provided by the *auxiliary library* (auxlib). All its definitions start with `luaL_` (e.g., `luaL_loadstring`). The auxiliary library uses the basic API provided by `lua.h` to provide a higher abstraction level, in particular with abstractions used by the standard libraries. The basic API strives for economy and orthogonality, whereas the auxiliary library strives for practicality for common tasks. Of course, it is very easy for your program to create other abstractions that it needs, too. Keep in mind that the auxiliary library has no access to the internals of Lua. It does its entire job through the official basic API. Whatever it does, your program can do.

The Lua library defines no global variables at all. It keeps all its state in the dynamic structure `lua_State`; all functions inside Lua receive a pointer to this structure as an argument. This implementation makes Lua reentrant and ready to be used in multithreaded code.

As its name implies, the `luaL_newstate` function creates a new Lua state. When `luaL_newstate` creates a fresh state, its environment contains no predefined functions, not even `print`. To keep Lua small, all standard libraries are provided as separate packages, so that you do not have to use them if you do not need to. The header file `lualib.h` defines functions to open the libraries. Function `luaL_openlibs` opens all standard libraries.

After creating a state and populating it with the standard libraries, it is time to interpret the user input. For each line the user enters, the program first calls luaL_loadstring to compile the code. If there are no errors, the call returns zero and pushes the resulting function on the stack. (Remember that we will discuss this "magic" stack in detail in the next section.) Then the program calls lua_pcall, which pops the function from the stack and runs it in protected mode. Like luaL_loadstring, lua_pcall returns zero if there are no errors. In case of an error, both functions push an error message on the stack; we get this message with lua_tostring and, after printing it, we remove it from the stack with lua_pop.

Notice that, in case of error, this program simply prints the error message to the standard error stream. Real error handling can be quite complex in C, and how to do it depends on the nature of your application. The Lua core never writes anything directly to any output stream; it signals errors by returning error messages. Each application can handle these messages in a way most appropriate for its needs. To simplify our discussions, we will assume for now a simple error handler like the following one, which prints an error message, closes the Lua state, and exits from the whole application:

```
#include <stdarg.h>
#include <stdio.h>
#include <stdlib.h>
void error (lua_State *L, const char *fmt, ...) {
  va_list argp;
  va_start(argp, fmt);
  vfprintf(stderr, fmt, argp);
  va_end(argp);
  lua_close(L);
  exit(EXIT_FAILURE);
}
```

Later we will discuss more about error handling in the application code.

Because you can compile Lua both as C and as C++ code, lua.h does not include this typical adjustment code that is present in several other C libraries:

```
#ifdef __cplusplus
extern "C" {
#endif
    ...
#ifdef __cplusplus
}
#endif
```

If you have compiled Lua as C code (the most common case) and are using it in C++, you can include lua.hpp instead of lua.h. It is defined as follows:

```
extern "C" {
#include "lua.h"
}
```

25.2 The Stack

We face two problems when trying to exchange values between Lua and C: the mismatch between a dynamic and a static type system and the mismatch between automatic and manual memory management.

In Lua, when we write a[k] = v, both k and v can have several different types; even a can have different types, due to metatables. If we want to offer this operation in C, however, any given settable function must have a fixed type. We would need dozens of different functions for this single operation (one function for each combination of types for the three arguments).

We could solve this problem by declaring some kind of union type in C — let us call it lua_Value — that could represent all Lua values. Then, we could declare settable as

```
void lua_settable (lua_Value a, lua_Value k, lua_Value v);
```

This solution has two drawbacks. First, it can be difficult to map such a complex type to other languages; we designed Lua to interface easily not only with C/C++, but also with Java, Fortran, C#, and the like. Second, Lua does garbage collection: if we keep a Lua table in a C variable, the Lua engine has no way to know about this use; it may (wrongly) assume that this table is garbage and collect it.

Therefore, the Lua API does not define anything like a lua_Value type. Instead, it uses an abstract stack to exchange values between Lua and C. Each slot in this stack can hold any Lua value. Whenever you want to ask for a value from Lua (such as the value of a global variable), you call Lua, which pushes the required value on the stack. Whenever you want to pass a value to Lua, you first push the value on the stack, and then you call Lua (which will pop the value). We still need a different function to push each C type on the stack and a different function to get each C type from the stack, but we avoid the combinatorial explosion. Moreover, because this stack lives inside Lua, the garbage collector knows which values C is using.

Nearly all functions in the API use the stack. As we saw in our first example, luaL_loadstring leaves its result on the stack (either the compiled chunk or an error message); lua_pcall gets the function to be called from the stack and leaves any occasional error message there too.

Lua manipulates this stack in a strict LIFO discipline (Last In, First Out). When you call Lua, it changes only the top part of the stack. Your C code has more freedom; specifically, it can inspect any element inside the stack and even insert and delete elements in any arbitrary position.

Pushing elements

The API has one push function for each C type that can be represented in Lua: lua_pushnil for the constant nil, lua_pushboolean for booleans (integers, in C), lua_pushnumber for doubles, lua_pushinteger for integers, lua_pushunsigned for unsigned integers, `lua_pushlstring` for arbitrary strings (a pointer to `char` plus a length), and `lua_pushstring` for zero-terminated strings:

```
void lua_pushnil     (lua_State *L);
void lua_pushboolean (lua_State *L, int bool);
void lua_pushnumber  (lua_State *L, lua_Number n);
void lua_pushinteger (lua_State *L, lua_Integer n);
void lua_pushunsigned (lua_State *L, lua_Unsigned n);
void lua_pushlstring (lua_State *L, const char *s, size_t len);
void lua_pushstring  (lua_State *L, const char *s);
```

There are also functions to push C functions and userdata values on the stack; we will discuss them later.

The type `lua_Number` is the numeric type in Lua. It is a double by default, but some installations can change it to a float or even a long integer, to accommodate Lua to restricted machines. The type `lua_Integer` is a signed integral type large enough to store the size of large strings. Usually, it is defined as the `ptrdiff_t` type. The type `lua_Unsigned`[3] is a 32-bit unsigned integral type in C; it is used by the bitwise library and related functions.

Strings in Lua are not zero-terminated; they can contain arbitrary binary data. In consequence, they must rely on an explicit length. The basic function to push a string onto the stack is `lua_pushlstring`, which requires an explicit length as an argument. For zero-terminated strings, you can use also `lua_pushstring`, which uses `strlen` to supply the string length. Lua never keeps pointers to external strings (or to any other external object except C functions, which are always static). For any string that it has to keep, Lua either makes an internal copy or reuses one. Therefore, you can free or modify your buffer as soon as these functions return.

Whenever you push an element onto the stack, it is your responsibility to ensure that the stack has space for it. Remember, you are a C programmer now; Lua will not spoil you. When Lua starts and any time that Lua calls C, the stack has at least 20 free slots. (The header file `lua.h` defines this constant as `LUA_MINSTACK`.) This space is more than enough for most common uses, so usually we do not even think about it. However, some tasks need more stack space, in particular if you have a loop pushing elements into the stack. In those cases, you may want to call `lua_checkstack`, which checks whether the stack has enough space for your needs:

```
int lua_checkstack (lua_State *L, int sz);
```

Querying elements

To refer to elements in the stack, the API uses *indices*. The first element pushed on the stack has index 1, the next one has index 2, and so on until the top. We can also access elements using the top of the stack as our reference, using negative indices. In this case, –1 refers to the element at the top (that is, the last

---

[3]This type is new in Lua 5.2.

element pushed), –2 to the previous element, and so on. For instance, the call
lua_tostring(L, -1) returns the value at the top of the stack as a string. As we
will see, there are several occasions when it is natural to index the stack from
the bottom (that is, with positive indices), and several other occasions when the
natural way is to use negative indices.

To check whether an element has a specific type, the API offers a family of
functions lua_is*, where the * can be any Lua type. So, there are lua_isnumber,
lua_isstring, lua_istable, and the like. All these functions have the same
prototype:

```
int lua_is* (lua_State *L, int index);
```

Actually, lua_isnumber does not check whether the value has that specific type,
but whether the value can be converted to that type; lua_isstring is similar: in
particular, any number satisfies lua_isstring.

There is also a function lua_type, which returns the type of an element in the
stack. Each type is represented by a constant defined in the header file lua.h:
LUA_TNIL, LUA_TBOOLEAN, LUA_TNUMBER, LUA_TSTRING, LUA_TTABLE, LUA_TTHREAD,
LUA_TUSERDATA, and LUA_TFUNCTION. We use this function mainly in conjunction
with a switch statement. It is also useful when we need to check for strings and
numbers without coercions.

To get a value from the stack, there are the lua_to* functions:

```
int          lua_toboolean (lua_State *L, int index);
const char  *lua_tolstring (lua_State *L, int index,
                                          size_t *len);
lua_Number   lua_tonumber  (lua_State *L, int index);
lua_Integer  lua_tointeger (lua_State *L, int index);
lua_Unsigned lua_tounsigned (lua_State *L, int idx);
```

The lua_toboolean converts any Lua value to a C boolean (0 or 1), following the
Lua rules for conditions: the values nil and **false** are false; any other value is
true.

It is OK to call any of the lua_to* functions even when the given element
does not have an appropriate type. Function lua_toboolean works for any
type; lua_tolstring returns NULL for non-string values. The numeric functions,
however, have no way to signal a wrong type, so they simply return zero. Usually
you would need to call lua_isnumber to check the type, but Lua 5.2 introduced
the following new functions:

```
lua_Number   lua_tonumberx (lua_State *L, int idx, int *isnum);
lua_Integer  lua_tointegerx (lua_State *L, int idx, int *isnum);
lua_Unsigned lua_tounsignedx (lua_State *L, int idx, int *isnum);
```

The out parameter isnum returns a boolean that indicates whether the Lua value
is a number. (You can call those functions with NULL as the last parameter, if you
do not need that value. The old lua_to* functions are now implemented as
macros using this facility.)

The `lua_tolstring` function returns a pointer to an internal copy of the
string and stores the string's length in the position given by `len`. You cannot
change this internal copy (there is a `const` there to remind you). Lua ensures
that this pointer is valid as long as the corresponding string value is in the stack.
When a C function called by Lua returns, Lua clears its stack; therefore, as a
rule, you should never store pointers to Lua strings outside the function that got
them.

Any string that `lua_tolstring` returns always has an extra zero at its end,
but it can have other zeros inside it. The size returned through the third
argument, `len`, is the real string's length. In particular, assuming that the value
at the top of the stack is a string, the following assertions are always valid:

```
size_t l;
const char *s = lua_tolstring(L, -1, &l);   /* any Lua string */
assert(s[l] == '\0');
assert(strlen(s) <= l);
```

You can call `lua_tolstring` with `NULL` as its third argument if you do not
need the length. Better yet, you can use the macro `lua_tostring`, which simply
calls `lua_tolstring` with a `NULL` third argument.

To illustrate the use of these functions, Listing 25.2 presents a useful helper
function that dumps the entire content of the stack. This function traverses
the stack from bottom to top, printing each element according to its type. It
prints strings between quotes; for numbers it uses a '%g' format; for other values
(tables, functions, etc.), it prints only their types. (`lua_typename` converts a type
code to a type name.)

Other stack operations

Besides the previous functions, which interchange values between C and the
stack, the API offers also the following operations for generic stack manipulation:

```
int  lua_gettop    (lua_State *L);
void lua_settop    (lua_State *L, int index);
void lua_pushvalue (lua_State *L, int index);
void lua_remove    (lua_State *L, int index);
void lua_insert    (lua_State *L, int index);
void lua_replace   (lua_State *L, int index);
void lua_copy      (lua_State *L, int fromidx, int toidx);
```

Function `lua_gettop` returns the number of elements in the stack, which is
also the index of the top element. Function `lua_settop` sets the top (that
is, the number of elements in the stack) to a specific value. If the previous
top was higher than the new one, the function discards the extra top values.

Listing 25.2. Dumping the stack:

```c
static void stackDump (lua_State *L) {
  int i;
  int top = lua_gettop(L);  /* depth of the stack */
  for (i = 1; i <= top; i++) {  /* repeat for each level */
    int t = lua_type(L, i);
    switch (t) {
      case LUA_TSTRING: {  /* strings */
        printf("'%s'", lua_tostring(L, i));
        break;
      }
      case LUA_TBOOLEAN: {  /* booleans */
        printf(lua_toboolean(L, i) ? "true" : "false");
        break;
      }
      case LUA_TNUMBER: {  /* numbers */
        printf("%g", lua_tonumber(L, i));
        break;
      }
      default: {  /* other values */
        printf("%s", lua_typename(L, t));
        break;
      }
    }
    printf("  ");  /* put a separator */
  }
  printf("\n");  /* end the listing */
}
```

Otherwise, it pushes nils on the stack to get the given size. As a particular case, lua_settop(L, 0) empties the stack. You can also use negative indices with lua_settop. Using this facility, the API offers the following macro, which pops n elements from the stack:

```c
#define lua_pop(L,n)  lua_settop(L, -(n) - 1)
```

The lua_pushvalue function pushes on the stack a copy of the element at the given index; lua_remove removes the element at the given index, shifting down all elements on top of this position to fill in the gap; lua_insert moves the top element into the given position, shifting up all elements on top of this position to open space; lua_replace pops a value from the top and sets it as the value of the given index, without moving anything; finally, lua_copy copies the value at one index to another, leaving the original untouched. Notice that the following operations have no effect on a non-empty stack:

```
lua_settop(L, -1);  /* set top to its current value */
lua_insert(L, -1);  /* move top element to the top */
lua_copy(L, x, x);  /* copy an element to its own position */
```

The program in Listing 25.3 uses stackDump (defined in Listing 25.2) to illustrate these stack operations.

25.3   Error Handling with the C API

All structures in Lua are dynamic: they grow as needed, and eventually shrink again when possible. This means that the possibility of a memory-allocation failure is pervasive in Lua. Almost any operation can face this eventuality. Moreover, many operations can raise other errors; for instance, an access to a global variable can trigger an __index metamethod and that metamethod may throw an error. Finally, operations that allocate memory eventually trigger the garbage collector, which may invoke finalizers, which can throw errors too. In fewer words, the vast majority of functions in the Lua API can result in errors.

Instead of using error codes for each operation in its API, Lua uses exceptions to signal errors. Unlike C++ or Java, the C language does not offer an exception handling mechanism. To circumvent this difficulty, Lua uses the setjmp facility from C, which results in a mechanism similar to exception handling. Therefore, most API functions can throw an error (that is, call longjmp) instead of returning.

When we write library code (that is, C functions to be called from Lua), the use of long jumps is almost as convenient as a real exception-handling facility, because Lua catches any occasional error. When we write application code (that is, C code that calls Lua), however, we must provide a way to catch those errors.

Error handling in application code

When your application calls functions in the Lua API, it is exposed to errors. As we just discussed, Lua usually signals these errors through long jumps. However, if there is no corresponding setjmp, the interpreter cannot do the jump. In that case, any error in the API causes Lua to call a panic function and, if that function returns, exit the application. You can set your own panic function with the lua_atpanic function, but there is not much that such a function can do.

To properly handle errors in your application code, you must call your code through Lua, so that it can set an appropriate context to catch errors (that is, it runs your code in the context of a setjmp). In the same way we can run Lua code in protected mode using pcall, we can run C code using lua_pcall. More specifically, we pack the C code in a function and call that function through Lua, using lua_pcall. (We will see the details of how to call C functions from Lua in Chapter 27.) With this setting, your C code will run in protected mode. Even in case of memory-allocation failure, lua_pcall returns a proper error code, leaving the interpreter in a consistent state.

Listing 25.3. Example of stack manipulation:

```
#include <stdio.h>
#include "lua.h"
#include "lauxlib.h"

static void stackDump (lua_State *L) {
  <as in Listing 25.2>
}

int main (void) {
  lua_State *L = luaL_newstate();

  lua_pushboolean(L, 1);
  lua_pushnumber(L, 10);
  lua_pushnil(L);
  lua_pushstring(L, "hello");

  stackDump(L);
                    /* true  10  nil  'hello'  */

  lua_pushvalue(L, -4); stackDump(L);
                    /* true  10  nil  'hello'  true  */

  lua_replace(L, 3); stackDump(L);
                    /* true  10  true  'hello'  */

  lua_settop(L, 6); stackDump(L);
                    /* true  10  true  'hello'  nil  nil  */

  lua_remove(L, -3); stackDump(L);
                    /* true  10  true  nil  nil  */

  lua_settop(L, -5); stackDump(L);
                    /* true  */

  lua_close(L);
  return 0;
}
```

Error handling in library code

Lua is a *safe* language. This means that no matter what you write in Lua, no matter how wrong it is, you can always understand the behavior of a program in terms of Lua itself. Moreover, errors are detected and explained in terms of Lua, too. You can contrast that with C, where the behavior of many wrong programs can be explained only in terms of the underlying hardware (e.g., error positions are given as instruction addresses).

Whenever you add new C functions to Lua, you can break its safety. For instance, a function like poke, which stores an arbitrary byte at an arbitrary memory address, can cause all sorts of memory corruption. You must strive to ensure that your add-ons are safe to Lua and provide good error handling.

As we discussed earlier, C programs have to set their error handling through lua_pcall. When you write library functions for Lua, however, usually they do not need to handle errors. Errors thrown by a library function will be caught either by a pcall in Lua or by a lua_pcall in the application code. So, whenever a function in a C library detects an error, it can simply call lua_error (or better yet luaL_error, which formats the error message and then calls lua_error). The lua_error function clears whatever needs to be cleared in Lua and jumps back to the protected call that originated that execution, passing along the error message.

Exercises

Exercise 25.1:   Compile and run the simple stand-alone interpreter (Listing 25.1).

Exercise 25.2: Assume the stack is empty. What will be its contents after the following sequence of calls?

```
lua_pushnumber(L, 3.5);
lua_pushstring(L, "hello");
lua_pushnil(L);
lua_pushvalue(L, -2);
lua_remove(L, 1);
lua_insert(L, -2);
```

Exercise 25.3: Use the simple stand-alone interpreter (Listing 25.1) and the stackDump function (Listing 25.2) to check your answer to the previous exercise.

26

Extending Your Application

An important use of Lua is as a *configuration* language. In this chapter, we will illustrate how we can use Lua to configure a program, starting with a simple example and evolving it to perform increasingly complex tasks.

26.1 The Basics

As our first task, let us imagine a simple configuration scenario: your C program has a window and you want the user to be able to specify the initial window size. Clearly, for such simple task, there are several options simpler than using Lua, such as environment variables or files with name-value pairs. But even using a simple text file, you have to parse it somehow; so, you decide to use a Lua configuration file (that is, a plain text file that happens to be a Lua program). In its simplest form, this file can contain something like the next lines:

```
-- define window size
width = 200
height = 300
```

Now, you must use the Lua API to direct Lua to parse this file, and then to get the values of the global variables `width` and `height`. Function `load`, in Listing 26.1, does the job. The function assumes that you have already created a Lua state, following what we saw in the previous chapter. It calls `luaL_loadfile` to load the chunk from file `fname`, and then calls `lua_pcall` to run the compiled chunk. In case of errors (e.g., a syntax error in your configuration file), these functions push the error message onto the stack and return a non-zero error code; our program then uses `lua_tostring` with index –1 to get the message from the top of the stack. (We defined the error function in Section 25.1.)

Listing 26.1. Getting user information from a configuration file:

```
void load (lua_State *L, const char *fname, int *w, int *h) {
  if (luaL_loadfile(L, fname) || lua_pcall(L, 0, 0, 0))
    error(L, "cannot run config. file: %s", lua_tostring(L, -1));
  lua_getglobal(L, "width");
  lua_getglobal(L, "height");
  if (!lua_isnumber(L, -2))
    error(L, "'width' should be a number\n");
  if (!lua_isnumber(L, -1))
    error(L, "'height' should be a number\n");
  *w = lua_tointeger(L, -2);
  *h = lua_tointeger(L, -1);
}
```

After running the chunk, the program needs to get the values of the global variables. For that, it calls `lua_getglobal` twice, whose single parameter (besides the omnipresent `lua_State`) is the variable name. Each call pushes the corresponding global value onto the stack, so that the width will be at index –2 and the height at index –1 (at the top). (Because the stack was previously empty, you could also index from the bottom, using the index 1 for the first value and 2 for the second. By indexing from the top, however, your code does not need to assume an empty stack.) Next, our example uses `lua_isnumber` to check whether each value is numeric. It then calls `lua_tointeger` to convert such values to integer, assigning them to their respective positions.

Is it worth using Lua for that task? As I said before, for such simple task, a simple file with only two numbers in it would be easier to use than Lua. Even so, the use of Lua brings some advantages. First, Lua handles all syntax details for you; your configuration file can even have comments! Second, the user is already able to do some complex configurations with it. For instance, the script may prompt the user for some information, or it can query an environment variable to choose a proper size:

```
-- configuration file
if getenv("DISPLAY") == ":0.0" then
  width = 300; height = 300
else
  width = 200; height = 200
end
```

Even in such simple configuration scenarios, it is hard to anticipate what users will want; but as long as the script defines the two variables, your C application works without changes.

A final reason for using Lua is that now it is easy to add new configuration facilities to your program; this easiness creates an attitude that results in programs that are more flexible.

26.2   Table Manipulation

Let us adopt that attitude: now, we want to configure a background color for the window, too. We will assume that the final color specification is composed of three numbers, where each number is a color component in RGB. Usually, in C, these numbers are integers in some range like $[0, 255]$. In Lua, because all numbers are real, we can use the more natural range $[0, 1]$.

A naive approach here is to ask the user to set each component in a different global variable:

```
-- configuration file
width = 200
height = 300
background_red = 0.30
background_green = 0.10
background_blue = 0
```

This approach has two drawbacks: it is too verbose (real programs may need dozens of different colors, for window background, window foreground, menu background, etc.); and there is no way to predefine common colors, so that, later, the user can simply write something like background=WHITE. To avoid these drawbacks, we will use a table to represent a color:

```
background = {r=0.30, g=0.10, b=0}
```

The use of tables gives more structure to the script; now it is easy for the user (or for the application) to predefine colors for later use in the configuration file:

```
BLUE = {r=0, g=0, b=1.0}
<other color definitions>

background = BLUE
```

To get these values in C, we can do as follows:

```
lua_getglobal(L, "background");
if (!lua_istable(L, -1))
  error(L, "'background' is not a table");

red = getcolorfield(L, "r");
green = getcolorfield(L, "g");
blue = getcolorfield(L, "b");
```

Listing 26.2. A particular `getcolorfield` implementation:

```
#define MAX_COLOR       255

/* assume that table is on the stack top */
int getcolorfield (lua_State *L, const char *key) {
  int result;
  lua_pushstring(L, key);  /* push key */
  lua_gettable(L, -2);  /* get background[key] */
  if (!lua_isnumber(L, -1))
    error(L, "invalid component in background color");
  result = (int)(lua_tonumber(L, -1) * MAX_COLOR);
  lua_pop(L, 1);  /* remove number */
  return result;
}
```

We first get the value of the global variable background and ensure that it is a table and then we use getcolorfield to get each color component.

Of course, the getcolorfield function is not part of the API; we must define it. Again, we face the problem of polymorphism: there are potentially many versions of getcolorfield functions, varying the key type, value type, error handling, etc. The Lua API offers one function, lua_gettable, that works for all types. It takes the position of the table in the stack, pops the key from the stack, and pushes the corresponding value. Our private getcolorfield, defined in Listing 26.2, assumes that the table is at the top of the stack; so, after pushing the key with lua_pushstring, the table will be at index –2. Before returning, getcolorfield pops the retrieved value from the stack, leaving the stack at the same level that it was before the call.

Because indexing a table with a string key is so common, Lua 5.1 introduced a specialized version of lua_gettable for this case: lua_getfield. Using this function, we can rewrite the two lines

```
lua_pushstring(L, key);
lua_gettable(L, -2);  /* get background[key] */
```

as

```
lua_getfield(L, -1, key);
```

(As we do not push the string onto the stack, the table index is still –1 when we call lua_getfield.)

We will extend our example a little further and introduce color names for the user. The user can still use color tables, but she can also use predefined names for the more common colors. To implement this feature, we need a color table in our C application:

```
struct ColorTable {
  char *name;
  unsigned char red, green, blue;
} colortable[] = {
  {"WHITE",   MAX_COLOR, MAX_COLOR, MAX_COLOR},
  {"RED",     MAX_COLOR,         0,         0},
  {"GREEN",           0, MAX_COLOR,         0},
  {"BLUE",            0,         0, MAX_COLOR},
  <other colors>
  {NULL, 0, 0, 0}  /* sentinel */
};
```

Our implementation will create global variables with the color names and initialize these variables using color tables. The result is the same as if the user had the following lines in her script:

```
WHITE = {r=1.0, g=1.0, b=1.0}
RED   = {r=1.0, g=0,   b=0}
<other colors>
```

To set the table fields, we define an auxiliary function, setcolorfield; it pushes the index and the field value on the stack, and then calls lua_settable:

```
/* assume that table is at the top */
void setcolorfield (lua_State *L, const char *index, int value) {
  lua_pushstring(L, index); /* key */
  lua_pushnumber(L, (double)value / MAX_COLOR);  /* value */
  lua_settable(L, -3);
}
```

Like other API functions, lua_settable works for many different types, so it gets all its operands from the stack. It takes the table index as an argument and pops the key and the value. The setcolorfield function assumes that before the call the table is at the top of the stack (index –1); after pushing the index and the value, the table will be at index –3.

Lua 5.1 also introduced a specialized version of lua_settable for string keys, called lua_setfield. Using this new function, we can rewrite our previous definition for setcolorfield as follows:

```
void setcolorfield (lua_State *L, const char *index, int value) {
  lua_pushnumber(L, (double)value / MAX_COLOR);
  lua_setfield(L, -2, index);
}
```

The next function, setcolor, defines a single color. It creates a table, sets the appropriate fields, and assigns this table to the corresponding global variable:

Listing 26.3. Colors as strings or tables:

```
lua_getglobal(L, "background");
if (lua_isstring(L, -1)) {    /* value is a string? */
  const char *name = lua_tostring(L, -1);   /* get string */
  int i;   /* search the color table */
  for (i = 0; colortable[i].name != NULL; i++) {
    if (strcmp(colorname, colortable[i].name) == 0)
      break;
  }
  if (colortable[i].name == NULL)   /* string not found? */
    error(L, "invalid color name (%s)", colorname);
  else {   /* use colortable[i] */
    red = colortable[i].red;
    green = colortable[i].green;
    blue = colortable[i].blue;
  }
} else if (lua_istable(L, -1)) {
  red = getcolorfield(L, "r");
  green = getcolorfield(L, "g");
  blue = getcolorfield(L, "b");
} else
    error(L, "invalid value for 'background'");
```

```
void setcolor (lua_State *L, struct ColorTable *ct) {
  lua_newtable(L);                    /* creates a table */
  setcolorfield(L, "r", ct->red);        /* table.r = ct->r */
  setcolorfield(L, "g", ct->green);      /* table.g = ct->g */
  setcolorfield(L, "b", ct->blue);       /* table.b = ct->b */
  lua_setglobal(L, ct->name);         /* 'name' = table */
}
```

The lua_newtable function creates an empty table and pushes it on the stack; the calls to setcolorfield set the table fields; finally, lua_setglobal pops the table and sets it as the value of the global with the given name.

With these previous functions, the following loop will register all colors for the configuration script:

```
int i = 0;
while (colortable[i].name != NULL)
  setcolor(L, &colortable[i++]);
```

Remember that the application must execute this loop before running the script.

Listing 26.3 shows another option for implementing named colors. Instead of global variables, the user can denote color names with strings, writing her settings as background="BLUE". Therefore, background can be either a table or a string. With this design, the application does not need to do anything before running the user's script. Instead, it needs more work to get a color. When it gets the value of variable background, it must test whether the value has type string, and then look up the string in the color table.

What is the best option? In C programs, the use of strings to denote options is not a good practice, because the compiler cannot detect misspellings. In Lua, however, the error message for a misspelling color probably will go to whom is writing the configuration "program". The distinction between programmer and user is blurred; the difference between a compilation error and a run-time error is not that big.

With strings, the value of background would be the misspelled string; so, the application can add this information to the error message. The application can also compare strings regardless of case, so that a user can write "white", "WHITE", or even "White". Moreover, if the user script is small and there are many colors, it may be odd to register hundreds of colors (and to create hundreds of tables and global variables) only for the user to choose a few. With strings, you avoid this overhead.

26.3 Calling Lua Functions

A great strength of Lua is that a configuration file can define functions to be called by the application. For instance, you can write an application to plot the graph of a function and use Lua to define the function to be plotted.

The API protocol to call a function is simple: first, you push the function to be called; second, you push the arguments to the call; then you use lua_pcall to do the actual call; finally, you get the results from the stack.

As an example, let us assume that your configuration file has a function like this:

```
function f (x, y)
  return (x^2 * math.sin(y)) / (1 - x)
end
```

You want to evaluate, in C, z=f(x,y) for given x and y. Assuming that you have already opened the Lua library and run the configuration file, function f in Listing 26.4 encapsulates this call.

The second and third arguments to lua_pcall are the number of arguments you are passing and the number of results you want. The fourth argument indicates an error-handling function; we will discuss it in a moment. As in a Lua assignment, lua_pcall adjusts the actual number of results to what you have asked for, pushing nils or discarding extra values as needed. Before pushing the results, lua_pcall removes from the stack the function and its arguments. When a function returns multiple results, the first result is pushed first; for

Listing 26.4. Calling a Lua function from C:

```
/* call a function 'f' defined in Lua */
double f (lua_State *L, double x, double y) {
  int isnum;
  double z;

  /* push functions and arguments */
  lua_getglobal(L, "f");  /* function to be called */
  lua_pushnumber(L, x);   /* push 1st argument */
  lua_pushnumber(L, y);   /* push 2nd argument */

  /* do the call (2 arguments, 1 result) */
  if (lua_pcall(L, 2, 1, 0) != LUA_OK)
    error(L, "error running function 'f': %s",
             lua_tostring(L, -1));

  /* retrieve result */
  z = lua_tonumberx(L, -1, &isnum);
  if (!isnum)
    error(L, "function 'f' must return a number");
  lua_pop(L, 1);  /* pop returned value */
  return z;
}
```

instance, if there are three results, the first one will be at index –3 and the last at index –1.

If there is any error while lua_pcall is running, lua_pcall returns an error code; moreover, it pushes the error message on the stack (but still pops the function and its arguments). Before pushing the message, however, lua_pcall calls the message handler function, if there is one. To specify a message handler function, we use the last argument of lua_pcall. A zero means no message handler function; that is, the final error message is the original message. Otherwise, this argument should be the index in the stack where the message handler function is located. In such cases, the handler must be pushed in the stack somewhere below the function to be called and its arguments.

For normal errors, lua_pcall returns the error code LUA_ERRRUN. Two special kinds of errors deserve different codes, because they never run the message handler. The first kind is a memory allocation error. For such errors, lua_pcall always returns LUA_ERRMEM. The second kind is an error while Lua is running the message handler itself. In this case, it is of little use to call the message handler again, so lua_pcall returns immediately with a code LUA_ERRERR. Lua 5.2 differentiates a third kind of error: when a finalizer throws an error, lua_pcall returns the code LUA_ERRGCMM (*error in a GC metamethod*). This code indicates that the error is not directly related to the call itself.

Listing 26.5. A generic call function:

```
#include <stdarg.h>

void call_va (lua_State *L, const char *func,
                            const char *sig, ...) {
  va_list vl;
  int narg, nres;  /* number of arguments and results */

  va_start(vl, sig);
  lua_getglobal(L, func);  /* push function */

  <push arguments (Listing 26.6)>

  nres = strlen(sig);  /* number of expected results */

  if (lua_pcall(L, narg, nres, 0) != 0)  /* do the call */
    error(L, "error calling '%s': %s", func,
                                       lua_tostring(L, -1));

  <retrieve results (Listing 26.7)>

  va_end(vl);
}
```

26.4 A Generic Call Function

As a more advanced example, we will build a wrapper for calling Lua functions, using the vararg facility in C. Our wrapper function, let us call it call_va, takes the name of the function to be called, a string describing the types of the arguments and results, then the list of arguments, and finally a list of pointers to variables to store the results; it handles all the details of the API. With this function, we could write our previous example simply like this:

```
call_va(L, "f", "dd>d", x, y, &z);
```

The string "dd>d" means "two arguments of type double, one result of type double". This descriptor can use the letters 'd' for double, 'i' for integer, and 's' for strings; a '>' separates arguments from the results. If the function has no results, the '>' is optional.

Listing 26.5 shows the implementation of function call_va. Despite its generality, this function follows the same steps of our first example: it pushes the function, pushes the arguments (Listing 26.6), does the call, and gets the results (Listing 26.7). Most of its code is straightforward, but there are some subtleties. First, it does not need to check whether func is a function; lua_pcall will trigger any error. Second, because it pushes an arbitrary number of arguments, it must check the stack space. Third, because the function can return strings, call_va

Listing 26.6. Pushing arguments for the generic call function:

```
for (narg = 0; *sig; narg++) {  /* repeat for each argument */

  /* check stack space */
  luaL_checkstack(L, 1, "too many arguments");

  switch (*sig++) {

    case 'd':  /* double argument */
      lua_pushnumber(L, va_arg(vl, double));
      break;

    case 'i':  /* int argument */
      lua_pushinteger(L, va_arg(vl, int));
      break;

    case 's':  /* string argument */
      lua_pushstring(L, va_arg(vl, char *));
      break;

    case '>':  /* end of arguments */
      goto endargs;

    default:
      error(L, "invalid option (%c)", *(sig - 1));
  }

}
endargs:
```

cannot pop the results from the stack. It is up to the caller to pop them, after it finishes using occasional string results (or after copying them to appropriate buffers).

Exercises

Exercise 26.1: Write a C program that reads a Lua file defining a function f from numbers to numbers and plots that function. (You do not need to do anything fancy; the program can plot the results printing ASCII asterisks as we did in Section 8.1.)

Exercise 26.2: Modify function call_va (Listing 26.5) to handle boolean values.

Exercise 26.3:   Let us suppose a program that needs to monitor several weather stations. Internally, it uses a four-byte string to represent each station,

Listing 26.7. Retrieving results for the generic call function:

```
nres = -nres;  /* stack index of first result */
while (*sig) {  /* repeat for each result */
  switch (*sig++) {

    case 'd': {  /* double result */
      int isnum;
      double n = lua_tonumberx(L, nres, &isnum);
      if (!isnum)
        error(L, "wrong result type");
      *va_arg(vl, double *) = n;
      break;
    }

    case 'i': {  /* int result */
      int isnum;
      int n = lua_tointegerx(L, nres, &isnum);
      if (!isnum)
        error(L, "wrong result type");
      *va_arg(vl, int *) = n;
      break;
    }

    case 's': {  /* string result */
      const char *s = lua_tostring(L, nres);
      if (s == NULL)
        error(L, "wrong result type");
      *va_arg(vl, const char **) = s;
      break;
    }

    default:
      error(L, "invalid option (%c)", *(sig - 1));
  }
  nres++;
}
```

and there is a configuration file to map each string to the actual URL of the corresponding station. A Lua configuration file could do this mapping in several ways:

- a bunch of global variables, one for each station;

- one table mapping string codes to URLs;

- one function mapping string codes to URLs.

Discuss the pros and cons of each option, considering things like the total number of stations, the regularity of the URLs (e.g., there may be a formation rule from codes to URLs), the kind of users, etc.

27

Calling C from Lua

When we say that Lua can call C functions, this does not mean that Lua can call any C function.[1] As we saw in the previous chapter, when C calls a Lua function, it must follow a simple protocol to pass the arguments and to get the results. Similarly, for Lua to call a C function, the C function must follow a protocol to get its arguments and to return its results. Moreover, for Lua to call a C function, we must register the function, that is, we must give its address to Lua in an appropriate way.

When Lua calls a C function, it uses the same kind of stack that C uses to call Lua. The C function gets its arguments from the stack and pushes the results on the stack.

An important concept here is that the stack is not a global structure; each function has its own private local stack. When Lua calls a C function, the first argument will always be at index 1 of this local stack. Even when a C function calls Lua code that calls the same (or another) C function again, each of these invocations sees only its own private stack, with its first argument at index 1.

27.1 C Functions

As a first example, let us see how to implement a simplified version of a function that returns the sine of a given number:

```
static int l_sin (lua_State *L) {
  double d = lua_tonumber(L, 1);  /* get argument */
  lua_pushnumber(L, sin(d));  /* push result */
  return 1;  /* number of results */
}
```

---

[1]There are packages that allow Lua to call any C function, but they are neither portable nor safe.

Any function registered with Lua must have this same prototype, defined as `lua_CFunction` in `lua.h`:

```
typedef int (*lua_CFunction) (lua_State *L);
```

From the point of view of C, a C function gets as its single argument the Lua state and returns an integer with the number of values it is returning in the stack. Therefore, the function does not need to clear the stack before pushing its results. After it returns, Lua automatically saves its results and clears its entire stack.

Before we can use this function from Lua, we must register it. We do this little magic with `lua_pushcfunction`: it gets a pointer to a C function and creates a value of type "`function`" that represents this function inside Lua. Once registered, a C function behaves like any other function inside Lua.

A quick-and-dirty way to test `l_sin` is to put its code directly into our basic interpreter (Listing 25.1) and add the following lines right after the call to `luaL_openlibs`:

```
lua_pushcfunction(L, l_sin);
lua_setglobal(L, "mysin");
```

The first line pushes a value of type function; the second line assigns it to the global variable `mysin`. After these modifications, you can use the new function `mysin` in your Lua scripts. (In the next section, we will discuss better ways to link new C functions with Lua.)

For a more professional sine function, we must check the type of its argument. Here, the auxiliary library helps us. The `luaL_checknumber` function checks whether a given argument is a number: in case of error, it throws an informative error message; otherwise, it returns the number. The modification to our function is minimal:

```
static int l_sin (lua_State *L) {
    double d = luaL_checknumber(L, 1);
    lua_pushnumber(L, sin(d));
    return 1;  /* number of results */
}
```

With the above definition, if you call `mysin('a')`, you get the message

```
bad argument #1 to 'mysin' (number expected, got string)
```

Notice how `luaL_checknumber` automatically fills the message with the argument number (#1), the function name ("mysin"), the expected parameter type (number), and the actual parameter type (string).

As a more complex example, let us write a function that returns the contents of a given directory. Lua does not provide this function in its standard libraries, because ANSI C does not have functions for this job. Here, we will assume that we have a POSIX compliant system. Our function—called `dir` in Lua, `l_dir` in C—gets as argument a string with the directory path and returns an array

with the directory entries. For instance, a call `dir("/home/lua")` may return the
table `{".", "..", "src", "bin", "lib"}`. In case of an error, the function returns
nil plus a string with the error message. The complete code for this function is in
Listing 27.1. Note the use of the `luaL_checkstring` function, from the auxiliary
library, which is the equivalent of `luaL_checknumber` for strings.

(In extreme conditions, this implementation of `l_dir` may cause a small
memory leak. Three of the Lua functions that it calls can fail due to insufficient
memory: `lua_newtable`, `lua_pushstring`, and `lua_settable`. If any of these
functions fails, it will raise an error and interrupt `l_dir`, which therefore will
not call `closedir`. As we discussed earlier, on many programs this is not a big
problem: if the program runs out of memory, the best it can do is to shut down
anyway. Nevertheless, in Chapter 30 we will see an alternative implementation
for a directory function that corrects this problem.)

27.2 Continuations

Through `lua_pcall` and `lua_call`, a C function called from Lua can call Lua
back. Several functions in the standard library do that: `table.sort` can call an
order function; `string.gsub` can call a replacement function; `pcall` and `xpcall`
call functions in protected mode. If we remember that the main Lua code was
itself called from C (the host program), we have a call sequence like C (host)
calls Lua (script) that calls C (library) that calls Lua (callback).

Usually, Lua handles these sequences of calls without problems; after all,
this integration with C is a hallmark of the language. There is one situation,
however, where this interlacement can cause difficulties: coroutines.

Each coroutine in Lua has its own stack, which keeps information about
the pending calls of the coroutine. Specifically, the stack stores the return
address, the parameters, and the local variables of each call. For calls to Lua
functions, the interpreter uses an appropriate data structure to implement the
stack, which is called *soft stack*. For calls to C functions, however, the interpreter
must use the C stack, too. After all, the return address and the local variables
of a C function live in the C stack.

It is easy for the interpreter to have multiple soft stacks, but the runtime
of ANSI C has only one internal stack. Therefore, coroutines in Lua cannot
suspend the execution of a C function: if there is a C function in the call path
from a resume to its respective yield, Lua cannot save the state of that C function
to restore it in the next resume. Consider the next example, in Lua 5.1:

```
co = coroutine.wrap(function (a)
              return pcall(function (x)
                          coroutine.yield(x[1])
                          return x[3]
                     end, a)
        end)
print(co({10, 3, -8, 15}))
    --> false    attempt to yield across metamethod/C-call boundary
```

Listing 27.1. A function to read a directory:

```
#include <dirent.h>
#include <errno.h>
#include <string.h>

#include "lua.h"
#include "lauxlib.h"

static int l_dir (lua_State *L) {
  DIR *dir;
  struct dirent *entry;
  int i;
  const char *path = luaL_checkstring(L, 1);

  /* open directory */
  dir = opendir(path);
  if (dir == NULL) {  /* error opening the directory? */
    lua_pushnil(L);  /* return nil... */
    lua_pushstring(L, strerror(errno));  /* and error message */
    return 2;  /* number of results */
  }

  /* create result table */
  lua_newtable(L);
  i = 1;
  while ((entry = readdir(dir)) != NULL) {
    lua_pushnumber(L, i++);  /* push key */
    lua_pushstring(L, entry->d_name);  /* push value */
    lua_settable(L, -3);
  }

  closedir(dir);
  return 1;  /* table is already on top */
}
```

The pcall function is a C function; therefore, Lua cannot suspend it, because there is no way in ANSI C to suspend a C function and resume it later.

Lua 5.2 ameliorated that difficulty with *continuations*. Lua 5.2 implements yields using long jumps, in the same way that it implements errors. A long jump simply throws away any information about C functions in the C stack, so it is impossible to resume those functions. However, a C function foo can specify a continuation function foo-c, which is another C function to be called when it is time to resume foo. That is, when the interpreter detects that it should resume foo, but that a long jump threw away the entry for foo in the C stack, it calls foo-c instead.

To make things a little more concrete, let us see an example: the implementation of pcall. In Lua 5.1, this function had the following code:

```
static int luaB_pcall (lua_State *L) {
  int status;
  luaL_checkany(L, 1);  /* at least one parameter */
  status = lua_pcall(L, lua_gettop(L) - 1, LUA_MULTRET, 0);
  lua_pushboolean(L, (status == 0));  /* status */
  lua_insert(L, 1);  /* status is first result */
  return lua_gettop(L);  /* return status + all results */
}
```

If the function being called through lua_pcall yielded, it would be impossible to resume luaB_pcall later. Therefore, the interpreter raised an error whenever we attempted to yield inside a protected call. Lua 5.2 implements pcall roughly like in Listing 27.2.[2] There are three differences from the Lua 5.1 version: first, the new version replaced the call to lua_pcall by a call to lua_pcallk; second, it grouped everything done after that call in a new auxiliary function finishpcall; the third difference is the function pcallcont, the last argument to lua_pcallk, which is the continuation function.

If there are no yields, lua_pcallk works exactly like lua_pcall. If there is a yield, then things are quite different. If a function called by lua_pcall tries to yield, Lua 5.2 raises an error, like Lua 5.1. But when a function called by lua_pcallk yields, there are no errors: Lua does a long jump and throws away the entry for luaB_pcall in the C stack, but it keeps in the soft stack of the coroutine a reference to the continuation function, pcallcont. Later, when the interpreter detects that it should return to luaB_pcall (which is impossible), it instead calls the continuation function pcallcont.

Unlike luaB_pcall, the continuation function pcallcont cannot get the return value from lua_pcallk. So, Lua provides a special function to return a status of the call: lua_getctx. When called from a regular Lua function (a case that does not happen in our example), lua_getctx returns LUA_OK. When called regularly from a continuation function, it returns LUA_YIELD. The continuation function can be called also in some cases of errors; in that case, lua_getctx returns the error status, which is the same value that lua_pcallk would return.

---

[2]The real code is a little more complex than shown here, because it has some parts shared with xpcall and it checks for stack overflow before pushing the extra boolean result.

Listing 27.2. Implementation of `pcall` with continuations:

```
static int finishpcall (lua_State *L, int status) {
    lua_pushboolean(L, status);  /* first result (status) */
    lua_insert(L, 1);  /* put first result in first slot */
    return lua_gettop(L);
}

static int pcallcont (lua_State *L) {
    int status = lua_getctx(L, NULL);
    return finishpcall(L, (status == LUA_YIELD));
}

static int luaB_pcall (lua_State *L) {
    int status;
    luaL_checkany(L, 1);
    status = lua_pcallk(L, lua_gettop(L) - 2, LUA_MULTRET, 0,
                        0, pcallcont);
    return finishpcall(L, (status == LUA_OK));
}
```

Besides the status of the call, `lua_getctx` can also return a *context* information (hence its name, from *get context*). The fifth parameter to `lua_pcallk` is an arbitrary integer that can be retrieved by the second parameter of `lua_getctx`, a pointer to integer. This integer value allows the original function to pass some arbitrary information directly to its continuation. It can pass additional information through the Lua stack. (Our example does not use this facility.)

The continuation system of Lua 5.2 is an ingenious mechanism to support yields, but it is not a panacea. Some C functions would need to pass too much context to their continuations. Examples include `table.sort`, which uses the C stack for recursion, and `string.gsub`, which must keep track of captures and a buffer for its partial result. Although it is possible to rewrite them in a "yieldable" way, the gains do not seem to be worth the extra complexity.

27.3   C Modules

A Lua module is a chunk that defines several Lua functions and stores them in appropriate places, typically as entries in a table. A C module for Lua mimics this behavior. Besides the definition of its C functions, it must also define a special function that plays the role of the main chunk in a Lua library. This function should register all C functions of the module and store them in appropriate places, again typically as entries in a table. Like a Lua main chunk, it should also initialize anything else that needs initialization in the module.

Lua perceives C functions through this registration process. Once a C function is represented and stored in Lua, Lua calls it through a direct reference to its address (which is what we give to Lua when we register a function). In other words, Lua does not depend on a function name, package location, or visibility rules to call a function, once it is registered. Typically, a C module has one single public (extern) function, which is the function that opens the library. All other functions can be private, declared as static in C.

When you extend Lua with C functions, it is a good idea to design your code as a C module, even when you want to register only one C function: sooner or later (usually sooner) you will need other functions. As usual, the auxiliary library offers a helper function for this job. The luaL_newlib macro takes a list of C functions with their respective names and registers all of them inside a new table. As an example, suppose we want to create a library with the l_dir function that we defined earlier. First, we must define the library functions:

```
static int l_dir (lua_State *L) {
  <as before>
}
```

Next, we declare an array with all functions in the module with their respective names. This array has elements of type luaL_Reg, which is a structure with two fields: a function name (a string) and a function pointer.

```
static const struct luaL_Reg mylib [] = {
  {"dir", l_dir},
  {NULL, NULL}  /* sentinel */
};
```

In our example, there is only one function (l_dir) to declare. The last pair in the array is always {NULL,NULL}, to signal its end. Finally, we declare a main function, using luaL_newlib:

```
int luaopen_mylib (lua_State *L) {
  luaL_newlib(L, mylib);
  return 1;
}
```

The call to luaL_newlib creates a new table and fills it with the pairs name–function specified by the array mylib. When it returns, luaL_newlib leaves on the stack the new table wherein it opened the library. The luaopen_mylib function then returns 1 to return this table to Lua.

After finishing the library, we must link it to the interpreter. The most convenient way to do it is with the dynamic linking facility, if your Lua interpreter supports this facility. In this case, you must create a dynamic library with your code (mylib.dll in Windows, mylib.so in Linux-like systems) and put it somewhere in the C path. After these steps, you can load your library directly from Lua, with require:

```
local mylib = require "mylib"
```

This call links the dynamic library `mylib` with Lua, finds the `luaopen_mylib` function, registers it as a C function, and calls it, opening the module. (This behavior explains why `luaopen_mylib` must have the same prototype as any other C function.)

The dynamic linker must know the name of the `luaopen_mylib` function in order to find it. It will always look for `luaopen_` concatenated with the name of the module. Therefore, if our module is called `mylib`, that function must be called `luaopen_mylib`.

If your interpreter does not support dynamic linking, then you have to re-compile Lua with your new library. Besides this recompilation, you need some way of telling the stand-alone interpreter that it should open this library when it opens a new state. A simple way to do this is to add `luaopen_mylib` into the list of standard libraries to be opened by `luaL_openlibs`, in file `linit.c`.

Exercises

Exercise 27.1: Write a `summation` function, in C, that computes the sum of its variable number of numeric arguments:

```
print(summation())                    -->    0
print(summation(2.3, 5.4))            -->    7.7
print(summation(2.3, 5.4, -34))       --> -26.3
print(summation(2.3, 5.4, {}))
   --> stdin:1: bad argument #3 to 'summation'
                    (number expected, got table)
```

Exercise 27.2: Implement a function equivalent to `table.pack`, from the standard library.

Exercise 27.3: Write a function that receives any number of parameters and returns them in reverse order.

```
print(reverse(1, "hello", 20))   --> 20    hello    1
```

Exercise 27.4: Write a function `foreach` that receives a table and a function and calls that function for each pair key–value in the table.

```
foreach({x = 10, y = 20}, print)
   --> x    10
   --> y    20
```

(Hint: check function `lua_next` in the Lua manual.)

Exercise 27.5: Rewrite function `foreach`, from the previous exercise, so that the function being called can yield.

Exercise 27.6: Create a C module with all functions from the previous exercises.

28

Techniques for Writing C Functions

Both the official API and the auxiliary library provide several mechanisms to help writing C functions. In this chapter, we cover the mechanisms for array manipulation, for string manipulation, and for storing Lua values in C.

28.1 Array Manipulation

"Array", in Lua, is just a name for a table used in a specific way. We can manipulate arrays using the same functions we use to manipulate tables, namely `lua_settable` and `lua_gettable`. However, the API provides special functions for array manipulation. One reason for these extra functions is performance: frequently we have an array-access operation inside the inner loop of an algorithm (e.g., sorting), so that any performance gain in this operation can have a big impact on the overall performance of the algorithm. Another reason is convenience: like string keys, integer keys are common enough to deserve special treatment.

The API provides two functions for array manipulation:

```
void lua_rawgeti (lua_State *L, int index, int key);
void lua_rawseti (lua_State *L, int index, int key);
```

The description of `lua_rawgeti` and `lua_rawseti` is a little confusing, as it involves two indices: `index` refers to where the table is in the stack; `key` refers to where the element is in the table. The call `lua_rawgeti(L, t, key)` is equivalent to the following sequence when `t` is positive (otherwise, you must compensate for the new item in the stack):

Listing 28.1. The map function in C:

```
int l_map (lua_State *L) {
  int i, n;

  /* 1st argument must be a table (t) */
  luaL_checktype(L, 1, LUA_TTABLE);

  /* 2nd argument must be a function (f) */
  luaL_checktype(L, 2, LUA_TFUNCTION);

  n = luaL_len(L, 1);  /* get size of table */

  for (i = 1; i <= n; i++) {
    lua_pushvalue(L, 2);     /* push f */
    lua_rawgeti(L, 1, i);    /* push t[i] */
    lua_call(L, 1, 1);       /* call f(t[i]) */
    lua_rawseti(L, 1, i);    /* t[i] = result */
  }

  return 0;  /* no results */
}
```

```
lua_pushnumber(L, key);
lua_rawget(L, t);
```

The call lua_rawseti(L, t, key) (again for t positive) is equivalent to this sequence:

```
lua_pushnumber(L, key);
lua_insert(L, -2);  /* put 'key' below previous value */
lua_rawset(L, t);
```

Note that both functions use raw operations. They are faster and, anyway, tables
used as arrays seldom use metamethods.

As a concrete example of the use of these functions, Listing 28.1 implements
the map function: it applies a given function to all elements of an array, replac-
ing each element by the result of the call. This example also introduces three
new functions: luaL_checktype, luaL_len, and lua_pcall.

The luaL_checktype function (from lauxlib.h) ensures that a given argument has a given type; otherwise, it raises an error.

The primitive lua_len (not used in the example) is equivalent to the '#'
operator. Because of metamethods, this operator may result in any kind of
object, not only numbers; therefore, lua_len returns its result in the stack.
The luaL_len function (the one used in the example, from the auxiliary library)
raises an error if the length is not a number; otherwise, it returns the length as
a C integer.

The `lua_call` function does an unprotected call. It is similar to `lua_pcall`, but it propagates errors, instead of returning an error code. When you are writing the main code in an application, you should not use `lua_call`, because you want to catch any errors. When you are writing functions, however, it is usually a good idea to use `lua_call`; if there is an error, just leave it to someone that cares about it.

28.2 String Manipulation

When a C function receives a string argument from Lua, there are only two rules that it must observe: not to pop the string from the stack while accessing it and never to modify the string.

Things get more demanding when a C function needs to create a string to return to Lua. Now, it is up to the C code to take care of buffer allocation/deallocation, buffer overflows, and the like. Nevertheless, the Lua API provides some functions to help with these tasks.

The standard API provides support for two of the most basic string operations: substring extraction and string concatenation. To extract a substring, remember that the basic operation `lua_pushlstring` gets the string length as an extra argument. Therefore, if you want to pass to Lua a substring of a string s ranging from position i to j (inclusive), all you have to do is this:

```
lua_pushlstring(L, s + i, j - i + 1);
```

As an example, suppose you want a function that splits a string according to a given separator (a single character) and returns a table with the substrings. For instance, the call `split("hi:ho:there", ":")` should return the table {"hi", "ho", "there"}. Listing 28.2 presents a simple implementation for this function. It needs no extra buffers and puts no constraints on the size of the strings it can handle. Lua takes care of all buffer needs.

To concatenate strings, Lua provides a specific function in its API, called `lua_concat`. It is equivalent to the concatenation operator .. in Lua: it converts numbers to strings and triggers metamethods when necessary. Moreover, it can concatenate more than two strings at once. The call `lua_concat(L, n)` will concatenate (and pop) the n values at the top of the stack, pushing the result on the top.

Another helpful function is `lua_pushfstring`:

```
const char *lua_pushfstring (lua_State *L, const char *fmt, ...);
```

It is somewhat similar to the C function `sprintf`, in that it creates a string according to a format string and some extra arguments. Unlike `sprintf`, however, you do not need to provide a buffer. Lua dynamically creates the string for you, as large as it needs to be. The function pushes the resulting string on the stack and returns a pointer to it. You do not have to worry about buffer overflows.

Listing 28.2. Splitting a string:

```
static int l_split (lua_State *L) {
  const char *s = luaL_checkstring(L, 1);  /* subject */
  const char *sep = luaL_checkstring(L, 2);  /* separator */
  const char *e;
  int i = 1;

  lua_newtable(L);  /* result table */

  /* repeat for each separator */
  while ((e = strchr(s, *sep)) != NULL) {
    lua_pushlstring(L, s, e-s);  /* push substring */
    lua_rawseti(L, -2, i++);  /* insert it in table */
    s = e + 1;  /* skip separator */
  }

  /* insert last substring */
  lua_pushstring(L, s);
  lua_rawseti(L, -2, i);

  return 1;  /* return the table */
}
```

Currently, this function accepts only the following directives:[1]

%s	inserts a zero-terminated string
%d	inserts an integer
%f	inserts a Lua number, that is, a double
%p	inserts a pointer
%c	inserts an integer as a character
%%	inserts the character '%'

It accepts no modifiers, such as width or precision.

Both `lua_concat` and `lua_pushfstring` are useful when we want to concatenate only a few strings. However, if we need to concatenate many strings (or characters) together, a one-by-one approach can be quite inefficient, as we saw in Section 11.6. Instead, we can use the buffer facility provided by the auxiliary library.

In its simpler usage, the buffer facility works with two functions: one gives you a buffer of any size where you can write your string; the other converts the contents of the buffer into a Lua string.[2] Listing 28.3 illustrates those functions with the implementation of the `string.upper` function, right from the source file `lstrlib.c`. The first step for using a buffer from the auxiliary

---

[1]The directive %p, for pointers, is new in Lua 5.2.
[2]These two functions are new in Lua 5.2.

Listing 28.3. The `string.upper` function:

```
static int str_upper (lua_State *L) {
  size_t l;
  size_t i;
  luaL_Buffer b;
  const char *s = luaL_checklstring(L, 1, &l);
  char *p = luaL_buffinitsize(L, &b, l);
  for (i = 0; i < l; i++)
    p[i] = toupper(uchar(s[i]));
  luaL_pushresultsize(&b, l);
  return 1;
}
```

library is to declare a variable with type `luaL_Buffer`. The next step is to call `luaL_buffinitsize` to get a pointer for a buffer with the given size; you can then use this buffer freely to create your string. The last step is to call `luaL_pushresultsize` to convert the buffer contents into a new Lua string on the top of the stack. The size in this second call is the final size of the string. (Often, as in our example, this size is equal to the size of the buffer, but it can be smaller. If you do not know the exact size of the resulting string, but have an upper bound, you can conservatively allocate a larger size.)

Note that function `luaL_pushresultsize` does not get a Lua state as its first argument. After the initialization, a buffer keeps a reference to the state, so we do not need to pass it when calling other functions that manipulate buffers.

We can also use these auxlib buffers without knowing any upper bound for the size of the final result. Listing 28.4 shows a simplified implementation for the `table.concat` function. In this function, we first call `luaL_buffinit` to initialize the buffer. We then add elements to the buffer one by one, in this example using `luaL_addvalue`. Finally, `luaL_pushresult` flushes the buffer and leaves the final string at the top of the stack.

The auxiliary library offers several functions to add things to a buffer: function `luaL_addvalue` adds a Lua string that is on the top of the stack; function `luaL_addlstring` adds strings with an explicit length; function `luaL_addstring` adds zero-terminated strings; and function `luaL_addchar` adds single characters. These functions have the following prototypes:

```
void luaL_buffinit   (lua_State *L, luaL_Buffer *B);
void luaL_addvalue   (luaL_Buffer *B);
void luaL_addlstring (luaL_Buffer *B, const char *s, size_t l);
void luaL_addstring  (luaL_Buffer *B, const char *s);
void luaL_addchar    (luaL_Buffer *B, char c);
void luaL_pushresult (luaL_Buffer *B);
```

When you use the auxlib buffer, you have to worry about one detail. After you initialize a buffer, it keeps some intermediate results in the Lua stack.

Listing 28.4. A simplified implementation for `table.concat`:

```
static int tconcat (lua_State *L) {
  luaL_Buffer b;
  int i, n;
  luaL_checktype(L, 1, LUA_TTABLE);
  n = luaL_len(L, 1);
  luaL_buffinit(L, &b);
  for (i = 1; i <= n; i++) {
    lua_rawgeti(L, 1, i);  /* get string from table */
    luaL_addvalue(b);  /* add it to the buffer */
  }
  luaL_pushresult(&b);
  return 1;
}
```

Therefore, you cannot assume that the stack top will remain where it was before you started using the buffer. Moreover, although you can use the stack for other tasks while using a buffer, the push/pop count for these uses must be balanced every time you access the buffer. The exception to this rule is function `luaL_addvalue`, that assumes that the string to be added to the buffer was pushed on the top of the stack.

28.3   Storing State in C Functions

Frequently, C functions need to keep some non-local data, that is, data that outlive their invocation. In C, we typically use global (`extern`) or static variables for this need. When you are programming library functions for Lua, however, global and static variables are not a good approach. First, you cannot store a generic Lua value in a C variable. Second, a library that uses such variables will not work with multiple Lua states.

A Lua function has two basic places to store non-local data: global variables and non-local variables. The C API also offers two basic places to store non-local data: the registry and upvalues.

The *registry* is a global table that can be accessed only by C code.[3] Typically, you use it to store data to be shared among several modules. If you need to store data private to a module or to a single function, you should use upvalues.

The registry

The registry is always located at a *pseudo-index*, whose value is defined by `LUA_REGISTRYINDEX`. A pseudo-index is like an index into the stack, except that

---

[3]Actually, we can access it from Lua using the debug function `debug.getregistry`.

its associated value is not in the stack. Most functions in the Lua API that accept indices as arguments also accept pseudo-indices — the exceptions being those functions that manipulate the stack itself, such as lua_remove and lua_insert. For instance, to get a value stored with key "Key" in the registry, you can use the following call:

```
lua_getfield(L, LUA_REGISTRYINDEX, "Key");
```

The registry is a regular Lua table. As such, you can index it with any Lua value but nil. However, because all C modules share the same registry, you must choose with care what values you use as keys, to avoid collisions. String keys are particularly useful when you want to allow other independent libraries to access your data, because all they need to know is the key name. For those keys, there is no bulletproof method of choosing names, but there are some good practices, such as avoiding common names and prefixing your names with the library name or something like it. (Prefixes like lua or lualib are not good choices.)

You should never use numbers as keys in the registry, because such keys are reserved for the *reference system*. This system comprises a couple of functions in the auxiliary library that allow you to store values in a table without worrying about how to create unique names. Function luaL_ref creates new references:

```
int r = luaL_ref(L, LUA_REGISTRYINDEX);
```

The previous call pops a value from the stack, stores it into the registry with a fresh integer key, and returns this key. We call this key a *reference*.

As the name implies, we use references mainly when we need to store a reference to a Lua value inside a C structure. As we have seen, we should never store pointers to Lua strings outside the C function that retrieved them. Moreover, Lua does not even offer pointers to other objects, such as tables or functions. So, we cannot refer to Lua objects through pointers. Instead, when we need such pointers, we create a reference and store it in C.

To push the value associated with a reference r onto the stack, we simply write this:

```
lua_rawgeti(L, LUA_REGISTRYINDEX, r);
```

Finally, to release both the value and the reference, we call luaL_unref:

```
luaL_unref(L, LUA_REGISTRYINDEX, r);
```

After this call, a new call to luaL_ref may return again this reference.

The reference system treats nil as a special case. Whenever we call luaL_ref for a nil value, it does not create a new reference, but instead returns the constant reference LUA_REFNIL. The next call has no effect:

```
luaL_unref(L, LUA_REGISTRYINDEX, LUA_REFNIL);
```

The next one pushes a nil, as expected:

```
lua_rawgeti(L, LUA_REGISTRYINDEX, LUA_REFNIL);
```

The reference system also defines the constant LUA_NOREF, which is an integer different from any valid reference. It is useful to mark references as invalid.

Another bulletproof method to create keys into the registry is to use as key the address of a static variable in your code: the C link editor ensures that this key is unique among all libraries. To use this option, you need the function lua_pushlightuserdata, which pushes on the Lua stack a value representing a C pointer. The following code shows how to store and retrieve a string from the registry using this method:

```
/* variable with a unique address */
static char Key = 'k';

/* store a string */
lua_pushlightuserdata(L, (void *)&Key);  /* push address */
lua_pushstring(L, myStr);  /* push value */
lua_settable(L, LUA_REGISTRYINDEX);  /* registry[&Key] = myStr */

/* retrieve a string */
lua_pushlightuserdata(L, (void *)&Key);  /* push address */
lua_gettable(L, LUA_REGISTRYINDEX);  /* retrieve value */
myStr = lua_tostring(L, -1);  /* convert to string */
```

We will discuss light userdata in more detail in Section 29.5.

To simplify the use of variable addresses as unique keys, Lua 5.2 introduced two new functions: lua_rawgetp and lua_rawsetp. They are similar to lua_rawgeti–lua_rawseti but, instead of integers, they use C pointers (translated to light userdata) as keys. With them, we can write the previous code like this:

```
static char Key = 'k';

/* store a string */
lua_pushstring(L, myStr);
lua_rawsetp(L, LUA_REGISTRYINDEX, (void *)&Key);

/* retrieve a string */
lua_rawgetp(L, LUA_REGISTRYINDEX, (void *)&Key);
myStr = lua_tostring(L, -1);
```

Both functions use raw accesses. As the registry usually does not have a metatable, a raw access has the same behavior of a regular access, and it is slightly more efficient.

Upvalues

While the registry offers global variables, the *upvalue* mechanism implements an equivalent of C static variables that are visible only inside a particular function. Every time you create a new C function in Lua, you can associate with it any number of upvalues; each upvalue can hold a single Lua value. Later, when the function is called, it has free access to any of its upvalues, using pseudo-indices.

We call this association of a C function with its upvalues a *closure*. A C closure is a C approximation to a Lua closure. In particular, you can create different closures using the same function code, but with different upvalues.

To see a simple example, let us create a newCounter function in C.[4] This function is a factory: it returns a new counter function each time it is called. Although all counters share the same C code, each one keeps its own independent counter. The factory function is like this:

```
static int counter (lua_State *L);  /* forward declaration */

int newCounter (lua_State *L) {
  lua_pushinteger(L, 0);
  lua_pushcclosure(L, &counter, 1);
  return 1;
}
```

The key function here is lua_pushcclosure, which creates a new closure. Its second argument is the base function (counter, in the example) and the third is the number of upvalues (1, in the example). Before creating a new closure, we must push on the stack the initial values for its upvalues. In our example, we push the number 0 as the initial value for the single upvalue. As expected, lua_pushcclosure leaves the new closure on the stack, so the closure is ready to be returned as the result of newCounter.

Now, let us see the definition of counter:

```
static int counter (lua_State *L) {
  int val = lua_tointeger(L, lua_upvalueindex(1));
  lua_pushinteger(L, ++val);  /* new value */
  lua_pushvalue(L, -1);  /* duplicate it */
  lua_replace(L, lua_upvalueindex(1));  /* update upvalue */
  return 1;  /* return new value */
}
```

Here, the key element is macro lua_upvalueindex, which produces the pseudo-index of an upvalue. In particular, the expression lua_upvalueindex(1) results in the pseudo-index of the first upvalue of the running function. Again, this pseudo-index is like any stack index, except that it does not live in the stack. So, the call to lua_tointeger retrieves the current value of the first (and only) upvalue as a number. Then, function counter pushes the new value ++val, makes a copy of it, and uses one of the copies to replace the upvalue's value. Finally, it returns the other copy as its return value.

As a more advanced example, we will implement tuples using upvalues. A *tuple* is a kind of constant record with anonymous fields; you can retrieve a

---

[4]We defined this same function in Lua in Section 6.1.

specific field with a numerical index, or you can retrieve all fields at once. In our implementation, we represent tuples as functions that store their values in their upvalues. When called with a numerical argument, the function returns that specific field. When called without arguments, it returns all its fields. The following code illustrates the use of tuples:

```
x = tuple.new(10, "hi", {}, 3)
print(x(1))     --> 10
print(x(2))     --> hi
print(x())      --> 10  hi  table: 0x8087878  3
```

In C, we represent all tuples by the same function t_tuple, presented in Listing 28.5. Because we can call a tuple with or without a numeric argument, t_tuple uses luaL_optint to get its optional argument. The luaL_optint function is similar to luaL_checkint, but it does not complain if the argument is absent; instead, it returns a given default value (0, in the example).

When we index a non-existent upvalue, the result is a pseudo-value whose type is LUA_TNONE. (When we access a stack index above the current top, we also get a pseudo-value with this type LUA_TNONE.) So, our t_tuple function uses lua_isnone to test whether it has a given upvalue. However, we should never call lua_upvalueindex with a negative index, so we must check for this condition when the user provides the index. The luaL_argcheck function checks any given condition, raising an error if necessary.

The function to create tuples, t_new (also in Listing 28.5), is trivial: because its arguments are already in the stack, it just has to call lua_pushcclosure to create a closure of t_tuple with all its arguments as upvalues. Finally, array tuplelib and function luaopen_tuple (also in Listing 28.5) are the standard code to create a library tuple with that single function new.

Shared upvalues

Frequently, we need to share some values or variables among all functions in a library. Although we can use the registry for that task, we can also use upvalues.

Unlike Lua closures, C closures cannot share upvalues. Each closure has its own independent upvalues. However, we can set the upvalues of different functions to refer to a common table, so that this table becomes a common environment where all those functions can share data.

Lua 5.2 offers a function that eases the task of sharing an upvalue among all functions of a library. We have been opening C libraries with luaL_newlib. Lua implements this function as the following macro:

```
#define luaL_newlib(L,l)  \
        (luaL_newlibtable(L,l), luaL_setfuncs(L,l,0))
```

The macro luaL_newlibtable just creates a new table for the library. (We could use lua_newtable as well, but this macro uses lua_createtable to create a table with a preallocated size optimal for the number of functions in the given library.)

Listing 28.5. An implementation of tuples:

```
int t_tuple (lua_State *L) {
  int op = luaL_optint(L, 1, 0);
  if (op == 0) {  /* no arguments? */
    int i;
    /* push each valid upvalue onto the stack */
    for (i = 1; !lua_isnone(L, lua_upvalueindex(i)); i++)
      lua_pushvalue(L, lua_upvalueindex(i));
    return i - 1;  /* number of values in the stack */
  }
  else {  /* get field 'op' */
    luaL_argcheck(L, 0 < op, 1, "index out of range");
    if (lua_isnone(L, lua_upvalueindex(op)))
      return 0;  /* no such field */
    lua_pushvalue(L, lua_upvalueindex(op));
    return 1;
  }
}

int t_new (lua_State *L) {
  lua_pushcclosure(L, t_tuple, lua_gettop(L));
  return 1;
}

static const struct luaL_Reg tuplelib [] = {
  {"new", t_new},
  {NULL, NULL}
};

int luaopen_tuple (lua_State *L) {
  luaL_newlib(L, tuplelib);
  return 1;
}
```

Function `luaL_setfuncs` adds the functions in the list `l` to that new table, which is on the top of the stack.

The third parameter to `luaL_setfuncs` is what we are interested here. It tells how many upvalues the new functions in the library will have. The initial value for these upvalues should be in the stack, as happens with `lua_pushcclosure`. Therefore, to create a library where all functions share a common table as their single upvalue, we can use the following code:

```
/* create library table ('lib' is its list of functions) */
luaL_newlibtable(L, lib);
/* create shared upvalue */
lua_newtable(L);
/* add functions in list 'lib' to the new library, sharing
   previous table as upvalue */
luaL_setfuncs(L, lib, 1);
```

The last call also removes the shared table from the stack, leaving there only the new library.

Exercises

Exercise 28.1: Implement a filter function in C. It should receive a list and a predicate and return a new list with all elements from the given list that satisfy the predicate:

```
t = filter({1, 3, 20, -4, 5}, function (x) return x < 5 end)
-- t = {1, 3, -4}
```

(A predicate is just a function that tests some condition, returning a boolean.)

Exercise 28.2:   Modify function `l_split` (from Listing 28.2) so that it can work with strings containing zeros. (Among other changes, it should use `memchr` instead of `strchr`.)

Exercise 28.3: Reimplement the `transliterate` function (Exercise 21.3) in C.

Exercise 28.4:   Implement a library with a modification of `transliterate` so that the transliteration table is not given as an argument, but instead is kept by the library. Your library should offer the following functions:

```
lib.settrans (table)   -- set the transliteration table
lib.gettrans ()        -- get the transliteration table
lib.tranliterate(s)    -- transliterate 's' according to the
                          current table
```

Use the registry to keep the transliteration table.

Exercise 28.5:   Repeat the previous exercise using an upvalue to keep the transliteration table.

Exercise 28.6: Do you think it is a good design to keep the transliteration table as part of the state of the library, instead of being a parameter to `tranliterate`?

29

User-Defined Types in C

In the previous chapter, we saw how to extend Lua with new functions written in C. Now, we will see how to extend Lua with new types written in C. We will start with a small example; through the chapter, we will extend it with metamethods and other goodies.

Our running example is a quite simple type: boolean arrays. The main motivation for this example is that it does not involve complex algorithms, so we can concentrate on API issues. Nevertheless, the example is useful by itself. Of course, we can use tables to implement arrays of booleans in Lua. But a C implementation, where we store each entry in one single bit, uses less than 3% of the memory used by a table.

Our implementation will need the following definitions:

```
#include <limits.h>

#define BITS_PER_WORD (CHAR_BIT*sizeof(unsigned int))
#define I_WORD(i)     ((unsigned int)(i) / BITS_PER_WORD)
#define I_BIT(i)      (1 << ((unsigned int)(i) % BITS_PER_WORD))
```

BITS_PER_WORD is the number of bits in an unsigned integer. The macro I_WORD computes the word that stores the bit corresponding to a given index, and I_BIT computes a mask to access the correct bit inside this word.

We will represent our arrays with the following structure:

```
typedef struct NumArray {
  int size;
  unsigned int values[1];  /* variable part */
} NumArray;
```

We declare the array `values` with size 1 only as a placeholder, because C 89 does not allow an array with size 0; we will set the actual size when we allocate the array. The next expression computes the total size for an array with n elements:

```
sizeof(NumArray) + I_WORD(n - 1)*sizeof(unsigned int)
```

(We subtract one from n because the original structure already includes space for one element.)

29.1   Userdata

Our first concern is how to represent the `NumArray` structure in Lua. Lua provides a basic type specifically for this: *userdata*. A userdatum offers a raw memory area, with no predefined operations in Lua, which we can use to store anything.

The `lua_newuserdata` function allocates a block of memory with the given size, pushes the corresponding userdatum on the stack, and returns the block address:

```
void *lua_newuserdata (lua_State *L, size_t size);
```

If for some reason you need to allocate memory by other means, it is very easy to create a userdatum with the size of a pointer and to store there a pointer to the real memory block. We will see examples of this technique in Chapter 30.

Using `lua_newuserdata`, the function that creates new boolean arrays is as follows:

```
static int newarray (lua_State *L) {
  int i;
  size_t nbytes;
  NumArray *a;

  int n = luaL_checkint(L, 1);
  luaL_argcheck(L, n >= 1, 1, "invalid size");
  nbytes = sizeof(NumArray) + I_WORD(n - 1)*sizeof(unsigned int);
  a = (NumArray *)lua_newuserdata(L, nbytes);

  a->size = n;
  for (i = 0; i <= I_WORD(n - 1); i++)
    a->values[i] = 0;  /* initialize array */

  return 1;  /* new userdatum is already on the stack */
}
```

(The `luaL_checkint` macro is only a type cast over `luaL_checkinteger`.) Once `newarray` is registered in Lua, you will be able to create new arrays with a statement like `a=array.new(1000)`.

To store an entry, we will use a call like `array.set(a,index,value)`. Later we will see how to use metatables to support the more conventional syntax `a[index]=value`. For both notations, the underlying function is the same. It assumes that indices start at 1, as is usual in Lua:

```
static int setarray (lua_State *L) {
  NumArray *a = (NumArray *)lua_touserdata(L, 1);
  int index = luaL_checkint(L, 2) - 1;

  luaL_argcheck(L, a != NULL, 1, "'array' expected");
  luaL_argcheck(L, 0 <= index && index < a->size, 2,
                   "index out of range");
  luaL_checkany(L, 3);

  if (lua_toboolean(L, 3))
    a->values[I_WORD(index)] |= I_BIT(index);   /* set bit */
  else
    a->values[I_WORD(index)] &= ~I_BIT(index);  /* reset bit */
  return 0;
}
```

Because Lua accepts any value for a boolean, we use `luaL_checkany` for the third parameter: it ensures only that there is a value (any value) for this parameter. If we call `setarray` with bad arguments, we get explanatory error messages:

```
array.set(0, 11, 0)
  --> stdin:1: bad argument #1 to 'set' ('array' expected)
array.set(a, 1)
  --> stdin:1: bad argument #3 to 'set' (value expected)
```

The next function retrieves an entry:

```
static int getarray (lua_State *L) {
  NumArray *a = (NumArray *)lua_touserdata(L, 1);
  int index = luaL_checkint(L, 2) - 1;

  luaL_argcheck(L, a != NULL, 1, "'array' expected");
  luaL_argcheck(L, 0 <= index && index < a->size, 2,
                   "index out of range");

  lua_pushboolean(L, a->values[I_WORD(index)] & I_BIT(index));
  return 1;
}
```

We define another function to retrieve the size of an array:

```
static int getsize (lua_State *L) {
  NumArray *a = (NumArray *)lua_touserdata(L, 1);
  luaL_argcheck(L, a != NULL, 1, "'array' expected");
  lua_pushinteger(L, a->size);
  return 1;
}
```

Finally, we need some extra code to initialize our library:

```
static const struct luaL_Reg arraylib [] = {
  {"new", newarray},
  {"set", setarray},
  {"get", getarray},
  {"size", getsize},
  {NULL, NULL}
};

int luaopen_array (lua_State *L) {
  luaL_newlib(L, arraylib);
  return 1;
}
```

Again, we use `luaL_newlib`, from the auxiliary library. It creates a table and fills it with the pairs name–function specified by the array `arraylib`.

After opening the library, we are ready to use our new type in Lua:

```
a = array.new(1000)
print(a)                 --> userdata: 0x8064d48
print(array.size(a))     --> 1000
for i = 1, 1000 do
  array.set(a, i, i%5 == 0)
end
print(array.get(a, 10))  --> true
```

29.2 Metatables

Our current implementation has a major security hole. Suppose the user writes something like `array.set(io.stdin,1,false)`. The value in `io.stdin` is a user-datum with a pointer to a stream (`FILE*`). Because it is a userdatum, `array.set` will gladly accept it as a valid argument; the probable result will be a memory corruption (with luck you can get an index-out-of-range error instead). Such behavior is unacceptable for any Lua library. No matter how you use a library, it should neither corrupt C data nor produce a core dump from Lua.

The usual method to distinguish one type of userdata from other userdata is to create a unique metatable for that type. Every time we create a userdata, we mark it with the corresponding metatable; every time we get a userdata, we check whether it has the right metatable. Because Lua code cannot change the metatable of a userdatum, it cannot fake our code.

We also need a place to store this new metatable, so that we can access it to create new userdata and to check whether a given userdatum has the correct type. As we saw earlier, there are two options for storing the metatable: in the registry or as an upvalue for the functions in the library. It is customary, in Lua, to register any new C type into the registry, using a *type name* as the index and the metatable as the value. As with any other registry index, we must choose a type name with care, to avoid clashes. Our example will use the name "LuaBook.array" for its new type.

As usual, the auxiliary library offers some functions to help us here. The new auxiliary functions we will use are these:

```
int   luaL_newmetatable (lua_State *L, const char *tname);
void  luaL_getmetatable (lua_State *L, const char *tname);
void *luaL_checkudata    (lua_State *L, int index,
                                        const char *tname);
```

The luaL_newmetatable function creates a new table (to be used as a metatable), leaves the new table on the top of the stack, and associates the table to the given name in the registry. The luaL_getmetatable function retrieves the metatable associated with tname from the registry. Finally, luaL_checkudata checks whether the object at the given stack position is userdata with a metatable that matches the given name. It raises an error if the object does not have the correct metatable or if it is not userdata; otherwise, it returns the userdata address.

Now we can start our implementation. The first step is to change the function that opens the library. The new version must create the metatable for arrays:

```
int luaopen_array (lua_State *L) {
  luaL_newmetatable(L, "LuaBook.array");
  luaL_newlib(L, arraylib);
  return 1;
}
```

The next step is to change newarray so that it sets this metatable in all arrays that it creates:

```
static int newarray (lua_State *L) {

  <as before>

  luaL_getmetatable(L, "LuaBook.array");
  lua_setmetatable(L, -2);

  return 1;  /* new userdatum is already on the stack */
}
```

The lua_setmetatable function pops a table from the stack and sets it as the metatable of the object at the given index. In our case, this object is the new userdatum.

Finally, setarray, getarray, and getsize have to check whether they got a valid array as their first argument. To simplify their tasks we define the following macro:

```
#define checkarray(L) \
          (NumArray *)luaL_checkudata(L, 1, "LuaBook.array")
```

Using this macro, the new definition for getsize is straightforward:

```
static int getsize (lua_State *L) {
  NumArray *a = checkarray(L);
  lua_pushinteger(L, a->size);
  return 1;
}
```

Because setarray and getarray also share code to check the index as their second argument, we factor out their common parts in the following function:

```
static unsigned int *getindex (lua_State *L,
                                unsigned int *mask) {
  NumArray *a = checkarray(L);
  int index = luaL_checkint(L, 2) - 1;

  luaL_argcheck(L, 0 <= index && index < a->size, 2,
                "index out of range");

  /* return element address */
  *mask = I_BIT(index);
  return &a->values[I_WORD(index)];
}
```

After the definition of getindex, setarray and getarray are straightforward:

```
static int setarray (lua_State *L) {
  unsigned int mask;
  unsigned int *entry = getindex(L, &mask);
  luaL_checkany(L, 3);
  if (lua_toboolean(L, 3))
    *entry |= mask;
  else
    *entry &= ~mask;

  return 0;
}

static int getarray (lua_State *L) {
  unsigned int mask;
  unsigned int *entry = getindex(L, &mask);
  lua_pushboolean(L, *entry & mask);
  return 1;
}
```

Now, if you try something like array.get(io.stdin, 10), you will get a proper error message:

```
error: bad argument #1 to 'get' ('array' expected)
```

29.3 Object-Oriented Access

Our next step is to transform our new type into an object, so that we can operate on its instances using the usual object-oriented syntax, like this:

```
a = array.new(1000)
print(a:size())      --> 1000
a:set(10, true)
print(a:get(10))     --> true
```

Remember that a:size() is equivalent to a.size(a). Therefore, we have to arrange for the expression a.size to return our getsize function. The key mechanism here is the __index metamethod. For tables, Lua calls this metamethod whenever it cannot find a value for a given key. For userdata, Lua calls it in every access, because userdata have no keys at all.

Assume that we run the following code:

```
local metaarray = getmetatable(array.new(1))
metaarray.__index = metaarray
metaarray.set = array.set
metaarray.get = array.get
metaarray.size = array.size
```

In the first line, we create an array only to get its metatable, which we assign to metaarray. (We cannot set the metatable of a userdata from Lua, but we can get it.) Then we set metaarray.__index to metaarray. When we evaluate a.size, Lua cannot find the key "size" in object a, because the object is a userdatum. Therefore, Lua tries to get this value from the field __index of the metatable of a, which happens to be metaarray itself. But metaarray.size is array.size, so a.size(a) results in array.size(a), as we wanted.

Of course, we can write the same thing in C. We can do even better: now that arrays are objects, with their own operations, we do not need to have these operations in the table array anymore. The only function that our library still has to export is new, to create new arrays. All other operations come only as methods. The C code can register them directly as such.

The operations getsize, getarray, and setarray do not change from our previous approach. What will change is how we register them. That is, we have to change the code that opens the library. First, we need two separate function lists: one for regular functions and one for methods.

```
static const struct luaL_Reg arraylib_f [] = {
  {"new", newarray},
  {NULL, NULL}
};

static const struct luaL_Reg arraylib_m [] = {
  {"set", setarray},
  {"get", getarray},
  {"size", getsize},
  {NULL, NULL}
};
```

The new version of the open function `luaopen_array` has to create the metatable, assign it to its own `__index` field, register all methods there, and create and fill the array table:

```
int luaopen_array (lua_State *L) {
  luaL_newmetatable(L, "LuaBook.array");

  /* metatable.__index = metatable */
  lua_pushvalue(L, -1);  /* duplicates the metatable */
  lua_setfield(L, -2, "__index");

  luaL_setfuncs(L, arraylib_m, 0);

  luaL_newlib(L, arraylib_f);
  return 1;
}
```

Here we use again `luaL_setfuncs`, to set the functions from the `arraylib_m` list into the metatable, which is on the top of the stack. Then we use `luaL_newlib` to create a new table and registers the functions from list `arraylib_f` there (only new, in this case).

As a final touch, we will add a `__tostring` method to our new type, so that `print(a)` prints "array" plus the size of the array inside parentheses; something like "array(1000)". The function itself is here:

```
int array2string (lua_State *L) {
  NumArray *a = checkarray(L);
  lua_pushfstring(L, "array(%d)", a->size);
  return 1;
}
```

The `lua_pushfstring` call formats the string and leaves it on the stack top. We also have to add `array2string` to the list `arraylib_m`, to include it in the metatable of array objects:

```
static const struct luaL_Reg arraylib_m [] = {
  {"__tostring", array2string},
  <other methods>
};
```

29.4 Array Access

An alternative to the object-oriented notation is to use a regular array notation to access our arrays. Instead of writing a:get(i), we could simply write a[i]. For our example, this is easy to do, because our functions setarray and getarray already receive their arguments in the order that they are given to the corresponding metamethods. A quick solution is to define these metamethods right into our Lua code:

```
local metaarray = getmetatable(array.new(1))
metaarray.__index = array.get
metaarray.__newindex = array.set
metaarray.__len = array.size
```

(We must run this code on the original implementation for arrays, without the modifications for object-oriented access.) That is all we need to use the standard syntax:

```
a = array.new(1000)
a[10] = true          -- 'setarray'
print(a[10])          -- 'getarray'    --> true
print(#a)             -- 'getsize'     --> 1000
```

If we prefer, we can register these metamethods in our C code. For this, we change again our initialization function:

```
static const struct luaL_Reg arraylib_f [] = {
  {"new", newarray},
  {NULL, NULL}
};

static const struct luaL_Reg arraylib_m [] = {
  {"__newindex", setarray},
  {"__index", getarray},
  {"__len", getsize},
  {"__tostring", array2string},
  {NULL, NULL}
};

int luaopen_array (lua_State *L) {
  luaL_newmetatable(L, "LuaBook.array");
  luaL_setfuncs(L, arraylib_m, 0);
  luaL_newlib(L, arraylib_f);
  return 1;
}
```

In this new version, again we have only one public function, new. All other functions are available only as metamethods for specific operations.

29.5   Light Userdata

The kind of userdata that we have been using until now is called *full userdata*. Lua offers another kind of userdata, called *light userdata*.

A light userdatum is a value that represents a C pointer (that is, a void* value). A light userdata is a value, not an object; we do not create them (in the same way that we do not create numbers). To put a light userdatum into the stack, we call lua_pushlightuserdata:

```
void lua_pushlightuserdata (lua_State *L, void *p);
```

Despite their common name, light userdata and full userdata are quite different things. Light userdata are not buffers, but single pointers. They have no metatables. Like numbers, light userdata are not managed by the garbage collector.

Sometimes we use light userdata as a cheap alternative to full userdata. This is not a typical use, however. First, light userdata do not have metatables, so there is no way to know their types. Second, despite the name, full userdata are inexpensive, too. They add little overhead compared to a malloc for the given memory size.

The real use of light userdata comes from equality. As a full userdata is an object, it is only equal to itself. A light userdata, on the other hand, represents a C pointer value. As such, it is equal to any userdata that represents the same pointer. Therefore, we can use light userdata to find C objects inside Lua.

We have already seen a typical use of light userdata, as keys in the registry (Section 28.3). There, the equality of light userdata was a fundamental ingredient. Every time we push the same address with lua_pushlightuserdata, we get the same Lua value and, therefore, the same entry in the registry.

Another typical scenario is the need to retrieve a full userdata given its C address. Suppose we are implementing a binding between Lua and a Window system. In this binding, we use full userdata to represent windows. Each userdatum can contain the whole window structure or only a pointer to a window created by the system. When there is an event inside a window (e.g., a mouse click), the system calls a specific callback, identifying the window by its address. To pass the callback to Lua, we must find the userdata that represents the given window. To find this userdata, we can keep a table where the indices are light userdata with the window addresses and the values are the full userdata that represent the windows in Lua. Once we have a window address, we push it into the API stack as a light userdata and use this userdata as an index into that table. (Probably that table should have weak values. Otherwise, those full userdata would never be collected.)

Exercises

Exercise 29.1: Modify the implementation of setarray so that it accepts only boolean values.

Exercise 29.2: We can see a boolean array as a set of integers (the indices with true values in the array). Add to the implementation of boolean arrays functions to compute the union and intersection of two arrays. These functions should receive two arrays and return a new one, without modifying its parameters.

Exercise 29.3: Modify the implementation of the __tostring metamethod so that it shows the full contents of the array in an appropriate way. Use the buffer facility (Section 28.2) to create the resulting string.

Exercise 29.4: Based on the example for boolean arrays, implement a small C library for integer arrays.

30

Managing Resources

In our implementation of boolean arrays in the previous chapter, we did not need to worry about managing resources. Those arrays need only memory. Each userdatum representing an array has its own memory, which is managed by Lua. When an array becomes garbage (that is, inaccessible by the program), Lua eventually collects it and frees its memory.

Life is not always that easy. Sometimes, an object needs other resources besides raw memory, such as file descriptors, window handles, and the like. (Often these resources are just memory too, but managed by some other part of the system.) In such cases, when the object becomes garbage and is collected, somehow these other resources must be released too.

As we have seen in Section 17.6, Lua provides finalizers in the form of the __gc metamethod. To illustrate the use of this metamethod in C and of the API as a whole, in this chapter we will develop two bindings from Lua to external facilities. The first example is another implementation for a function to traverse a directory. The second (and more substantial) example is a binding to *Expat*, an open source XML parser.

30.1 A Directory Iterator

In Section 27.1, we implemented a dir function that returned a table with all files from a given directory. Our new implementation will return an iterator that returns a new entry each time it is called. With this new implementation, we will be able to traverse a directory with a loop like this:

```
for fname in dir.open(".") do
  print(fname)
end
```

To iterate over a directory, in C, we need a `DIR` structure. Instances of `DIR` are created by `opendir` and must be explicitly released with a call to `closedir`. Our previous implementation of `dir` kept its `DIR` instance as a local variable and closed this instance after retrieving the last file name. Our new implementation cannot keep this `DIR` instance in a local variable, because it must query this value over several calls. Moreover, it cannot close the directory only after retrieving the last name; if the program breaks the loop, the iterator will never retrieve this last name. Therefore, to make sure that the `DIR` instance is always released, we store its address in a userdatum and use the `__gc` metamethod of this userdatum to release the directory structure.

Despite its central role in our implementation, this userdatum representing a directory does not need to be visible from Lua. The `dir` function returns an iterator function; this function is what Lua sees. The directory can be an upvalue of the iterator function. As such, the iterator function has direct access to this structure, but Lua code has not (and does not need to).

In all, we need three C functions. First, we need the `dir.open` function, a factory that Lua calls to create iterators; it must open a `DIR` structure and create a closure of the iterator function with this structure as an upvalue. Second, we need the iterator function. Third, we need the `__gc` metamethod, which closes a `DIR` structure. As usual, we also need an extra function to make initial arrangements, such as to create and initialize a metatable for directories.

Let us start our code with the `dir.open` function, shown in Listing 30.1. A subtle point in this function is that it must create the userdatum before opening the directory. If it first opens the directory, and then the call to `lua_newuserdata` raises a memory error, the function loses and leaks the `DIR` structure. With the correct order, the `DIR` structure, once created, is immediately associated with the userdatum; whatever happens after that, the `__gc` metamethod will eventually release the structure.

The next function is `dir_iter` (in Listing 30.2), the iterator itself. Its code is straightforward. It gets the `DIR`-structure address from its upvalue and calls `readdir` to read the next entry.

Function `dir_gc` (also in Listing 30.2) is the `__gc` metamethod. This metamethod closes a directory, but it must take one precaution: because we create the userdatum before opening the directory, this userdatum will be collected whatever the result of `opendir`. If `opendir` fails, there will be nothing to close.

The last function in Listing 30.2, `luaopen_dir`, is the function that opens this one-function library.

This complete example has an interesting subtlety. At first, it may seem that `dir_gc` should check whether its argument is a directory. Otherwise, a malicious user could call it with another kind of userdata (a file, for instance), with disastrous consequences. However, there is no way for a Lua program to access this function: it is stored only in the metatable of directories, which in

Listing 30.1. The dir.open factory function:

```
#include <dirent.h>
#include <errno.h>
#include <string.h>

#include "lua.h"
#include "lauxlib.h"

/* forward declaration for the iterator function */
static int dir_iter (lua_State *L);

static int l_dir (lua_State *L) {
  const char *path = luaL_checkstring(L, 1);

  /* create a userdatum to store a DIR address */
  DIR **d = (DIR **)lua_newuserdata(L, sizeof(DIR *));

  /* set its metatable */
  luaL_getmetatable(L, "LuaBook.dir");
  lua_setmetatable(L, -2);

  /* try to open the given directory */
  *d = opendir(path);
  if (*d == NULL)  /* error opening the directory? */
    luaL_error(L, "cannot open %s: %s", path, strerror(errno));

  /* creates and returns the iterator function;
     its sole upvalue, the directory userdatum,
     is already on the top of the stack */
  lua_pushcclosure(L, dir_iter, 1);
  return 1;
}
```

turn are stored as upvalues of the iteration functions. Lua programs cannot access these directories.

30.2   An XML Parser

Now we will look at a simplified implementation of a binding between Lua and Expat, which we will call lxp. Expat is an open source XML 1.0 parser written in C. It implements SAX, the *Simple API for XML*. SAX is an event-based API. This means that a SAX parser reads an XML document and, as it goes, reports to the application what it finds, through callbacks. For instance, if we instruct Expat to parse a string like "<tag cap="5">hi</tag>", it will generate three events: a *start-element* event, when it reads the substring "<tag cap="5">"; a

Listing 30.2. Other functions for the `dir` library:

```c
static int dir_iter (lua_State *L) {
  DIR *d = *(DIR **)lua_touserdata(L, lua_upvalueindex(1));
  struct dirent *entry;
  if ((entry = readdir(d)) != NULL) {
    lua_pushstring(L, entry->d_name);
    return 1;
  }
  else return 0;   /* no more values to return */
}

static int dir_gc (lua_State *L) {
  DIR *d = *(DIR **)lua_touserdata(L, 1);
  if (d) closedir(d);
  return 0;
}

static const struct luaL_Reg dirlib [] = {
  {"open", l_dir},
  {NULL, NULL}
};

int luaopen_dir (lua_State *L) {
  luaL_newmetatable(L, "LuaBook.dir");

  /* set its __gc field */
  lua_pushcfunction(L, dir_gc);
  lua_setfield(L, -2, "__gc");

  /* create the library */
  luaL_newlib(L, dirlib);
  return 1;
}
```

text event (also called a *character data* event), when it reads "hi"; and an *end-element* event, when it reads "</tag>". Each of these events calls an appropriate *callback handler* in the application.

Here we will not cover the entire Expat library. We will concentrate only on those parts that illustrate new techniques for interacting with Lua. Although Expat handles more than a dozen different events, we will consider only the three events that we saw in the previous example (start elements, end elements, and text).[1]

The part of the Expat API that we need for this example is small. First, we need the functions to create and destroy an Expat parser:

```
XML_Parser XML_ParserCreate (const char *encoding);
void XML_ParserFree (XML_Parser p);
```

The encoding argument is optional; we will use NULL in our binding.

After we have a parser, we must register its callback handlers:

```
void XML_SetElementHandler(XML_Parser p,
                           XML_StartElementHandler start,
                           XML_EndElementHandler end);

void XML_SetCharacterDataHandler(XML_Parser p,
                                 XML_CharacterDataHandler hndl);
```

The first function registers handlers for start and end elements. The second function registers handlers for text (*character data*, in XML parlance).

All callback handlers receive some user data as their first parameter. The start-element handler receives also the tag name and its attributes:

```
typedef void (*XML_StartElementHandler)(void *uData,
                                        const char *name,
                                        const char **atts);
```

The attributes come as a NULL-terminated array of strings, where each pair of consecutive strings holds an attribute name and its value. The end-element handler has only one extra parameter, the tag name:

```
typedef void (*XML_EndElementHandler)(void *uData,
                                      const char *name);
```

Finally, a text handler receives only the text as an extra parameter. This text string is not null-terminated; instead, it has an explicit length:

```
typedef void (*XML_CharacterDataHandler)(void *uData,
                                         const char *s,
                                         int len);
```

To feed text to Expat, we use the following function:

```
int XML_Parse (XML_Parser p, const char *s, int len, int isLast);
```

---

[1]The package LuaExpat offers a quite complete interface to Expat.

Expat receives the document to be parsed in pieces, through successive calls
to XML_Parse. The last argument to XML_Parse, isLast, informs Expat whether
that piece is the last one of a document. Notice that each piece of text does
not need to be zero terminated; instead, we supply an explicit length. The
XML_Parse function returns zero if it detects a parse error. (Expat also provides
functions to retrieve error information, but we will ignore them here, for the
sake of simplicity.)

The last function we need from Expat allows us to set the user data that will
be passed to the handlers:

```
void XML_SetUserData (XML_Parser p, void *uData);
```

Now let us have a look at how we can use this library in Lua. A first approach
is a direct approach: simply export all those functions to Lua. A better approach
is to adapt the functionality to Lua. For instance, because Lua is untyped, we
do not need different functions to set each kind of callback. Better yet, we can
avoid the callback registering functions altogether. Instead, when we create a
parser, we give a callback table that contains all callback handlers, each with
an appropriate key. For instance, if we want to print a layout of a document, we
could use the following callback table:

```
local count = 0

callbacks = {
  StartElement = function (parser, tagname)
    io.write("+ ", string.rep("  ", count), tagname, "\n")
    count = count + 1
  end,

  EndElement = function (parser, tagname)
    count = count - 1
    io.write("- ", string.rep("  ", count), tagname, "\n")
  end,
}
```

Fed with the input "<to> <yes/> </to>", these handlers would print this output:

```
+ to
+   yes
-   yes
- to
```

With this API, we do not need functions to manipulate callbacks. We manipulate them directly in the callback table. Thus, the whole API needs only three
functions: one to create parsers, one to parse a piece of text, and one to close a
parser. Actually, we will implement the last two functions as methods of parser
objects. A typical use of the API could be like this:

```
local lxp = require"lxp"
```

```
p = lxp.new(callbacks)          -- create new parser
for l in io.lines() do          -- iterate over input lines
  assert(p:parse(l))            -- parse the line
  assert(p:parse("\n"))         -- add newline
end
assert(p:parse())               -- finish document
p:close()
```

Now let us turn our attention to the implementation. The first decision is how to represent a parser in Lua. It is quite natural to use a userdatum, but what do we need to put inside it? At least, we must keep the actual Expat parser and the callback table. We cannot store a Lua table inside a userdatum (or inside any C structure), but Lua allows each userdata to have a *user value*, which can be any Lua table, associated to it.[2] We must store also a Lua state into a parser object, because these parser objects are all that an Expat callback receives, and the callbacks need to call Lua. Therefore, the definition for a parser object is as follows:

```
#include <stdlib.h>
#include "expat.h"
#include "lua.h"
#include "lauxlib.h"

typedef struct lxp_userdata {
  XML_Parser parser;          /* associated expat parser */
  lua_State *L;
} lxp_userdata;
```

The next step is the function that creates parser objects, lxp_make_parser. Listing 30.3 shows its code. This function has four main steps:

- Its first step follows a common pattern: it first creates a userdatum; then it pre-initializes the userdatum with consistent values; and finally sets its metatable. The reason for the pre-initialization is subtle: if there is any error during the initialization, we must make sure that the finalizer (the __gc metamethod) will find the userdata in a consistent state.

- In step 2, the function creates an Expat parser, stores it in the userdatum, and checks for errors.

- Step 3 ensures that the first argument to the function is actually a table (the callback table), and sets it as the user value for the new userdatum.

- The last step initializes the Expat parser. It sets the userdatum as the object to be passed to callback functions and it sets the callback functions. Notice that these callback functions are the same for all parsers; after all, it is impossible to dynamically create new functions in C. Instead, those fixed C functions will use the callback table to decide which Lua functions they should call each time.

---

[2]In Lua 5.1, the userdata's environment fills the role of the user value.

Listing 30.3. Function to create XML parser objects:

```
/* forward declarations for callback functions */
static void f_StartElement (void *ud,
                            const char *name,
                            const char **atts);
static void f_CharData (void *ud, const char *s, int len);
static void f_EndElement (void *ud, const char *name);

static int lxp_make_parser (lua_State *L) {
  XML_Parser p;

  /* (1) create a parser object */
  lxp_userdata *xpu = (lxp_userdata *)lua_newuserdata(L,
                                    sizeof(lxp_userdata));

  /* pre-initialize it, in case of error */
  xpu->parser = NULL;

  /* set its metatable */
  luaL_getmetatable(L, "Expat");
  lua_setmetatable(L, -2);

  /* (2) create the Expat parser */
  p = xpu->parser = XML_ParserCreate(NULL);
  if (!p)
    luaL_error(L, "XML_ParserCreate failed");

  /* (3) check and store the callback table */
  luaL_checktype(L, 1, LUA_TTABLE);
  lua_pushvalue(L, 1);  /* put table on the stack top */
  lua_setuservalue(L, -2);   /* set it as the user value */

  /* (4) configure Expat parser */
  XML_SetUserData(p, xpu);
  XML_SetElementHandler(p, f_StartElement, f_EndElement);
  XML_SetCharacterDataHandler(p, f_CharData);
  return 1;
}
```

Listing 30.4. Function to parse an XML fragment:

```
static int lxp_parse (lua_State *L) {
  int status;
  size_t len;
  const char *s;
  lxp_userdata *xpu;

  /* get and check first argument (should be a parser) */
  xpu = (lxp_userdata *)luaL_checkudata(L, 1, "Expat");

  /* check whether it is not closed */
  luaL_argcheck(L, xpu->parser != NULL, 1, "parser is closed");

  /* get second argument (a string) */
  s = luaL_optlstring(L, 2, NULL, &len);

  /* put callback table at stack index 3 */
  lua_settop(L, 2);
  lua_getuservalue(L, 1);
  xpu->L = L;   /* set Lua state */

  /* call Expat to parse string */
  status = XML_Parse(xpu->parser, s, (int)len, s == NULL);

  /* return error code */
  lua_pushboolean(L, status);
  return 1;
}
```

The next step is the parse method `lxp_parse` (Listing 30.4), which parses a piece of XML data. It gets two arguments: the parser object (the *self* of the method) and an optional piece of XML data. When called without any data, it informs Expat that the document has no more parts.

When `lxp_parse` calls `XML_Parse`, the latter function will call the handlers for each relevant element that it finds in the given piece of document. These handlers will need to access the callback table, so `lxp_parse` puts this table at stack index 3 (right after the parameters). There is one more detail in the call to `XML_Parse`: remember that the last argument to this function tells Expat whether the given piece of text is the last one. When we call parse without an argument, s will be NULL, so this last argument will be true.

Now let us turn our attention to the callback functions `f_StartElement`, `f_EndElement`, and `f_CharData`. All these three functions have a similar structure: each checks whether the callback table defines a Lua handler for its specific event and, if so, prepares the arguments and then calls this Lua handler.

Let us first see the `f_CharData` handler, in Listing 30.5. Its code is quite

Listing 30.5. Handler for character data:

```
static void f_CharData (void *ud, const char *s, int len) {
  lxp_userdata *xpu = (lxp_userdata *)ud;
  lua_State *L = xpu->L;

  /* get handler */
  lua_getfield(L, 3, "CharacterData");
  if (lua_isnil(L, -1)) {  /* no handler? */
    lua_pop(L, 1);
    return;
  }

  lua_pushvalue(L, 1);  /* push the parser ('self') */
  lua_pushlstring(L, s, len);  /* push Char data */
  lua_call(L, 2, 0);  /* call the handler */
}
```

simple. The handler receives a `lxp_userdata` structure as its first argument,
due to our call to `XML_SetUserData` when we created the parser. After retrieving
the Lua state, the handler can access the callback table at stack index 3, set by
`lxp_parse`, and the parser itself at stack index 1. Then it calls its corresponding handler in Lua (when present), with two arguments: the parser and the
character data (a string).

The `f_EndElement` handler is quite similar to `f_CharData`; see Listing 30.6. It
also calls its corresponding Lua handler with two arguments — the parser and
the tag name (again a string, but now null-terminated).

Listing 30.7 shows the last handler, `f_StartElement`. It calls Lua with three
arguments: the parser, the tag name, and a list of attributes. This handler is a
little more complex than the others, because it needs to translate the tag's list
of attributes into Lua. It uses a quite natural translation, building a table that
associates attribute names to their values. For instance, a start tag like

```
<to method="post" priority="high">
```

generates the following table of attributes:

```
{method = "post", priority = "high"}
```

The last method for parsers is `close`, in Listing 30.8. When we close a parser,
we have to free its resources, namely the Expat structure. Remember that, due
to occasional errors during its creation, a parser may not have this resource.
Notice how we keep the parser in a consistent state as we close it, so there is
no problem if we try to close it again or when the garbage collector finalizes it.
Actually, we will use exactly this function as the finalizer. This ensures that
every parser eventually frees its resources, even if the programmer does not
close it.

Listing 30.6. Handler for end elements:

```
static void f_EndElement (void *ud, const char *name) {
  lxp_userdata *xpu = (lxp_userdata *)ud;
  lua_State *L = xpu->L;

  lua_getfield(L, 3, "EndElement");
  if (lua_isnil(L, -1)) {  /* no handler? */
    lua_pop(L, 1);
    return;
  }

  lua_pushvalue(L, 1);  /* push the parser ('self') */
  lua_pushstring(L, name);  /* push tag name */
  lua_call(L, 2, 0);  /* call the handler */
}
```

Listing 30.7. Handler for start elements:

```
static void f_StartElement (void *ud,
                            const char *name,
                            const char **atts) {
  lxp_userdata *xpu = (lxp_userdata *)ud;
  lua_State *L = xpu->L;

  lua_getfield(L, 3, "StartElement");
  if (lua_isnil(L, -1)) {  /* no handler? */
    lua_pop(L, 1);
    return;
  }

  lua_pushvalue(L, 1);  /* push the parser ('self') */
  lua_pushstring(L, name);  /* push tag name */

  /* create and fill the attribute table */
  lua_newtable(L);
  for (; *atts; atts += 2) {
    lua_pushstring(L, *(atts + 1));
    lua_setfield(L, -2, *atts);  /* table[*atts] = *(atts+1) */
  }

  lua_call(L, 3, 0);  /* call the handler */
}
```

Listing 30.8. Method to close an XML parser:

```
static int lxp_close (lua_State *L) {
  lxp_userdata *xpu =
                (lxp_userdata *)luaL_checkudata(L, 1, "Expat");

  /* free Expat parser (if there is one) */
  if (xpu->parser)
    XML_ParserFree(xpu->parser);
  xpu->parser = NULL;  /* avoids closing it again */
  return 0;
}
```

Listing 30.9 is the final step: it shows luaopen_lxp, which opens the library putting all previous parts together. We use here the same scheme that we used in the object-oriented boolean-array example from Section 29.3: we create a metatable, make its __index field point to itself, and put all methods inside it. For that, we need a list with the parser methods (lxp_meths). We also need a list with the functions of this library (lxp_funcs). As is common with object-oriented libraries, this list has a single function, which creates new parsers.

Exercises

Exercise 30.1: Modify the dir_iter function in the directory example so that it closes the DIR structure when it reaches the end of the traversal. With this change, the program does not need to wait for a garbage collection to release a resource that it knows it will not need anymore.

(When you close the directory, you should set the address stored in the userdatum to NULL, to signal to the finalizer that the directory is already closed. Also, function dir_iter will have to check whether the directory is not closed before using it.)

Exercise 30.2: In the lxp example, the handler for start elements receives a table with the element attributes. In that table, the original order in which the attributes appear inside the element is lost. How can you pass this information to the callback?

Exercise 30.3:   In the lxp example, we used user values to associate the callback table with the userdatum that represents a parser. This choice created a small problem, because what the C callbacks receive is the lxp_userdata structure, and that structure does not offer direct access to the table. We solved this problem by storing the callback table at a fixed stack index during the parse of each fragment.

An alternative design would be to associate the callback table with the userdatum through references (Section 28.3): we create a reference to the callback

Listing 30.9. Initialization code for the `lxp` library:

```
static const struct luaL_Reg lxp_meths[] = {
  {"parse", lxp_parse},
  {"close", lxp_close},
  {"__gc", lxp_close},
  {NULL, NULL}
};

static const struct luaL_Reg lxp_funcs[] = {
  {"new", lxp_make_parser},
  {NULL, NULL}
};

int luaopen_lxp (lua_State *L) {
  /* create metatable */
  luaL_newmetatable(L, "Expat");

  /* metatable.__index = metatable */
  lua_pushvalue(L, -1);
  lua_setfield(L, -2, "__index");

  /* register methods */
  luaL_setfuncs(L, lxp_meths, 0);

  /* register functions (only lxp.new) */
  luaL_newlib(L, lxp_funcs);
  return 1;
}
```

table and store the reference (an integer) in the `lxp_userdata` structure. Implement this alternative. Do not forget to release the reference when closing the parser.

31

Threads and States

Lua does not support true multithreading, that is, preemptive threads sharing memory. There are two reasons for this lack of support: The first reason is that ANSI C does not offer it, and so there is no portable way to implement this mechanism in Lua. The second and stronger reason is that we do not think multithreading is a good idea for Lua.

Multithreading was developed for low-level programming. Synchronization mechanisms like semaphores and monitors were proposed in the context of operating systems (and seasoned programmers), not application programs. It is very hard to find and correct bugs related to multithreading, and some of these bugs can lead to security breaches. Moreover, multithreading can lead to performance penalties related to the need of synchronization in some critical parts of a program, such as the memory allocator.

The problems with multithreading arise from the combination of preemptive threads and shared memory, so we can avoid them either using non-preemptive threads or not sharing memory. Lua offers support for both. Lua threads (also known as coroutines) are collaborative, and therefore avoid the problems created by unpredictable thread switching. Lua states share no memory, and therefore form a good base for concurrency in Lua. We will cover both options in this chapter.

31.1 Multiple Threads

A *thread* is the essence of a coroutine in Lua. We can think of a coroutine as a thread plus a nice interface, or we can think of a thread as a coroutine with a lower-level API.

From the C API perspective, you may find it useful to think of a thread as a stack — which is what a thread actually is, from an implementation point of view. Each stack keeps information about the pending calls of a thread and the parameters and local variables of each call. In other words, a stack has all the information that a thread needs to continue running. So, multiple threads mean multiple independent stacks.

When we call most functions from the Lua–C API, that function operates on a specific stack. For instance, `lua_pushnumber` must push the number on a specific stack; `lua_pcall` needs a call stack. How does Lua know which stack to use? What do we do to push a number on a different stack? The secret is that the type `lua_State`, the first argument to these functions, represents not only a Lua state, but also a thread within that state. (Many people argue that this type should be called `lua_Thread`.)

Whenever you create a Lua state, Lua automatically creates a new thread within this state and returns a `lua_State` representing this thread. This *main thread* is never collected. It is released together with the state, when you close the state with `lua_close`.

You can create other threads in a state calling `lua_newthread`:

```
lua_State *lua_newthread (lua_State *L);
```

This function returns a `lua_State` pointer representing the new thread, and also pushes the new thread on the stack, as a value of type "thread". For instance, after the statement

```
L1 = lua_newthread(L);
```

we have two threads, L1 and L, both referring internally to the same Lua state. Each thread has its own stack. The new thread L1 starts with an empty stack; the old thread L has the new thread on the top of its stack:

```
printf("%d\n", lua_gettop(L1));          --> 0
printf("%s\n", luaL_typename(L, -1));    --> thread
```

Except for the main thread, threads are subject to garbage collection, like any other Lua object. When you create a new thread, the value pushed on the stack ensures that the thread is not garbage. You should never use a thread that is not properly anchored in the state. (The main thread is internally anchored, so you do not have to worry about it.) Any call to the Lua API may collect a non-anchored thread, even a call using this thread. For instance, consider the following fragment:

```
lua_State *L1 = lua_newthread (L);
lua_pop(L, 1);          /* L1 now is garbage for Lua */
lua_pushstring(L1, "hello");
```

The call to `lua_pushstring` may trigger the garbage collector and collect L1 (crashing the application), despite the fact that L1 is in use. To avoid this, always keep a reference to the threads you are using, for instance in the stack of an anchored thread or in the registry.

Once we have a new thread, we can use it like the main thread. We can push on and pop elements from its stack, we can use it to call functions, and the like. For instance, the following code does the call f(5) in the new thread and then moves the result to the old thread:

```
lua_getglobal(L1, "f");     /* assume a global function 'f' */
lua_pushinteger(L1, 5);
lua_call(L1, 1, 1);
lua_xmove(L1, L, 1);
```

The lua_xmove function moves Lua values between two stacks in the same state. A call like lua_xmove(F,T,n) pops n elements from the stack F and pushes them on T.

For these uses, however, we do not need a new thread; we could just use the main thread as well. The main point of using multiple threads is to implement coroutines, so that we can suspend their executions and resume them later. For that, we need the lua_resume function:

```
int lua_resume (lua_State *L, lua_State *from, int narg);
```

To start running a coroutine, we use lua_resume as we use lua_pcall: we push the function to be called, push its arguments, and call lua_resume passing in narg the number of arguments. (The from parameter is the thread that is doing the call.) The behavior is also much like lua_pcall, with three differences. First, lua_resume does not have a parameter for the number of wanted results; it always returns all results from the called function. Second, it does not have a parameter for a message handler; an error does not unwind the stack, so you can inspect the stack after the error. Third, if the running function yields, lua_resume returns a special code LUA_YIELD and leaves the thread in a state that can be resumed later.

When lua_resume returns LUA_YIELD, the visible part of the thread's stack contains only the values passed to yield. A call to lua_gettop will return the number of yielded values. To move these values to another thread, we can use lua_xmove.

To resume a suspended thread, we call lua_resume again. In such calls, Lua assumes that all values in the stack are to be returned by the call to yield. For instance, if you do not touch the thread's stack between a return from lua_resume and the next resume, yield will return exactly the values it yielded.

Typically, we start a coroutine with a Lua function as its body. This Lua function can call other functions, and any of these functions can occasionally yield, finishing the call to lua_resume. For instance, assume the following definitions:

```
function foo (x)  coroutine.yield(10, x)  end

function fool (x)  foo(x + 1); return 3  end
```

Now, we run this C code:

```
lua_State *L1 = lua_newthread(L);
lua_getglobal(L1, "foo1");
lua_pushinteger(L1, 20);
lua_resume(L1, L, 1);
```

The call to lua_resume will return LUA_YIELD, to signal that the thread yielded.
At this point, the L1 stack has the values given to yield:

```
printf("%d\n", lua_gettop(L1));           --> 2
printf("%d\n", lua_tointeger(L1, 1));     --> 10
printf("%d\n", lua_tointeger(L1, 2));     --> 21
```

When we resume the thread again, it continues from where it stopped (the call
to yield). From there, foo returns to foo1, which in turn returns to lua_resume:

```
lua_resume(L1, L, 0);
printf("%d\n", lua_gettop(L1));           --> 1
printf("%d\n", lua_tointeger(L1, 1));     --> 3
```

This second call to lua_resume will return LUA_OK, which means a normal return.

A coroutine can also call C functions, which can call back other Lua functions.
We have already discussed how to use continuations to allow those Lua functions
to yield (Section 27.2). A C function itself can yield, too. In that case, it also must
provide a continuation function to be called when the thread resumes. To yield,
a C function must call the following function:

```
int lua_yieldk (lua_State *L, int nresults, int ctx,
                              lua_CFunction k);
```

We should always use this function in a return statement, such as here:

```
static inf myCfunction (lua_State *L) {
  ...
    return lua_yieldk(L, nresults, ctx, k);
}
```

This call immediately suspends the running coroutine. The nresults parameter
is the number of values in the stack to be returned to the respective lua_resume;
ctx is the context information to be passed to the continuation; and k is the
continuation function. When the coroutine resumes, control goes directly to the
continuation function k. After yielding, myCfunction cannot do anything else; it
must delegate any further work to its continuation.

Let us see a typical hypothetical example. Assume we want to code a function
that reads some data, yielding while the data is not available. We may write the
function in C like this:

```
int prim_read (lua_State *L) {
  if (nothing_to_read())
    return lua_yieldk(L, 0, 0, &prim_read);
  lua_pushstring(L, read_some_data());
  return 1;
}
```

If the function has some data to read, it reads and returns this data. Otherwise, if it has nothing to read, it yields. When the thread resumes, it calls the continuation function. In this example, the continuation function is `prim_read` itself, so the thread calls `prim_read` again and tries again to read some data. (This pattern of the function calling `lua_yieldk` being the continuation function is not uncommon.)

If a C function has nothing else to do after yielding, it can call `lua_yieldk` without a continuation function or use the macro `lua_yield`:

```
return lua_yield(L, nres);
```

After this call, when the thread resumes again, control returns to the function that called `myCfunction`.

31.2 Lua States

Each call to `luaL_newstate` (or to `lua_newstate`, as we will see in Chapter 32) creates a new Lua state. Different Lua states are completely independent of each other. They share no data at all. This means that no matter what happens inside a Lua state, it cannot corrupt another Lua state. This also means that Lua states cannot communicate directly; we have to use some intervening C code. For instance, given two states L1 and L2, the following command pushes in L2 the string at the top of the stack in L1:

```
lua_pushstring(L2, lua_tostring(L1, -1));
```

Because data must pass through C, Lua states can exchange only types that are representable in C, like strings and numbers. Other types, such as tables, must be serialized to be transferred.

In systems that offer multithreading, an interesting architecture is to create an independent Lua state for each thread. This architecture results in threads similar to UNIX processes, where we have concurrency without shared memory. In this section, we will develop a prototype implementation for multithreading following this approach. I will use POSIX threads (`pthreads`) for this implementation. It should not be difficult to port the code to other thread systems, as it uses only basic facilities.

The system we are going to develop is very simple. Its main purpose is to show the use of multiple Lua states in a multithreading context. After you have it up and running, you can add several advanced features on top of it. We will call our library `lproc`. It offers only four functions:

`lproc.start(chunk)` starts a new process to run the given chunk (a string). The library implements a Lua *process* as a C *thread* plus its associated Lua state.

`lproc.send(channel, val1, val2, ...)` sends all given values (which should be strings) to the given channel (identified by its name, also a string).

`lproc.receive(channel)` receives the values sent to the given channel.

`lproc.exit()` finishes a process. Only the main process needs this function. If this process ends without calling `lproc.exit`, the whole program terminates, without waiting for the end of the other processes.

The library identifies channels by strings and uses them to match senders and receivers. A send operation can send any number of string values, which are returned by the matching receive operation. All communication is synchronous: a process sending a message to a channel blocks until there is a process receiving from this channel, while a process receiving from a channel blocks until there is a process sending to it.

Like its interface, the implementation of `lproc` is also simple. It uses two circular double-linked lists, one for processes waiting to send a message and another for processes waiting to receive a message. It uses one single mutex to control the access to these lists. Each process has an associated condition variable. When a process wants to send a message to a channel, it traverses the receiving list looking for a process waiting for that channel. If it finds one, it removes the process from the waiting list, moves the message's values from itself to the found process, and signals the other process. Otherwise, it inserts itself into the sending list and waits on its condition variable. To receive a message it does a symmetrical operation.

A main element in the implementation is the structure that represents a process:

```
#include <pthread.h>
#include "lua.h"

typedef struct Proc {
  lua_State *L;
  pthread_t thread;
  pthread_cond_t cond;
  const char *channel;
  struct Proc *previous, *next;
} Proc;
```

The first two fields represent the Lua state used by the process and the C thread that runs the process. The other fields are used only when the process has to wait for a matching send/receive. The third field, `cond`, is the condition variable that the thread uses to block itself; the fourth field stores the channel that the process is waiting; and the last two fields, `previous` and `next`, are used to link the process structure in a waiting list.

The following code declares the two waiting lists and the associated mutex:

```
static Proc *waitsend = NULL;
static Proc *waitreceive = NULL;

static pthread_mutex_t kernel_access = PTHREAD_MUTEX_INITIALIZER;
```

Each process needs a `Proc` structure, and it needs access to this structure whenever its script calls `send` or `receive`. The only parameter that these functions receive is the process' Lua state; therefore, each process should store its `Proc` structure inside its Lua state. In our implementation, each state keeps its corresponding `Proc` structure as a full userdata in the registry, associated with the key "_SELF". The auxiliary function `getself` retrieves the `Proc` structure associated with a given state:

```
static Proc *getself (lua_State *L) {
  Proc *p;
  lua_getfield(L, LUA_REGISTRYINDEX, "_SELF");
  p = (Proc *)lua_touserdata(L, -1);
  lua_pop(L, 1);
  return p;
}
```

The next function, `movevalues`, moves values from a sender process to a receiver process:

```
static void movevalues (lua_State *send, lua_State *rec) {
  int n = lua_gettop(send);
  int i;
  for (i = 2; i <= n; i++)   /* move values to receiver */
    lua_pushstring(rec, lua_tostring(send, i));
}
```

It moves to the receiver all values in the sender stack but the first, which will be the channel.

Listing 31.1 defines `searchmatch`, which traverses a waiting list looking for a process waiting for a given channel. If it finds one, the function removes the process from the list and returns it; otherwise, the function returns NULL.

The last auxiliary function, defined in Listing 31.2, is called when a process cannot find a match. In this case, the process links itself at the end of the appropriate waiting list and waits until another process matches with it and wakes it up. (The loop around `pthread_cond_wait` protects from spurious wakeups allowed in POSIX threads.) When a process wakes up another, it sets the other process' field `channel` to NULL. So, if `p->channel` is not NULL, it means that nobody matched process p, so it has to keep waiting.

With these auxiliary functions in place, we can write `send` and `receive` (Listing 31.3). The `send` function starts checking for the channel. Then it locks the mutex and searches for a matching receiver. If it finds one, it moves its values to this receiver, marks the receiver as ready, and wakes it up. Otherwise, it puts itself on wait. When it finishes the operation, it unlocks the mutex and returns with no values to Lua. The `receive` function is similar, but it has to return all received values.

Now let us see how to create new processes. A new process needs a new POSIX thread, and a new thread needs a body to run. We will define this body later; here is its prototype, dictated by pthreads:

Listing 31.1. Function to search for a process waiting for a channel:

```
static Proc *searchmatch (const char *channel, Proc **list) {
  Proc *node = *list;
  if (node == NULL) return NULL;   /* empty list? */
  do {
    if (strcmp(channel, node->channel) == 0) {   /* match? */
      /* remove node from the list */
      if (*list == node)   /* is this node the first element? */
        *list = (node->next == node) ? NULL : node->next;
      node->previous->next = node->next;
      node->next->previous = node->previous;
      return node;
    }
    node = node->next;
  } while (node != *list);
  return NULL;   /* no match */
}
```

Listing 31.2. Function to add a process to a waiting list:

```
static void waitonlist (lua_State *L, const char *channel,
                                     Proc **list) {
  Proc *p = getself(L);

  /* link itself at the end of the list */
  if (*list == NULL) {   /* empty list? */
    *list = p;
    p->previous = p->next = p;
  }
  else {
    p->previous = (*list)->previous;
    p->next = *list;
    p->previous->next = p->next->previous = p;
  }

  p->channel = channel;

  do {   /* waits on its condition variable */
    pthread_cond_wait(&p->cond, &kernel_access);
  } while (p->channel);
}
```

Listing 31.3. Functions to send and receive messages:

```
static int ll_send (lua_State *L) {
  Proc *p;
  const char *channel = luaL_checkstring(L, 1);

  pthread_mutex_lock(&kernel_access);

  p = searchmatch(channel, &waitreceive);

  if (p) {  /* found a matching receiver? */
    movevalues(L, p->L);  /* move values to receiver */
    p->channel = NULL;  /* mark receiver as not waiting */
    pthread_cond_signal(&p->cond);  /* wake it up */
  }
  else
    waitonlist(L, channel, &waitsend);

  pthread_mutex_unlock(&kernel_access);
  return 0;
}

static int ll_receive (lua_State *L) {
  Proc *p;
  const char *channel = luaL_checkstring(L, 1);
  lua_settop(L, 1);

  pthread_mutex_lock(&kernel_access);

  p = searchmatch(channel, &waitsend);

  if (p) {  /* found a matching sender? */
    movevalues(p->L, L);  /* get values from sender */
    p->channel = NULL;  /* mark sender as not waiting */
    pthread_cond_signal(&p->cond);  /* wake it up */
  }
  else
    waitonlist(L, channel, &waitreceive);

  pthread_mutex_unlock(&kernel_access);

  /* return all stack values but channel */
  return lua_gettop(L) - 1;
}
```

Listing 31.4. Function to create new processes:

```
static int ll_start (lua_State *L) {
  pthread_t thread;
  const char *chunk = luaL_checkstring(L, 1);
  lua_State *L1 = luaL_newstate();

  if (L1 == NULL)
    luaL_error(L, "unable to create new state");

  if (luaL_loadstring(L1, chunk) != 0)
    luaL_error(L, "error starting thread: %s",
                  lua_tostring(L1, -1));

  if (pthread_create(&thread, NULL, ll_thread, L1) != 0)
    luaL_error(L, "unable to create new thread");

  pthread_detach(thread);
  return 0;
}
```

```
static void *ll_thread (void *arg);
```

To create and run a new process, the system must create a new Lua state, start a new thread, compile the given chunk, call the chunk, and finally free its resources. The original thread does the first three tasks, and the new thread does the rest. (To simplify error handling, the system only starts the new thread after it has successfully compiled the given chunk.)

Function ll_start creates a new process (Listing 31.4). This function creates a new Lua state L1 and compiles the given chunk in this new state. In case of an error, it signals the error to the original state L. Then it creates a new thread (using pthread_create) with body ll_thread, passing the new state L1 as the argument to the body. The call to pthread_detach tells the system that we will not want any final answer from this thread.

The body of each new thread is the ll_thread function (Listing 31.5). It receives its corresponding Lua state (created by ll_start), with only the pre-compiled main chunk on the stack. The new thread opens the standard Lua libraries, opens the lproc library, and then calls its main chunk. Finally, it destroys its condition variable (which was created by luaopen_lproc) and closes its Lua state.

(Note the use of luaL_requiref to open the lproc library.[1] This function is somewhat equivalent to require but, instead of searching for a loader, it uses the given function (luaopen_lproc, in our case) to open the library. After calling the open function, luaL_requiref registers the result in the package.loaded table, so that future calls to require the library will not try to open it again. With true

[1]This function is new in Lua 5.2.

Listing 31.5. Body for new threads:

```
int luaopen_lproc (lua_State *L);

static void *ll_thread (void *arg) {
  lua_State *L = (lua_State *)arg;
  luaL_openlibs(L);  /* open standard libraries */
  luaL_requiref(L, "lproc", luaopen_lproc, 1);
  lua_pop(L, 1);
  if (lua_pcall(L, 0, 0, 0) != 0)  /* call main chunk */
    fprintf(stderr, "thread error: %s", lua_tostring(L, -1));
  pthread_cond_destroy(&getself(L)->cond);
  lua_close(L);
  return NULL;
}
```

as its last parameter, it also registers the library in the corresponding global variable (lproc, in our case).)

The last function from the module, exit, is quite simple:

```
static int ll_exit (lua_State *L) {
  pthread_exit(NULL);
  return 0;
}
```

Only the main process needs to call this function when it finishes, to avoid the immediate end of the whole program.

Our last step is to define the open function for the lproc module. The open function luaopen_lproc (Listing 31.6) must register the module functions, as usual, but it also has to create and initialize the Proc structure of the running process.

As I said earlier, this implementation of processes in Lua is a very simple one. There are endless improvements you can make. Here I will briefly discuss some of them.

A first obvious improvement is to change the linear search for a matching channel. A nice alternative is to use a hash table to find a channel and to use independent waiting lists for each channel.

Another improvement relates to the efficiency of process creation. The creation of new Lua states is a light operation. However, the opening of all standard libraries is not that light, and most processes probably will not need all standard libraries. We can avoid the cost of opening a library by using the pre-registration of libraries we discussed in Section 15.1. With this approach, instead of calling luaL_requiref for each standard library, we just put the library opening function into the package.preload table. If the process calls require"lib", then — and only then — require will call the associated function to open the library. Function registerlib, in Listing 31.7, does this registration.

Listing 31.6. Open function for the `lproc` module:

```
static const struct luaL_reg ll_funcs[] = {
  {"start", ll_start},
  {"send", ll_send},
  {"receive", ll_receive},
  {"exit", ll_exit},
  {NULL, NULL}
};

int luaopen_lproc (lua_State *L) {
  /* create own control block */
  Proc *self = (Proc *)lua_newuserdata(L, sizeof(Proc));
  lua_setfield(L, LUA_REGISTRYINDEX, "_SELF");
  self->L = L;
  self->thread = pthread_self();
  self->channel = NULL;
  pthread_cond_init(&self->cond, NULL);
  luaL_register(L, "lproc", ll_funcs);  /* open library */
  return 1;
}
```

Listing 31.7. Registering libraries to be opened on demand:

```
static void registerlib (lua_State *L, const char *name,
                                       lua_CFunction f) {
  lua_getglobal(L, "package");
  lua_getfield(L, -1, "preload");  /* get 'package.preload' */
  lua_pushcfunction(L, f);
  lua_setfield(L, -2, name);  /* package.preload[name] = f */
  lua_pop(L, 2);  /* pop 'package' and 'preload' tables */
}

static void openlibs (lua_State *L) {
  luaL_requiref(L, "_G", luaopen_base, 1);
  luaL_requiref(L, "package", luaopen_package, 1);
  lua_pop(L, 2);  /* remove results from previous calls */
  registerlib(L, "io", luaopen_io);
  registerlib(L, "os", luaopen_os);
  registerlib(L, "table", luaopen_table);
  registerlib(L, "string", luaopen_string);
  registerlib(L, "math", luaopen_math);
  registerlib(L, "debug", luaopen_debug);
}
```

It is always a good idea to open the basic library. You also need the package library; otherwise, you will not have require available to open other libraries. (You will not have even the package.preload table.) All other libraries can be optional. Therefore, instead of calling luaL_openlibs, we can call our own openlibs function (shown also in Listing 31.7) when opening new states. Whenever a process needs one of these libraries, it requires the library explicitly, and require will call the corresponding luaopen_* function.

Other improvements involve the communication primitives. For instance, it would be useful to provide limits on how long lproc.send and lproc.receive should wait for a match. As a particular case, a zero limit would make these functions non-blocking. With POSIX threads, we could implement this facility using pthread_cond_timedwait.

Exercises

Exercise 31.1: As we saw, if a function calls lua_yield (the version with no continuation), control returns to the function that called it when the thread resumes again. What values does the calling function receive as results from that call?

Exercise 31.2: Modify the lproc library so that it can send and receive other primitive types such as booleans and numbers. (Hint: you only have to modify the movevalues function.)

Exercise 31.3: Implement in the lproc library a non-blocking send operation.

32

Memory Management

Lua allocates all its data structures dynamically. All these structures grow when needed, and eventually shrink or disappear.

Lua keeps a tight control over its memory use. When we close a Lua state, Lua explicitly frees all its memory. Moreover, all objects in Lua are subject to garbage collection: not only tables and strings, but also functions, threads, and modules (as they are actually tables).

The way Lua manages memory is convenient for most applications. Some special applications, however, may require adaptations, for instance to run in memory-constrained environments or to reduce garbage-collection pauses to a minimum. Lua allows these adaptations in two levels. In the low level, we can set the allocation function used by Lua. In a higher level, we can set some parameters that control its garbage collector, or we can even get direct control over the collector. In this chapter, we will cover these facilities.

32.1 The Allocation Function

The Lua core does not assume anything about how to allocate memory. It calls neither malloc nor realloc to allocate memory. Instead, it does all its memory allocation and deallocation through one single *allocation function*, which the user must provide when she creates a Lua state.

Function luaL_newstate, which we have been using to create states, is an auxiliary function that creates a Lua state with a default allocation function. This default allocation function uses the standard malloc–realloc–free functions from the C standard library, which are (or should be) good enough for regular applications. However, it is quite easy to get full control over Lua allocation, by creating your state with the primitive lua_newstate:

```
lua_State *lua_newstate (lua_Alloc f, void *ud);
```

This function receives two arguments: an allocation function and a user data. A state created in this way does all its memory allocation and deallocation by calling f. (Even the structure lua_State itself is allocated by f.)

The type lua_Alloc of the allocation function is defined as follows:

```
typedef void * (*lua_Alloc) (void *ud,
                             void *ptr,
                             size_t osize,
                             size_t nsize);
```

The first parameter is always the user data we provided to lua_newstate; the second parameter is the address of the block being reallocated or released; the third parameter is the original block size; and the last parameter is the requested block size.

Lua ensures that, if ptr is not NULL, then it was previously allocated with size osize.

Lua identifies NULL with blocks of size zero. When nsize is zero, the allocation function must free the block pointed to by ptr and return NULL, which corresponds to a block of the required size (zero). When ptr is NULL, the function must allocate and return a block with the given size; if it cannot allocate the given block, it must return NULL. If both ptr is NULL and nsize is zero, both previous descriptions apply: the net result is that the allocation function does nothing and returns NULL.

Finally, when both ptr is not NULL and nsize is not zero, the allocation function should reallocate the block, like realloc, and return the new address (which may or may not be the same as the original). Again, in case of errors, it must return NULL. Lua assumes that the allocation function never fails when the new size is smaller than or equal to the old one. (Lua shrinks some structures during garbage collection, and it is unable to recover from errors there.)

The standard allocation function used by luaL_newstate has the following definition (extracted directly from file lauxlib.c):

```
void *l_alloc (void *ud, void *ptr, size_t osize, size_t nsize) {
  if (nsize == 0) {
    free(ptr);
    return NULL;
  }
  else
    return realloc(ptr, nsize);
}
```

It assumes that free(NULL) does nothing and that realloc(NULL, size) is equivalent to malloc(size). The ANSI C standard assures both behaviors.

You can get the memory allocator of a Lua state by calling lua_getallocf:

```
lua_Alloc lua_getallocf (lua_State *L, void **ud);
```

If ud is not NULL, the function sets *ud with the value of the user data for this allocator. You can change the memory allocator of a Lua state by calling lua_setallocf:

```
void lua_setallocf (lua_State *L, lua_Alloc f, void *ud);
```

Keep in mind that any new allocator will be responsible for freeing blocks that were allocated by the previous one. More often than not, the new function is a wrapper around the old one, for instance to trace allocations or to synchronize accesses to the heap.

Internally, Lua does not cache free memory blocks for reuse. It assumes that the allocation function does this caching; good allocators do. Lua also does not attempt to minimize fragmentation. Studies show that fragmentation is more the result of poor allocation strategies than of program behavior; good allocators do not create much fragmentation.

It is difficult to beat a well-implemented allocator, but sometimes you may try. For instance, Lua gives you the old size of any block it frees or reallocates. Therefore, a specialized allocator does not need to keep information about the block size, reducing the memory overhead for each block.

Another situation where you can improve memory allocation is in multi-threading systems. Such systems typically demand synchronization for their memory-allocation functions, as they use a global resource (memory). However, the access to a Lua state must be synchronized too — or, better yet, restricted to one thread, as in our implementation of lproc in Chapter 31. So, if each Lua state allocates memory from a private pool, the allocator can avoid the costs of extra synchronization.

32.2 The Garbage Collector

Until version 5.0, Lua always used a simple mark-and-sweep garbage collector (GC). This collector is sometimes called a "stop-the-world" collector. This means that, from time to time, Lua stops interpreting the main program to perform a whole garbage-collection cycle. Each cycle comprises three phases: *mark*, *cleaning*, and *sweep*.

Lua starts the mark phase marking as alive its *root set*, which comprises the objects that Lua has direct access to: the registry and the main thread. Any object stored in a live object is reachable by the program, and therefore is marked as alive too. The mark phase ends when all reachable objects are marked as alive.

Before starting the sweep phase, Lua performs the cleaning phase, which is related to finalizers and weak tables. First, it traverses all objects marked for finalization looking for non-marked objects. Those objects are marked as alive (resurrected) and put in a separate list, to be used in the finalization phase. Second, Lua traverses its weak tables and removes from them all entries wherein either the key or the value is not marked.

The sweep phase traverses all Lua objects. (To allow this traversal, Lua keeps all objects it creates in a linked list.) If an object is not marked as alive, Lua collects it. Otherwise, Lua clears its mark, in preparation for the next cycle. During the sweep phase, Lua also calls the finalizers of the objects that were separated in the cleaning phase.

With version 5.1 Lua got an *incremental collector*. This incremental collector performs the same steps as the old one, but it does not need to stop the world while it runs. Instead, it runs interleaved with the interpreter. Every time the interpreter allocates some amount of memory, the collector runs a small step. This means that, while the collector works, the interpreter may change an object's reachability. To ensure the correctness of the collector, some operations in the interpreter have barriers that detect dangerous changes and correct the marks of the objects involved.

Garbage-collector's API

Lua offers an API that allows us to exert some control over the garbage collector. From C we use `lua_gc`:

```
int lua_gc (lua_State *L, int what, int data);
```

From Lua we use the `collectgarbage` function:

```
collectgarbage(what [, data])
```

Both offer the same functionality. The `what` argument (an enumeration value in C, a string in Lua) specifies what to do. The options are:

LUA_GCSTOP ("stop"): stops the collector until another call to `collectgarbage` (or to `lua_gc`) with the option "restart".

LUA_GCRESTART ("restart"): restarts the collector.

LUA_GCCOLLECT ("collect"): performs a complete garbage-collection cycle, so that all unreachable objects are collected and finalized. This is the default option for `collectgarbage`.

LUA_GCSTEP ("step"): performs some garbage-collection work. The amount of work is equivalent to what the collector would do after allocating `data` bytes.

LUA_GCCOUNT ("count"): returns the number of kilobytes of memory currently in use by Lua. The count includes dead objects that were not collected yet.

LUA_GCCOUNTB (*not available*): returns the fraction of the number of kilobytes of memory currently in use by Lua. In C, the next expression computes the total number of bytes (assuming that it fits in an `int`):

```
(lua_gc(L, LUA_GCCOUNT, 0) * 1024)
    + lua_gc(L, LUA_GCCOUNTB, 0)
```

In Lua, the result of `collectgarbage("count")` is a floating-point number, and the total number of bytes can be computed as follows:

```
collectgarbage("count") * 1024
```

So, `collectgarbage` has no equivalent to this option.

LUA_GCSETPAUSE ("setpause"): sets the collector's pause parameter. The value is given by data in percentage points: when data is 100 the parameter is set to 1 (100%).

LUA_GCSETSTEPMUL ("setstepmul"): sets the collector's step multiplier (`stepmul`) parameter. The value is given by data also in percentage points.

Any garbage collector trades memory for CPU time. In one extreme, the collector might not run at all. It would spend no CPU time at all, at the price of a huge memory consumption. In the other extreme, the collector might do a complete cycle for every change in the accessibility graph. The program would use exactly the minimum memory it needed, at the price of a huge CPU consumption. Real garbage collectors try to find a good balance between those two extremes.

Like its allocator function, Lua's garbage collector is good enough for most applications. In some scenarios, however, it is worth trying to optimize the collector. The two parameters `pause` and `stepmul` allow some control over the collector's character.

The `pause` parameter controls how long the collector waits between finishing a collection and starting a new one. A pause of zero makes Lua start a new collection as soon as the previous one ends. A pause of 200% waits for memory usage to double before starting the collector. You can set a lower pause if you want to trade more CPU time for lower memory usage. Typically, you should keep this value between 0 and 200%.

The step-multiplier parameter (`stepmul`) controls how much work the collector does for each kilobyte of memory allocated. The higher this value the less incremental is the collector. A huge value like 100 000 000% makes the collector work like a non-incremental collector. The default value is 200%. Values lower than 100% make the collector so slow that it may never finish a collection.

The other options of `lua_gc` give you control over when the collector runs. Games are typical clients for this kind of control. For instance, if you do not want any garbage-collection work during some periods, you can stop it with a call `collectgarbage("stop")` and then restart it with `collectgarbage("restart")`. In systems where you have periodic idle phases, you can keep the collector stopped and call `collectgarbage("step",n)` during the idle time. To set how much work to do at each idle period, you can either choose experimentally an appropriate value for n or call `collectgarbage` in a loop, with n set to zero (meaning small steps), until the period expires.

Exercises

Exercise 32.1: Write a library that allows a script to limit the total amount of memory used by its Lua state. It may offer a single function, `setlimit`, to set that limit.

The library should set its own allocation function. This function, before calling the original allocator, checks the total memory in use and returns `NULL` if the requested memory exceeds the limit.

(Hint: the library can use `lua_gc` to initialize its byte count when it starts. It also can use the user data of the allocation function to keep its state: the byte count, the current memory limit, etc.; remember to use the original user data when calling the original allocation function.)

Exercise 32.2: For this exercise, you need at least one Lua script that uses lots of memory. If you do not have one, write it. (It can be as simple as a loop creating tables.)

- Run your script with different GC parameters. How they affect the performance of the script?

- What happens if you set the GC pause to zero? What happens if you set the GC pause to 1000?

- What happens if you set the step multiplier to zero? What happens if you set the step multiplier to 1 000 000?

- Adapt your script so that it keeps full control over the garbage collector. It should keep the collector stopped and call it from time to time to do some work.

  Can you improve the performance of your script with this approach?

Index

CPSIA information can be obtained at www.ICGtesting.com
Printed in the USA
LVOW110450100113

315156LV00006B/142/P